Flora Roy

The Practical Vision
Essays in English Literature in Honour of Flora Roy

The Practical Vision

Essays in English Literature
in Honour of Flora Roy

Edited by

Jane Campbell
James Doyle

Canadian Cataloguing in Publication Data

Main entry under title:

The practical vision

ISBN 0-88920-066-1

1. English literature - History and criticism -
Addresses, essays, lectures.   I. Campbell, Jane,
1934-   II. Doyle, James, 1937-   III. Roy,
Flora.

PR14.P75   820'.9   C78-001190-2

Copyright © 1978

Wilfrid Laurier University Press
Waterloo, Ontario, Canada
N2L 3C5

Contents

Introduction

The essays in this volume are offered as a tribute, on the occasion of her retirement, to an outstanding Canadian university teacher of English, Dr. Flora Roy. It has become conventional recently in academic circles to avoid this use of the title "Doctor," presumably out of deference to the medical profession, but Dr. Roy has thus been known on the campus of her university for so long that it strikes us as incongruous to use any other form of address or reference. It is worth recalling, furthermore, that the original meaning of the word "doctor" is *teacher*; and no one is worthier of that designation than Flora Roy. Dr. Roy has been a teacher—an inspired and distinguished one—virtually all her adult life; and for the past thirty years she has been professor and head of the English Department at the institution known successively as Waterloo College, Waterloo Lutheran University, and (since 1973) Wilfrid Laurier University, in Waterloo, Ontario.

Although her career has thus been centred in southern Ontario, Dr. Roy is a prairie westerner born and bred, as she never tires of reminding her less fortunate colleagues from the east. When occasionally expressing her regret for the decline of academic standards in the predominantly urban and therefore sybaritic east, she will mention her own solid educational grounding, in the days when hardy and conscientious young prairie teachers drilled their students in the three "r's," and at more advanced levels, in the principles of grammar, rhetoric, and literary appreciation, as well as the rudiments of the social and physical sciences. But even dedicated westerners like Flora Roy, before the modern explosion of higher education across Canada, had to defer to the forces which traditionally located the centre of Canadian culture east of the Ontario-Manitoba border. After completing her B.A. and M.A. at the University of Saskatchewan, she came to the University of Toronto in 1944 to begin studies toward a doctorate. These were the golden years of English studies at Toronto: the legendary A. S. P. Woodhouse was head of department, E. J. Pratt was teaching modern poetry at Victoria College, F. E. L. Priestley and Northrop Frye were young instructors, and the graduate students included several subsequently renowned scholars, such as William Blissett, Milton Wilson, Hugh Maclean, and Millar McClure.

Several lines of influence converged at this time to assist Flora Roy in developing a liberalized multi-disciplinary approach to literary studies, which she put into practice by writing a dissertation on "Berkeley and the Eighteenth Century." The title sounds as if the project ought to have been done in the philosophy department; but these were the days before the evolution of that rigid compartmentalization of disciplines which sometimes provokes legitimate complaints against the narrowness and absurd specialization of scholarly research. E. J. Pratt had done graduate study and teaching in theology and psychology before entering the English department as a lecturer; Northrop Frye, like Pratt, was an ordained minister; and Flora Roy's thesis supervisor, F. E. L. Priestley, was interested in everything from the physics of Newton to the social reform essays and fiction of William Godwin.

This intellectual environment, Flora Roy must have immediately recognized, was merely a more sophisticated version of the omnibus approach to education professed by her prairie teachers of earlier years. In a larger sense, this environment also reflected a reaching after those universal ideals of thought and practice which are associated with the English Renaissance and Enlightenment. In fixing on Bishop Berkeley as the subject of her thesis, Flora Roy indicated her empathy with the early eighteenth-century British Empiricists, who continued and elaborated upon Renaissance intellectual and spiritual optimism by expounding an epistemology which was simultaneously grounded in the inescapable realities of sense experience and inspired by the transcendental aspirations of Christian mysticism. British Empiricism ultimately led to the total skepticism of Hume; but before Hume came out with his ruthless dissection of Empiricist logic, Berkeley presented to the world an irresistible vision of what the truth ought to be for men who want to believe in a personal deity as well as in the reliability of their own senses. He compoudned his gift to posterity, furthermore, by presenting this vision in superb English prose. Literary scholars need to be reminded from time to time that the British Empiricists, and especially Berkeley, were outstanding writers—perhaps even better writers than thinkers, although the discipline of English Studies has been traditionally content to leave their literary bones to the discipline of Philosophy. Besides responding to the intellectual optimism of Berkeley, Flora Roy recognized the literary virtues of the bishop's writings, and her dissertation effectively surveyed and united both these topics.

Dr. Roy's study of Berkeley was a comprehensive examination of his thought, style, and influence, but one aspect of his work particularly engaged her attention: his vision of the ideal university. In accordance with the optimism of his Empiricist philosophy, Berkeley conceived a

Utopian vision of an educational institution "designed to teach mankind the most refined luxury, to raise the mind to its due perfection, and give it a taste for those entertainments which afford the highest transport." This sort of description has become something of a cliché to the cynical twentieth century, when university administrators are more and more obliged to concern themselves with financial and managerial matters rather than academic ideals, and harassed instructors find their days numbingly consumed by lectures, the marking of papers, interviews with students, and frantic efforts to keep up with the explosion of information in their specialized fields. Yet as almost everyone engaged in the academic profession will acknowledge, there are distinguished spirits who seem to rise calmly and easily above the petty routine of workaday life and invoke with serene efficiency an approximation of the academic ideals of Bishop Berkeley. Everyone who knows Dr. Roy, furthermore, will recognize immediately that to place her in this exclusive company is no mere flattering and meaningless overstatement. Those of us who have seen her year after year bringing order out of what appears to lesser mortals as academic or administrative chaos, and have listened to her hold forth on one or more of her many scholarly enthusiasms, must unreservedly express our recognition of her outstanding abilities. Her professional career reflects, in brief, the successful combination of imaginative vision and practical action. Precisely appropriate to her own life and work are the words she used to describe Bishop Berkeley, who "saw visions and . . . dreamed dreams . . . then . . . set out in the most realistic and shrewd way to make them come true."

Like Berkeley and her University of Toronto mentors, Dr. Roy's educational and administrative policies have always been informed by a confidence in the unity of truth and in the competence of the sincere intellectual inquirer to grasp this unity amid the constant flux of empirical fact and theory. Accordingly, in the thirty years devoted to building an undergraduate English programme which has been widely recognized as a model of comprehensiveness and balance, Dr. Roy's visions and labours have appeared to take her far beyond her initial fields of concentration. She has taught courses in almost every traditional field of specialization recommended to the English honours and major students, and has been particularly noted for her courses in twentieth-century literature and world literature in translation. In addition, she has ensured that the English programmes under her administration have continued to offer the best of tradition and innovation. Old English Language and Literature, the Renaissance, and the Enlightenment and post-Enlightenment periods have all been the focus of her interest and attention. She introduced into the curriculum and taught courses in the Literature of the United States. At a time when many Canadian universities were still vehemently debating the now self-evident merits of Canadian literature, she introduced courses in this area. In more recent years, her department was among the first in Canada to begin offering a programme in the serious critical study of the film. Dr. Roy made this film study programme possible by simultaneously creating a facility of audio-visual resources, which was ultimately expanded under her direction to serve the whole university community. Also in recent years, her energies have been particularly devoted to building a programme of courses in practical writing and speaking skills, appropriately labeled Communication courses, and effectively designed to deal with the increasingly evident problem of impaired linguistic abilities in a proportion of students entering university.

This sense of simultaneous ideality and practicality, which characterizes both the literary interests and administrative activities of Dr. Roy, is reflected in the various essays of the present volume. All the authors represented here are aware of the responsibility of the English teacher and critic to demonstrate constantly the relationship between literature and the perennial human urge to achieve understanding and control of both the subjective and objective worlds. At the same time, the authors are all obviously inspired by the Aristotelian intrinsic desire to know, to follow out a line of thought for its own sake; or rather, for the self-justifying beauty which emerges from the pursuit and discovery of truth.

Most of the contributions, it will be noted, deal with the post-Enlightenment modern literary period, where Dr. Roy's interests have been particularly engaged, but there are also essays here on Old English, medieval, and Renaissance writings, which reflect Dr. Roy's constant devotion to the concept of a great tradition of English literature. Indeed, the rather eclectic subject matter of this volume is deliberately intended to reflect the variety of Dr. Roy's own intellectual attitudes. At the same time, however, the volume is loosely unified by certain recurrent or pervasive features which reflect the more specific elements of Dr. Roy's scholarly interests. Many of the essays, for instance, offer the fruits of research into comparatively obscure or ostensibly minor works, and show how this research illuminates or relates to more prominent works in the literary tradition. Thus Margaret Allen effectively shows the connection between Spenser's *Faerie Queene* and the anonymous Middle English metrical romance, *The Squyr of Lowe Degre*, and Hugh Maclean investigates the relationship between Spenser's great poem and the ancient tradition of the complaint. Similarly, William Blissett offers an intriguing summary of the "Wagnerite" background to T. S. Eliot's *The Waste Land*, and Michael Ballin explores a revealing analogy between D. H. Lawrence's use of the horse symbol and comparable symbolism in the mystical writings of Maurice Maeterlinck. On the other hand, in a discussion of the comparatively little known Canadian writer Richard B. Wright, James Doyle reverses the paradigm by discussing the importance of such authors as Yeats, Dylan Thomas, and Saul Bellow to Wright's literary vision. Not all the comparisons are between the "prominent" and the "obscure": F. E. L. Priestley discusses the connection between Berkeley and Newton, two figures of roughly equal stature in the history of ideas; Elizabeth Dipple's interest is in two figures in the forefront of modern English literature, Vladimir Nabokov and Iris Murdoch; and Paul Tiessen's subject is the intriguing (but hitherto little known) artistic encounter between Malcolm Lowry and the fiction of F. Scott Fitzgerald. Some of the essays, such as Jane Campbell's study of Margaret Drabble and Larry McKill's discussion of Old English *Genesis II*, are more concisely focused on the works of individual authors. But in all the essays presented here, there is a consistent attempt to see specific works in terms of a comprehensive and coherent tradition: a tradition of literature related to the unified intellectual experience postulated by Bishop Berkeley.

If the essays in this volume all reflect to some degree the attitudes and interests of Dr. Roy, this is partly because all the scholars here represented have been directly and personally influenced by her. Professor F. E. L. Priestley, her thesis supervisor of thirty years ago, has been a friend and intellectual associate for as many years. Professors William Blissett and Hugh Maclean were fellow graduate students with Dr. Roy. Three of the contributors to this volume, Larry McKill, Elizabeth Dipple, and Paul Tiessen, are former students of Dr. Roy; Margaret Allen is a former colleague, and Jane Campbell, Michael Ballin, Paul Tiessen and James Doyle are all current colleagues. All unreservedly acknowledge the immense influence, both personal and intellectual, which Dr. Roy has had on them. It is in grateful recognition of this influence, and as an acknowledgement of Dr. Roy's indisputable membership in the community of scholars, that the editors and authors present the tribute of the following essays.

— James Doyle

Notes on Contributors

MARGARET J. ALLEN is a Fellow of St. John's College at the University of Manitoba, where she teaches English. Her area of specialization is Malory and mediaeval romance.

MICHAEL BALLIN teaches English at Wilfrid Laurier University. His main research interest is in the relationship between the occult traditions and the writings of D. H. Lawrence.

WILLIAM BLISSETT, Professor of English at the University of Toronto, has published many articles on a wide range of topics, including the music of Wagner, the literature of the English Renaissance, and twentieth-century English literature. He is the co-editor of a recently published collection of essays, *A Celebration of Ben Jonson*. Professor Blissett was editor of the *University of Toronto Quarterly* from 1965 to 1976.

JANE CAMPBELL teaches English Romantic and Victorian literature at Wilfrid Laurier University, and is the author of *The Retrospective Review (1820-28) and the Revival of Seventeenth-Century Poetry*.

ELIZABETH DIPPLE teaches English at Northwestern University, Evanston, Illinois. A graduate of Waterloo College, Ms. Dipple's research interests include sixteenth- and twentieth-century English literature.

JAMES DOYLE teaches English at Wilfrid Laurier University. He has published articles on Canadian and American literature in *Canadian Literature, Canadian Review of American Studies*, and other journals.

LARRY N. McKILL teaches English and is director of the remedial writing programme at the University of Alberta. As an undergraduate at Waterloo Lutheran University, he developed his interest in Old English language and literature.

HUGH MACLEAN, Professor of English at the State University of New York (Albany), has published widely on Spenser and seventeenth-century English literature. He is the editor of the Norton Critical Editions of *Edmund Spenser's Poetry* and *Ben Jonson and the Cavalier Poets.*

F. E. L. PRIESTLEY, retired Professor of English at the University of Toronto, is well known in Canadian academic circles as an author, editor, and teacher. Among his numerous publications, two of the most recent are *Language and Structure in Tennyson's Poetry,* and the *Report of Commission on Undergraduate Studies in English in Canadian Universities.*

PAUL TIESSEN teaches English at Wilfrid Laurier University. He has published several critical and review articles on various aspects of literature and film, and has written the Introduction to Malcolm Lowry's *Notes on a Screenplay for F. Scott Fitzgerald's Tender Is the Night.*

The Offering of Isaac and the Artistry of Old English *Genesis A*

L. N. McKILL

Genesis A, the first poem of the *Junius Manuscript*, has fared poorly in literary criticism, largely because of the greater immediate appeal of the interpolated *Genesis B* (lines 235-851) which suits more readily the modern predilection for psychological realism. W. P. Ker's preference for the later *Genesis B* and his hasty dismissal of *Genesis A* is typical of most critical assessment even today:

> The poem is easily detected as by different hands. Milton patched upon Blackmore and Glover might represent in more modern terms the incongruity of it. Great part [sic] of *Genesis* is mere flat commonplace, interesting as giving the average literary taste and the commonplace poetical stock of a dull educated man. But some of it—the story of *Paradise Lost* in it—is magnificent.[1]

Ker then leaves *Genesis A* and goes on to praise the later work. Similarly, in his edition of *Genesis B* (1948), B. J. Timmer comments, "but there is a very great difference in poetical quality: *Genesis A* is dull, L. G. [*Later Genesis*] on the other hand, lively and dramatic."[2]

Few have found much to admire in the earlier *Genesis*. Benjamin Thorpe, the poem's second editor after Junius (1655), writes in his 1832 preface that "the First Book of the poem [the *Junius Manuscript*], being a paraphrase of parts of the Old Testament and Apocrypha, needs no analysis, and its merits and defects must speak for themselves."[3] Thorpe concludes his preface on a note of apology:

> Those readers who may rise disappointed from the perusal should reflect, that he is our earliest poet; that he lived (himself a herds-

[1] W. P. Ker, *The Dark Ages* (1904; rpt. London: Thomas Nelson, 1955), p. 256.

[2] B. J. Timmer, ed., *The Later Genesis* (Oxford: Scrivener, 1948), p. 55.

[3] Benjamin Thorpe, ed., *Cædmon's Metrical Paraphrase of Parts of the Holy Scriptures* (London: Society of Antiquaries, 1832), p. xiv.

man,) when all around him was barbarism; and that these his mangled remains are all that Time has spared to us.[4]

Thorpe's lack of analysis and his interest mainly in authorship have modern parallels. In his *Study of Old English Literature* (1967), C. L. Wrenn has little to say about *Genesis A,* although he ascribes some interest to the poem "because of its apparently genuine echoes of the authentic Cædmon."[5] J. E. Cross (1970) similarly points to the work's "antiquarian interest" but finds little else to admire in it.[6]

Ever since Junius gave the heading "Paraphrasis" to the manuscript, critics of the early Genesis have used the term "paraphrase" disparagingly to describe it,[7] for the most part dismissing it as a fragment, as a crude and slavish metrical versification of the Vulgate, devoid of structure and unity, and lacking in imagination or artistry. Significantly, however, there has been little close analysis to substantiate any of these serious charges. Most late nineteenth- and early twentieth-century criticism has been limited to problems of dating, textual analysis, and philology, and to questions about the unity of authorship and possible apocryphal, patristic, and liturgical influences. Bede's remark that Cædmon, our first named poet, *canebat autem de creatione mundi et origine humani generis, et tota Genesis historia* "sang about the creation of the world, the origin of the human race, and the whole history of Genesis"[8] has generated more critical speculation and investigation about authorship than about the poem's literary merits.

Part of the notion that *Genesis A* is a fragment arises from Bede's statement that Cædmon "sang about the whole history of Genesis," part from the fact that the next poems of the *Junius Manuscript, Exodus* and *Daniel,* use only selected portions of chapters from their biblical sources and give evidence of a freer reorganization of materials. Although nothing precludes Cædmonian authorship, there is no solid evidence either for assuming that Cædmon composed *Genesis A* or that the poem of the manuscript represents only a fragment. No reason compels us to believe *Genesis A* incomplete, or that the poet intended to

[4] Ibid., p. xvi.

[5] C. L. Wrenn, *A Study of Old English Literature* (New York: Norton, 1967), p. 102.

[6] J. E. Cross, "The Old English Period," in *History of Literature in the English Language,* ed. W. F. Bolton (London: Barrie and Jenkins, 1970), I, 23.

[7] For example, W. L. Renwick and H. Orton refer to the poem as a "mere biblical paraphrase" in their *Beginnings of English Literature to Skelton, 1509,* 3rd ed., rev. M. F. Wakelin, Vol. 1 of *Introductions to English Literature,* ed. B. Dobrée (London: Cresset Press, 1966), p. 208. In his introduction to *Exodus,* G. P. Krapp writes: "For *Exodus* is not in intent merely a paraphrase of the second book of the Old Testament as *Genesis* is of the first." See *The Junius Manuscript,* in *The Anglo-Saxon Poetic Records,* Vol. 1 (1931; rpt. New York: Columbia University Press, 1969), p. xxvii.

[8] Bede, *Bede's Ecclesiastical History of the English People,* ed. B. Colgrave and R. A. B. Mynors (Oxford: Clarendon Press, 1969), pp. 418-19.

retell the whole book of the biblical Genesis. The manuscript itself gives no evidence of missing leaves between the end of the poem at line 2936 and the beginning of *Exodus*; moreover, the careful planning of the manuscript, its provision for illustrations, and the lack of any evidence of being terminally fragmented all lend support to accepting the given ending as intentional. Although the poem largely parallels the biblical text, one cannot therefore conclude that the poet intended to tell the whole story of Genesis.[9] Rather than hypothesizing about a possible longer poem and about the poet's intentions, a better critical stance, in my opinion, is to deal with the poem given us in the manuscript. A close analysis of the Offering of Isaac episode demonstrates not only the essential unity of *Genesis A* but the conscious artistry of a poet who was no mere versifier.

The poem's beginning and ending with praise to God lends partial support to arguments for unity. In words of exhortation, the narrator urges,

> Us is riht micel   ðæt we rodera weard,
> wereda wuldorcining,   wordum herigen,
> modum lufien!   He is mægna sped,
> heafod ealra   heahgesceafta,
> frea ælmihtig.[10]

(1-5a: It is very fitting for us that we should praise in words, love in our spirits, the Guardian of heavens, the Glory-King of hosts! He is the fullness of power, the head of all noble creations, the Lord Almighty.) The poem ends as well on a note of praise, as Abraham sacrifices the ram that God has provided in place of Isaac:

>   sægde leana þanc
> and ealra þara sælða   þe he him sið and ær
> gifena drihten,   forgifen hæfde.

(2934b-2936: He said thanks for all the rewards and blessings which He, the Lord of gifts, had given him before and after.) But the unity of

---

[9] Lawrence Mason, one of the poem's early translators, for example, asserts in his footnote to line 2935 that "as 28 Chapters of the Biblical Genesis are passed over, it seems probable that several pages in the MS. of the poem have been lost or were not translated." Mason, *Genesis A Translated from the Old English*, Yale Studies in English, 48 (New York: Holt, 1915), p. 201; facsimile reprinted in A. S. Cook et al., *Translations from the Old English* (New York: Archon Books, 1970). In his introduction to *The Junius Manuscript*, Krapp writes that *Genesis* represents "in effect, a versification of the first book of the Old Testament, though it carries the story only from the Creation to the sacrifice of Isaac, that is through the 13th verse of the 22d chapter. But there is no telling how much more may have been contained in the poem as originally written, and how much may possibly have been lost" (pp. xxiv-xxv).

[10] Krapp, ed., *The Junius Manuscript*, verses 1-5a. All quotations in Old English are from *The Anglo-Saxon Poetic Records*, 6 vols. (New York: Columbia University Press, 1931-1942), and will be cited by line number only following the quotation.

Genesis A does not reside in this one structural tie any more than *Beowulf*'s unity depends upon its beginning and ending with a funeral. The important episode of the Offering of Isaac follows a long sequence of scenes of sacrifice and thanksgiving. Cain and Abel both make sacrifices (975b-979a); Adam praises God for giving him Seth in place of the slain Abel (1110b-1116); Noah makes a sacrifice when he leaves the ark (1497-1510a); and Abraham makes several sacrifices to God, especially after successful journeys (1790a-1793a, 1805-1810, 1885-1889, 2840-2845). The poet makes clear the necessity of praising God in his introductory exhortation, and he reiterates his theme by giving examples of those who do fittingly praise God and remain faithful and obedient, and by showing the consequences of God's wrath upon those who are faithless and disobedient.

Numerous references to praise and sacrifice suggest that Abraham's words of praise following Isaac's liberation form merely part of a series of similar episodes, that the poet could have ended his poem with Noah's sacrifice, for example, or continued past Genesis 22:13 to a sacrifice further along in his biblical source without violating his unity. One might argue, therefore, that Abraham's sacrifice and praise following Isaac's release form no better conclusion than *any* scene of thanksgiving, and consequently, that the poem represents an incomplete paraphrase whose narrative structure rests solely in its biblical source. The Offering of Isaac episode is pre-eminent among other scenes of sacrifice, however, both in its rich typological and liturgical significance, and in terms of its dramatic and climactic effect suitable for a conclusion. Typological commentary pointing out the prefiguration of Christ's sacrifice in the Offering of Isaac is abundant, as J. Daniélou clearly shows in his study of biblical typology, *From Shadows to Reality*.[11] Quoting Tertullian, Daniélou writes, " 'That is why, in the first place, when Isaac was delivered by his father, he carried the wood himself, signifying in this way the death of Christ who is accepted by the Father as a victim and who carried the wood of his cross.' "[12] Daniélou comments,

> The symbolism here [Tertullian's exegesis] is quite straightforward. Isaac, sacrificed by his father, and carrying the wood, typifies Christ offered by the Father and carrying his cross.... This text needs certain clarifications. On the one hand it is important with regard to the doctrine of typology. A type is an event which offers likeness to something in the future, but yet does not really fulfil this something.... The ram was offered in his place and so became literally the type of the sacrifice.[13]

[11] J. Daniélou, *From Shadows to Reality*, trans. Dom Wulstan Hibberd (London: Burns and Oates, 1960). See especially Book III, pp. 115-30.

[12] Ibid., p. 124.

[13] Ibid., pp. 124-25.

B. F. Huppé's *Doctrine and Poetry* suggests that the poet may have intended the Offering of Isaac as his conclusion because of its symbolic meaning. The poem's purpose, like Hilary's *Genesis*, is "through figurative interpretation of a portion of Genesis, to set forth man's duty to praise God."[14] R. P. Creed lends support to Huppé's overall thesis of a completed poem with his discussion of line 2887b: *wudu bær sunu*. Creed argues that the ambiguous verse "can be caught both ways: 'son bore wood' and 'wood bore son': or 'the Son bore the Cross,' and 'the Cross bore the Son.' In this remarkable punning line the Offering of Isaac not only prefigures the crucifixion of Christ, it sharply figures —images—the later drama of Christianity. Isaac becomes the Son sacrificed in order to mediate between man and God."[15]

The typology of the Offering of Isaac contributes to a recognition of the relationship between the concluding figural sacrifice and the introduction to the poem which closely echoes the liturgical *Praefatio* to the Mass: "*Vere dignum et justum est, aequum et salutare, nos tibi semper et ubique gratias agere, Domine sancte, Pater omnipotens, æterne Deus* 'It is truly meet and just, right and available to salvation, always and in all places to give thee thanks, O holy Lord, almighty Father, eternal God.'"[16] In the words of the Old English poem,

Us is riht micel   ðæt we rodera weard,
wereda wuldorcining,   wordum herigen,
modum lufien!

(1-3a: It is very fitting for us that we should praise in words, love in our spirits, the Glory-King of hosts!) In overall structural terms, the sacrifice which ends the poem admirably follows the traditional words of the *Praefatio*. As L. Michel suggests, "It was an exhortation to the faithful to join with the companies of the blessed in their song of praise; it emphasized the fitness and justness of assuming such a disposition in preparation for the great and solemn representation to follow."[17]

Studies in the relationship of the liturgy, especially the readings for Holy Week, the Paschal Vigil in particular, reinforce the claim that the Offering of Isaac forms an intentional conclusion to *Genesis A*. As early as 1912, J. W. Bright had pointed to the relationship of *Exodus* to the

---

[14] B. F. Huppé, "The Cædmonian *Genesis*," in *Doctrine and Poetry: Augustine's Influence on Old English Poetry* (New York: State University of New York, 1959), p. 135.

[15] R. P. Creed, "The Art of the Singer: Three Old English Tellings of The Offering of Isaac," in his *Old English Poetry: Fifteen Essays* (Providence, R.I.: Brown University Press, 1967), p. 80.

[16] P. Guéranger, *The Liturgical Year: Passiontide and Holy Week*, trans. L. Shepherd (1886; rpt. London: Burns and Oates, 1929), p. 190.

[17] L. Michel, "*Genesis A* and the *Praefatio*," *MLN* 62 (1947), 550. The relationship is also cited by F. Holthausen, ed., *Die ältere Genesis* (Heidelberg, 1914), p. 91, and is mentioned briefly by B. F. Huppé in *Doctrine and Poetry*, p. 134.

liturgy.[18] The prophetic readings of the Paschal Vigil all come from the Old Testament, and they closely parallel the key episodes not only of *Genesis A*, but of the next two poems in the manuscript, *Exodus* and *Daniel*. The prophecies traditionally jump from Genesis 22 (the Offering of Isaac) to Exodus 14 (the departure of the children of Israel from Egypt),[19] the same break in narrative in Ms. Junius XI. M. M. Larès suggests a direct parallel between the liturgy and the order and essence of the Old Testament narratives of the *Junius Manuscript*: "C'est dans l'usage de Jérusalem au ve siècle pendant la Semaine sainte que nous avons trouvé un même ordre de lectures empruntées à la Genèse, à l'Exode, au Livre de Daniel, avec des reprises de thèmes qui pourraient précisément expliquer certaines «interpolations» ou «digressions» figurant dans le manuscrit."[20]

The close parallel of the introductory lines of the poem to the *Preface* to the Mass, and the relationship of the liturgical readings of Holy Week to *Genesis A* provide important corroborative evidence of the poem's unity, but they lack sufficient grounds in themselves to argue indisputably for a unified narrative structure. In the first place, although the key episodes of *Genesis A* (the Creation, the Fall, the Flood, the Offering of Isaac) form the major readings of the Paschal Vigil, the poem contains much more than these episodes. We are told, for example, almost the whole account of Abraham's journeys, and the stories of Lot's capture and eventual rescue and the destruction of Sodom and Gomorrah are related fully. Secondly, J. W. Tyrer's historical survey of Holy Week indicates a large number of Old Testament lessons, only some of which might be selected for use.[21] His list, moreover, includes a reading from Genesis 27, the story of how Jacob wins Esau's birthright. The poet, one might argue, could just as well have continued beyond Genesis 22:13 to the end of his biblical source without destroying the unity of his work. But the Offering of Isaac, prefiguring Christ's passion and resurrection logically concludes a poem that begins with echoes of the *Preface* to the Mass. In addition, the Offering ends the poem with a highly dramatic and moving episode. God's promise to Abraham, that from him would come a mighty nation, can now be realized with Isaac's redemption from the sacrificial altar; the covenant remains secure.

[18] J. W. Bright, "The Relationship of the Cædmonian *Exodus* to the Liturgy," *MLN* 27 (1912), 97-103.

[19] Guéranger, "Holy Saturday: Morning Service," in *Passiontide and Holy Week*, pp. 520-25.

[20] M. M. Larès, "Echos d'un rite hierosolymitain dans un manuscrit du haut Moyen Age anglais," *Revue de l'histoire des Religions* 165 (1964), 34. See also G. C. Thornley, "The Accents and Points of Manuscript Junius XI," *Transactions of the Philological Society* (1953), 178-205.

[21] J. W. Tyrer, *Historical Survey of Holy Week: Its Services and Ceremonial* (Oxford: Oxford University Press, 1932), p. 156.

Evidence of careful artistic shaping can be seen in a close analysis of the text itself, for not only does Isaac prefigure Christ, but Abraham shows himself to be a fitting hero to conclude a poem whose major theme concerns God's rewards to the obedient and destruction of the disobedient. Immediately prior to the Offering of Isaac episode, Sarah begs Abraham to banish Ishmael, his son by Hagar. Abraham becomes *weorce on mode þæt he on wræc drife | his selfes sunu* "worked up in his mind that he should drive his own son into exile" (2792-2793a). The metrical collocation between *weorce* "worked up" and *wræc* "exile" effectively reinforces the relationship between the source of Abraham's grief and his troubled spirit; in addition, paronomasia links the two words by the mere metathesis of *r* with the vowel. Obeying his Ruler, Abraham drives away the *dreorigmod tu* "sorrowful-minded pair" (2805b).

The narrator's addition to his source, *and his agen bearn* (2806b), contrasting with the same formula used by Sarah just a few lines above in reference to Isaac (2789a), transforms the biblical source even more significantly than does the exile imagery. With the addition of this formulaic verse, we know for certain that Abraham will, indeed, carry out his Lord's order to sacrifice Isaac, even though Isaac is his *agen bearn* (2852a). The poem forces us to admire, rather than condemn Abraham for his deeds, however, because he acts obediently, yet not without believable human emotion in carrying out his Lord's commands. He becomes "worked up in his mind" over having to expel Ishmael, *his selfes sunu* "his own son" (2793a) from his dwelling. Consequently, the poet need not state explicitly Abraham's grief now at having to sacrifice the long-awaited heir, Isaac, who should break treasure after him.

By indicating Abraham's genuine compassion and human feelings in the Ishmael episode, the poet can emphasize his hero's perfect obedience in the account of the Offering of Isaac without making Abraham appear heartless and unconcerned to sacrifice his child. The whole episode is cast as an opportunity for the hero Abraham to make known his heroic courage:

> Þa þæs rinces   se rica ongan
> cyning costigan,   cunnode georne
> hwilc þæs æðelinges   ellen wære,

(2846-2849: Then the powerful King began to make a test of the warrior, earnestly tried what this nobleman's courage might be.) Nobility and heroic courage are linked here, as in *Beowulf,* line 3: *hu ða æþelingas ellen fremedon* "how the noblemen performed deeds of heroic courage"; the two are inseparable. Abraham's test represents the supreme trial of loyalty to one's lord, for the faithful retainer places obedience to his Lord over blood ties, even though Isaac signifies the fulfillment of years of longing for a son.

This ultimate test of Abraham's faith provides a suitably dramatic conclusion to the narrative. The deeply moving account of the biblical Genesis becomes even more poignant in the Old English telling. While retaining the laconic style of the Old Testament story, the *Genesis*-poet intensifies the drama and points to the significance of the action by adding brief narrative comments. Each addition emphasizes Abraham's firm trust and obedience, and reinforces the overall theme of the poem that God will reward with gifts and protection all those who remain faithful to Him. After Abraham responds immediately to God's command to sacrifice Isaac, the narrator remarks, *Him wæs frean engla | word ondrysne and his waldend leof* "To him the word of the Lord of angels was awesome, and his Ruler dear" (2861b-2862). And two lines later he adds, *Nalles nergendes | hæse wiðhogode* "In no wise did he resist the command of the Saviour" (2864b-2865a). Before Abraham's response to Isaac about the need for something to sacrifice, the poet says, *hæfde on an gehogod | þæt he gedæde swa hine drihten het* "he had decided on one thing only, that he should do as the Lord ordered him" (2893b-2894). *Swa him bebead metod* "as the Measurer commanded him" (2872b); *swa hine drihten het* "as the Lord had ordered him" (2894b); *swa him se eca bebead* "as the Eternal One commanded him" (2898b): like a refrain, the narrative additions underscore Abraham's complete obedience to his Lord.

It is especially through his diction that the poet demonstrates fine structural control. By employing the same words for both God's command and the narration of Abraham's response, the poet increases our sense of the patriarch's perfect obedience. The order to depart *ofestlice* "hastily" (2850a) is fulfilled in the word *efste* "he hastened" (2873a). God's commands, *and þe læde mid | þin agen bearn* "and lead with you your own child" (2851b-2852a) and sacrifice *sunu ðinne* "your son" (2853a), are met in verse 2871b with the verb *lædan* "to lead" and in the frequent use of the phrase "his own son."[22] Each occurrence of the words "own" or "only" increases both the pathos of the situation and our awe at Abraham's unquestioning obedience, especially since his desire for a son has been so keenly emphasized by the narrator, even more than in the biblical Genesis. The poet uses the word "own" in other places too: God tells Abraham to climb the hill *up þinum agnum fotum* "upon your own feet" (2856a); and Abraham leaves *from his agenum hofe* "from his own dwelling" (2871a). In their accumulative power, both instances of the adjective "own" serve to intensify our

---

[22] Verses 2852a, 2869b, 2885b, 2914b, 2931b. In addition, the very accumulation of these words keeps the fact of Isaac's being the only son constantly before us and makes Abraham's prompt obedience even more impressive and pathetic.

response to Abraham's obedience. Even the ram, Isaac's replacement provided by God, stands *ænne* "alone" (2928b), caught in the brambles. The narrator also describes Isaac as *unweaxen* "not fully grown up" (2872a) and *geongne* "young" (2905a), without scriptural support, but with strong connotations for us.[23] There is even a suggestion of the contrasting fate of Isaac about to be killed, though young, with the two *geongne* "young" (2868b) men accompanying father and son. The two young men are servants, not sole heirs, yet they do not face Isaac's destiny. Once more, the Bible gives no indication of the servants' ages, but the poet has seen the dramatic potential in the contrast.

Abraham's quick response to God's command is accelerated in the *Genesis* poem, and thereby sharpens the fact of the faithful man's obedience. *Ne forsæt he þy siðe, ac sona ongann | fysan to fore* "He did not delay in that exploit; on the contrary, he immediately began to hasten on that journey" (2860-2861a). Unlike the biblical account, in which Abraham rises at dawn, the *Genesis*-poet has him give up his *nihtreste* "night's rest" (2864a). He departs *fus* "quickly | eagerly | willingly" (2870b). *Efste þa swiðe and onette | forð foldwege* "He hurried exceedingly and hastened forth on the land's way" (2873-2874a). And he seizes the sword *ædre* "quickly" (2905b) to kill Isaac. The poet constantly points to his singleness of thought to obey the Lord's command.

The whole episode compares to a battle, for from the outset we learn that the powerful King wishes to *costigan* "make trial of" the warrior, to *cunnian* "test" his *ellen* "heroic courage" (2846-2848). The *Beowulf*-poet, for example, employs the verb *cunnian* in the description of Beowulf's heroic tests with Breca (508b) and against Grendel's mother (1500b).

God's command is expressed much like a leader's exhortation in an approach-to-battle type-scene.[24] Abraham *gyrde grægan sweorde* "gird[s] himself with a grey sword" (2866a) for his "battle," and like a hero, responds promptly and obediently to his Lord's command. The indication of the warrior's "intention" is suggested in the words which describe Abraham's purpose: *and þa ædre gegrap | sweord be gehil-*

---

[23] The youthful Isaac of *Genesis A*, as in the Towneley and Chester plays, however, works counter to the exegetical tradition in which Isaac is a man of Christ's age. See Arnold Williams, "Typology and the Cycle Plays: Some Criteria," *Speculum* 43 (1968), 677-84.

[24] The nine details are cited by Lee C. Ramsey, "The Theme of Battle in Old English Poetry," Diss., Indiana University, 1965; *DA* 26 (1965), 2758. He describes the details as follows: "the central action is the *advance* to the field, and the supplementary actions are the *command* to advance, the *preparations* for advancing, and the *assembly.* . . . Other details include the statement of *intention*, which follows a reference to the advance . . . ; the *beasts of battle* . . . ; *hastening* . . . ; *the bearing of equipment* . . . ; and various details about the *attitude* of the warriors, which can come almost anywhere" (p. 72).

tum, wolde his sunu cwellan / folmum sinum "and then quickly he grasped the sword by the hilt, intended to kill his son with his own hands" (2905b-2907a). Abraham's intention, expressed by the verb *wolde*, seems certain, for like all good heroes, he will achieve his heroic pledge. Throughout the long narrative describing Abraham's journeys we have witnessed his complete faithfulness to God's *wære* "covenant/pledge"; we have observed his obedience in sending *his agen bearn* "his own child [Ishmael]" (2806b) into exile. Now, we fully expect him to perform his *ellen* "deeds of valour" by sacrificing Isaac at his Lord's command.

In contrast to the verbs and modifiers expressing action and haste comes the dramatic calm after the angel calls out *hlude* "loudly" (2909b) to Abraham: *He stille gebad* "He awaited silently/motionless" (2910b). No corresponding phrase occurs in the Vulgate. In addition, the poet merely says, Abraham *þam engle oncwæð* "replied to the angel" (2911b); he does not break the dramatic silence with the direct response indicated in the biblical Genesis 22:11, *Adsum* "I am here." The poet effectively employs repeated diction when he describes Abraham's haste in placing the ram this time, and not his son, on the altar: Abraham moves *ofestum miclum* "with great haste" (2931a). This contrast between *ofestum* in this circumstance compared with God's command at the outset (2850a) and with Abraham's journey (2873a), dramatically serves to heighten our sense of Abraham's joy in having Isaac restored to him *cwicne* "alive" (2915a).

We expect Isaac's death when we read that Abraham *Ongan þa ad hladan, æled weccan* began then to load the pyre and to kindle a fire" (2902); *ad stod onæled* "the pyre stood lighted" (2923a) the poet says later. Suspense and drama increase with the poet's description of the actual fire and Isaac's being bound *fet and honda* "feet and hands" (2903b). No mention of the fire is made in the Bible which merely states that Abraham *alligasset Isaac* "bound Isaac" (gen. 22:9). However, by placing a significant adject just before Abraham fetters his son and places him on the pyre, the narrator subtly foreshadows that everything will turn out all right. Prior to the lines describing Abraham's action, the poet tells us that the father and his heir stood on the ridge where the *wærfæst metod wordum tæhte* "pledge-firm Measurer had directed with words" (2901). The "pledge-firm Measurer" has previously promised that a mighty nation will arise from Isaac (2325b-2337, 2353-2369). For a moment the lighted pyre stands in opposition to the pledge, but only temporarily, for God's angel speaks to him, *ofstum* "hastily" (2912a) from heaven. Abraham, once more called *leofa* "dear" (2914a), has proved his *ellen* "heroic courage."

Although the episode concludes with the biblical Genesis 22:13, there is some indication that the poet has incorporated verses 15 and 16, the angel's second announcement to Abraham, into the single speech of *Genesis* 2908b-2922. Genesis 22:16 gives God's promise, through the words of the angel, of rich rewards. The angel speaks of Abraham's willingness to give up his son for God's sake in both Genesis 22:12 and 16, and one might argue that the authority of verse 12 is sufficient. But only verse 16 makes mention of rewards. Lines 2917-2922 concern the rewards that Abraham will obtain. Like a successful warrior in battle, Abraham receives the promise of *soðum sigorleanum* "true victory-rewards" (2919a). By his structural manoeuvring, if we grant that the heroic idea of rewards for valour and obedience needs the scriptural authority provided by verse 16, the poet can once more point to the blessings received by the faithful and yet end his poem on the note of praise with which he began.

Functioning as a dénouement after the high and dramatic tension of Abraham's heroic test, the scene of sacrifice closing the poem suitably points to Abraham's constant thanks for all the good things his Lord has provided. Unlike the wicked people of Sodom and Gomorrah, who forgot their Lord who gave them *dugeða ..., blæd on burgum* "good things ..., prosperity in the cities" (2584b-2585a), Abraham turns at once, even at this time of emotional stress, to thank his Lord:

sægde leana þanc
and ealra þara sælða   þe he him sið and ær,
gifena drihten,   forgifen hæfde.

(2934b-2936: He said thanks for all the rewards and blessings which He, the Lord of gifts, had given him before and after.) Coming after a scene of great tension and drama, the closing words of the poem recall the narrator's opening exhortation.

The Offering of Isaac represents the epitome of faith and obedience; it is both the crown of Abraham's noble life and the assurance that God's pledge of a mighty nation will be realized. To have continued with Sarah's death and Abraham's subsequent remarriage would have been anti-climactic to the event which powerfully emphasizes the theme of *Genesis*. The Offering, dramatically effective and rich in typological and liturgical significance, provides a fit conclusion to a poem revealing in concrete terms both sure punishment for the *wærlogan* "pledge-betrayers" and rewards for the *wærfæst* "pledge-firm" dear to God.

The Harlot and the Mourning Bride

MARGARET J. ALLEN

It is frequently remarked that one of the difficulties in reading the literature of earlier centuries is that we are prone to apply to it standards with which its authors would have had little sympathy. Often such warnings precede criticism that character and plot are not convincing; that speeches, though long, do not engage the reader in the emotions of the speakers; that stock characters and familiar motifs argue a lack of originality on the part of the author. It would therefore seem necessary, if we are to make a just evaluation of a literature that exhibits such characteristics, to ascertain the function of plot and character, of speech, monologue and motif in them, which allowed the author to dispense with qualities that are the hallmarks of excellence in modern writers.

That many motifs convey more than their surface or ostensible meaning because they are drawn out of a body of associated material which author and reader have in common is another observation so widely recognized as to be hardly worth remarking. Nevertheless, anything which helps to piece together the background against which works of an earlier period were written will assist us in our goal of reading each "with the same spirit that its author writ." With this objective in view, therefore, I should like first to examine the story of her life which Spenser's Duessa tells the Red Cross Knight. There, it will be remembered, Duessa calls herself a wretched woman who

> Was, (O what now availeth that I was?)
> Borne the sole daughter of an emperour,
> He that the wide west under his rule has,
> And high hath set his throne where Tiberis doth pas.

> 'He, in the first flowre of my freshest age,
> Betrothed me unto the onely haire
> Of a most mighty king, most rich and sage;
> Was never prince so faithfull and so faire,

Was never prince so meeke and debonaire;
But ere my hoped day of spousall shone,
My dearest lord fell from high honors staire,
Into the hands of hys accursed fone,
And cruelly was slaine, that shall I ever mone.

'His blessed body, spoild of lively breath,
Was afterward, I know not how, convaid
And fro me hid: of whose most innocent death
When tidings came to mee, unhappy maid,
O how great sorrow my sad soule assaid!
Then forth I went his woefull corse to find,
And many yeares throughout the world I straid,
A viigin widow, whose deepe wounded mind
With love, long time did languish as the striken hind.

(*F.Q.* I, ii, 22-24)[1]

Here we have a princess who is betrothed to a noble youth; but, before their wedding can take place, the bridegroom has vanished, slain, the bride believes, by his foes. The reader, however, senses that she is mistaken in thinking that the body hidden from her is, in fact, a corpse, and sees that her unremitting search is doomed to failure because it is guided by error.

In addition we notice that Spenser has put this sad story into the mouth of one who seems totally unlike the princess who has suffered this tragic fate. Nothing in the dress or demeanour of Duessa as she rides along with Sansfoy in "mirth and wanton play" suggests that she is inconsolable.

Another feature is worthy of note. Both Duessa and Fidessa are in error and reprehensibly so. William Nelson distinguishes between their errors when he says that Duessa "knows that Christ is dead, but she does not know, or pretends not to know, that He lives again."[2] Duessa, if she does know that Christ lives again, obviously believes that her power—or the source of her power—is great enough to triumph over the risen Christ and that, therefore, for all practical purposes He is dead. Fidessa, however, if we may for the moment grant her a separate existence, is genuinely mistaken and is guilty only in being ignorant of that which she ought to know. She pays heavily for her ignorance as for many years she strays through the world, languishing as the stricken hind. Until she discovers that her bridegroom is alive, she will continue to grieve.

In all this Fidessa conforms to the figure I have called the mourning bride, and Duessa to the figure many have called the harlot. The two

---

[1] Passages from *The Faerie Queene* are quoted from the R. E. Neil Dodge edition, *The Complete Poetical Works of Spenser* (Cambridge, Mass.: Riverside Press, 1908, rpt. 1936).

[2] William Nelson, *The Poetry of Edmund Spenser: A Study* (New York and London: Columbia University Press, 1963), p. 149.

women are not least conventional in appearing juxtaposed, for, despite differences which would seem to ensure that they would rarely meet, they come together, as I hope to show, rather frequently in literature. It is also in conformity with tradition that the mislaid bridegroom should be, in an allegorical sense, Christ, or should have Christ-like characteristics attributed to him. He does so, if I am correct, because the mourning bride has as her archetype the redeemed harlot, Mary Magdalene.

She, too, it will be recalled, sought the body of her dearest Lord whom she believed incorrectly to be dead. What Duessa claims to do, the Magdalene in fact does. She weeps not only for the death of her Lord but also, as she tells the angels, "Because they have taken away my Lord, and I know not where they have laid him" (John 20:13).[3] Later when she is asked by Jesus, Whom she mistakes for the gardener, "Woman, why weepest thou? whom seekest thou?" she replies, "Sir, if thou have borne him hence, tell me where thou hast laid him, and I will take him away" (20:15).

The Bible itself provides grounds for considering the Magdalene not above reproach in her ignorance. The tempered criticism of Fidessa implied by Nelson's remark is also implicit in Luke's account of the Magdalene's part in the resurrection scene. There, she has come with Joanna and Mary the mother of James to anoint the body of Jesus, and the angels in the sepulchre say to the women,

> Why seek ye the living among the dead? He is not here, but is risen: remember how he spake unto you when he was yet in Galilee, saying, The Son of man must be delivered into the hands of sinful men, and be crucified, and the third day rise again. (Luke 24:5-7)

The Church Fathers, while they praise Mary Magdalene for her faithfulness, identify her lack of understanding as a failing. Jerome, for example, says,

> When the women, Mary Magdalene and Mary the mother of James and Joseph [sic], pious and well-meaning women, to be sure, but mistaken, were looking for God in the tomb, He accepted, indeed, their good desire, but the angel who rolled back the stone made known to them their error.[4]

The *Glossa Ordinaria* chides her mildly by saying that because she grieved too much she could not believe her eyes. The angel's "Why weepest thou?" is interpreted in part as *Noli peccare* and the gloss says

---

[3] Biblical passages are quoted from the Authorized Version but I have compared them with earlier translations and the Vulgate to make sure that substantially the same material was available at the time the various works were written.

[4] *The Homilies of Saint Jerome*, trans. Sr. Marie Liguori Ewald, Vol. II, *The Fathers of the Church*, Vol. LVII (Washington: The Catholic University of America Press, 1966), p. 219.

that she failed to recognize Jesus because she had her back turned "to the one she did not believe raised from the dead; because she loved and wavered, saw and did not recognize."[5] Rabanus Maurus sees her as "mourning inestimably over the corporeal absence of her beloved lover,"[6] the word "corporeal" suggesting a limitation in an otherwise virtuous attitude. In harsher tones Ambrose compares her unfavourably with Stephen who, during his martyrdom, fixed his eyes on heaven and saw God and Jesus standing at His right hand (Acts 7:55). On this Ambrose comments, "Thus Stephen did not seek on earth, yet saw the Lord. . . . But Mary Magdalene sought Him on earth and was not able to touch Him."[7] Similarly Peter Comestor in the *Historia Scholastica* interprets Christ's "Touch me not" (John 20:17) as meaning that "the one whom you seek dead, you are not worthy living to touch; whom you consider to be a corpse borne away, not a Son equal to the Father."[8]

Mary recognizes her error when she hears her master pronounce her name, but other mourning brides must serve a longer apprenticeship to wisdom. The seven years of grief to which the King of Hungary in *The Squyr of Lowe Degre* subjects his Daughter, although he could at any moment correct her mistake, give her an opportunity to become capable of a similar realization.

The Princess, it will be remembered, had entered into a secret betrothal with the Squire, secret because the difference in rank made it dangerous to the squire to have their love known. However, the wicked Steward who lurks in so many medieval romances, having overheard their vows, reports them with embellishments[9] to the King. The news does not stir the King to the anger which the parties involved expect, he being willing to countenance the wedding if the Squire can prove himself worthy. However, he grants the Steward permission and men-at-arms to protect the Princess from dishonour, permission the Steward uses to attack the Squire in force when he comes alone to bid farewell to his sweetheart. Virtue prevails and the Squire kills the Steward but is himself taken prisoner and stripped of his clothes which are then put on

---

[5] J. P. Migne's *Patrologia Latina*, CXIV, 422-23. The translations from the *Patrologia* are my own.

[6] *P.L.,* CXII, 1485-86.

[7] *P.L.,* XV, 1937-38.

[8] *P.L.,* CXCVIII, 1638.

[9] The Steward reports their conversation and adds:

> Had I not come in, verayly,
> The squyer had layne her by,
> But whan he was ware of me,
> Full fast away can he fle.
> (ll. 349-52)

Neither the Princess nor the Squire is aware that the Steward has overheard their conversation. Here and throughout I quote from William Edward Mead's edition, *The Squyr of Lowe Degre: A Middle English Metrical Romance* (Boston: Ginn & Co., 1904).

the Steward's corpse. The face is hacked beyond recognition and the body left at the chamber door of the King's Daughter.

Thus it seems that, like Fidessa, she makes an honest mistake when she assumes that the faceless body dressed in the clothes of the Squire is, in fact, the Squire. However, like the Magdalene's ignorance of the resurrection, her mistake reflects a flaw in her. The knowledge is there for her to grasp if she will but perceive it. In this connection it may be helpful to remember the commonly accepted view that Una's veil is really over the eyes of those who see her veiled, and represents the inability of fallen man to perceive Truth clearly.[10] It is the King's Daughter whose spiritual condition is symbolized in the marred face which makes it impossible for her to distinguish between the Squire and the Steward. When she looks at the body, her own marred identity obscures her vision and, if she is to learn her mistake, she must find her true identity through her bereavement.

Curiously enough, bereft of their beloved before their "hoped day of spousal shone," Fidessa and the Princess of Hungary resemble once again Mary Magdalene. In this case it is unlikely that she is the source of the tradition of the virgin widow. Rather it might seem that, established as the grieving woman who seeks the corpse of her beloved, Mary Magdalene was herself drawn back into the tradition of the harlot and the mourning bride which had sprung from her but had acquired the new feature of the imminent wedding. As Mary's story grew in the telling, she was provided with a situation which attributed to her this additional facet.

An unknown fourteenth-century Italian writer attributed to Jerome the story that Mary Magdalene was the spouse of St. John the

---

[10] See for example Robert Kellogg and Oliver Steele in their "Introduction" to *Edmund Spenser, Books I and II of "The Faerie Queene", "The Mutability Cantos" and Selections from the Minor Poetry* (New York: The Odyssey Press, 1965), p. 16. The transference can be traced to II Cor. 3:13-15: "Not as Moses, which put a vail over his face, that the children of Israel could not stedfastly look to the end of that which is abolished: But their minds were blinded: for until this day remaineth the same vail untaken away in the reading of the old testament: which vail is done away in Christ. But even unto this day, when Moses is read, the vail is upon their heart." Paul refers to the veil which Moses put over his face to protect his people from the brightness with which it shone after he had talked with God (Ex. 34:29-33).

The embalming rites with which the King's Daughter cares for the supposed corpse of her Squire suggest that the story owes its origin to a non-Christian source. The disemboweling, bandaging and preserving are like those practised in Ancient Egypt (see Siegfried Morenz, *Egyptian Religion*, trans. Ann E. Keep (Ithaca, N.Y.: Cornell University Press, 1960), pp. 199-200). The enclosing of the body "in a maser tre" suggests the incident in the Osiris legend where the coffer in which the evil Set has enclosed him comes to shore at Byblos, and rests against a tamarisk tree which instantly grows up and encloses coffer, Osiris and all (see E. A. Wallis Budge, *The Book of the Dead* [New York: Dover Publications, 1967], pp. xlix-l).

Evangelist,[11] but it is highly unlikely that it is of so early an origin. It probably antedates Jacobus de Voragine (d. 1298), however, for it is to be found in his *Golden Legend* which, in Caxton's 1483 translation, reads in part, "Some say that S. Mary Magdalene was wedded to S. John the Evangelist when Christ called him from the wedding."[12]

This apocryphal story enjoyed wide currency, for we read in *Mirk's Festial*, "Then, as mony bokys tellyth, when Ion the Ewangelyst schuld haue weddyd her, Cryst bade Ion Sewe hym, and lyf yn maydynhode; and soo he dyd."[13] The *Cursor Mundi*[14] adds another detail, making John and Mary Magdalene the bride and bridegroom of the wedding feast in Cana at which Christ performed His first miracle:

> Than left the bridgrom his bride,
> And folud iesum fra that tide,
> Ne lai he neuer bi hir side,
> Bot left hir and all werldes pride,
> O wijf for-sok he hand-band
> And turnd him to the better hand.

(ll. 13,424-29)

Deprived of her bridegroom by his own choice rather than by death, Mary Magdalene does not linger in her role of mourning bride but turns swiftly to that of harlot, as *The Golden Legend* continues, "and when he was called from her, she had thereof indignation that her husband was taken from her, and went and gave herself to all delight;"[15] or as in *Mirk's Festial*, "Herfore Mary was wrath, and gaf her al to synne and namely to lechery, yn so moch that scho lost the name of Mawdelen, and was callyd the synfull woman."[16]

With less provocation, Duessa has obviously given herself to all sin since she is adorned with jewels, "the which her lavish lovers to her gave," and when she enters the tale we learn that

> With faire disport and courting dalliaunce
> She intertainde her lover all the way.

(*F.Q.* I, ii, 14)

[11] *The Life of Saint Mary Magdalen: Translated from the Italian of an Unknown Fourteenth Century Writer* by Valentina Hawtrey (London and New York: Bodley Head, 1904), p. 2.

[12] *The Golden Legend or Lives of the Saints as Englished by William Caxton*, ed. F. S. Ellis (London: J. M. Dent & Co., 1900), IV, 87.

[13] *Mirk's Festial: A Collection of Homilies, Part I*, ed. Theodor Erbe, EETS, ES 96 (London: K. Paul, Trench, Trübner & Co., 1905), p. 203. Archaic characters have been modernized.

[14] *Cursor Mundi*, ed. R. Morris, EETS OS 62 (London: K. Paul, Trench, Trübner & Co., 1876), p. 770. Archaic characters have been modernized.

[15] *The Golden Legend*, IV, 87.

[16] *Mirk's Festial*, p. 203.

Bennett and Hankins[17] have shown that she and her *alter ego* Lucifera borrow the imagery by which the sinfulness of their lives is presented from the whore of Babylon in the Book of Revelation. They owe to "the woman . . . arrayed in purple and scarlet colour and decked with gold and precious stones and pearls" (Rev. 17:4) their purple and scarlet clothing and their gems (*F.Q.* I, ii, 13 and iv, 8). Lucifera inherits her coach, Hankins suggests, from the scarlet beast on which the whore rides (Rev. 17:3), which had been previously converted by Dante into the coach of the Church in which a harlot, rather than a more suitable figure, rides.[18]

However, if Spenser has made liberal use of the whore of Babylon, the author of *The Squyr* has drawn still more lavishly upon her characteristics in devising the pleasures which the King of Hungary offers his Daughter in an effort to entice her to take up again her former demeanour as "the meriest in chamber comyng" (716). She shall, he offers, ride "in a chare, / It shalbe covered with veluet reede" (ll. 740-41). She shall, if she wishes, have

> . . . clothes of fyne golde al about your hed,
> With damaske, white and asure blewe,
> Wel dyapred with lyllyes newe;
> Your pomelles shalbe ended with gold,
> Your chaynes enameled many a folde;
> Your mantel of ryche degre,
> Purpyl palle and armyne fre.

(ll. 742-48)

Like the whore of Babylon over whose fall the merchants weep and mourn (Rev. 18:11), she shall have gold, silver, precious stones and pearls, fine linen, purple silk and scarlet (see ll. 783-86 and 835-44). Like Babylon's, too, her appetite and her nostrils shall be delighted by spices, good and fine (ll. 825-28 and 846-49). The finest of foods shall be accompanied by wines imported from many lands (ll. 753-64) such as the merchants provided for Babylon (Rev. 18:13). She shall ride Jennettes of Spayne (l. 749), medieval equivalents of the horses that the merchants sell to Babylon (Rev. 18:13). The voice of the harpers, musicians and pipers which will be silenced when Babylon falls (Rev. 18:22) shall sound in the ears of the King's Daughter if she will only agree that it will give her pleasure (l. 813 and possibly ll. 778-80, 789-92, 851-52).

Thus the King offers his Daughter the luxuries of a harlot such as Spenser provides for Duessa and Lucifera, luxuries which they accept

[17] Josephine Waters Bennett, *The Evolution of "The Faerie Queene"* (Chicago: University of Chicago Press, 1942), pp. 108-23; and John E. Hankins, "Spenser and the Revelation of St. John," *PMLA* 60 (1945), 364-81.

[18] Hankins, "Spenser and the Revelation of St. John," p. 368.

but she refuses. The King even offers her the opportunity to play the harlot literally (if mildly), volunteering to ennoble any man of poor fame, or to purchase any man of exalted rank whom she has a mind to wed (ll. 725-32), and promising she shall be wedded to a king (l. 976), presumably that she may conform to the pattern established by Babylon with whom "the kings of the earth have committed fornication" (Rev. 18:3). Technically, since the Princess and the Squire have not actually been married, and in any case the Squire is to all appearance dead, the laws of both church and state would permit the widow to re-marry. However, in keeping with the allegorical significance of the two characters, the virgin widow would be committing adultery if she were to slacken in her devotion to her lost love and enter into a second marriage.

The false picture Duessa draws of herself represents a choice she had when her "dearest Lord" was slain. She might have chosen the role of virgin widow as she claims she has. Instead she rides proudly, and if she is not actually crowned, her mitre is garnished with crowns. Lucifera, also borrowing from the whore of Babylon,

> ... made her selfe a queene, and crownd to be;
> Yet rightfull kingdome she had none at all,
> Ne heritage of native soveraintie,
> But did usurpe with wrong and tyrannie
> Upon the scepter, which she now did hold.

(F.Q. I, iv, 12)

That is, like the whore of Babylon, she says in her heart, "I sit a queen, and am no widow, and shall see no sorrow" (Rev. 18:7). For this Fidessa's appearance can provide no correcting exemplum and we must turn to Una for one. The latter might legitimately have claimed the right to ride with pomp and assurance since she is descended from kings and queens "that had of yore / Their scepters stretcht from east to westerne shore" (*F.Q.* I, i, 5). Instead she rode

> Upon a lowly asse more white then snow,
> Yet she much whiter, but the same did hide
> Under a vele, that wimpled was full low
> And over all a blacke stole shee did throw:
> As one that inly mournd, so was she sad,
> And heavie sate upon her palfrey slow:
> Seemed in heart some hidden care she had.

(F.Q. I, i, 4)

Recognizing the correct model for her behaviour in the "negative" of Babylon's self-assertion, she says in her heart, "I sit as a widow and am no queen." So, too, does the King's Daughter who devotes herself to mourning rites over the body she believes to be that of the Squire and, as her father comments, wears clothes of black (l. 723).

The quality of Una's grief will have to be considered more closely later because it does not conform to the pattern for a mourning bride which makes her capacity to be mistaken on a point of great importance the cause of her distress. Fidessa does not know that the body of her "dearest Lord" has not been conveyed and hidden from her but is alive again. The Princess must rely on externals to distinguish the surly Steward from her Squire. However, the author of *The Squyr of Lowe Degre* is a good deal more explicit about the nature of the malady that separates the King's Daughter from her true love, as it separates her and all men from Christ. To elaborate this point he patterns her choices on two figures who may be regarded as sub-types of the virgin widow and the harlot, namely the Bride of the Song of Solomon and the Church of the Laodiceans (Rev. 3:14-21).

In his dire struggle with his foes outside the King's Daughter's chamber, the Squire cries out to her in words that become a refrain, "Undo thy dore!" (Repeated with variations, ll. 534, 539, 541, 545). This refrain was so important, either to the author or to the early editors, that, as has been pointed out by others, [19] it appears as the title for the romance in the Wynkyn de Worde fragments and as an alternative title in the *explicit* of the Copeland text. [20]

It is possible that, with these words, the poet was making an allusion to a fourteenth-century poem found in the Commonplace Book of John Grimestone (d. 1372), or if not quoting it, was alluding to the same verse of scripture it uses for its opening. It is the poem to which Carleton Brown has given the title *Ecce sto ad hostium et pulso* (Rev. 3:20), a portion of the reproach of Christ to the lukewarm Church of the Laodiceans. In this lyric the poet has combined the tardiness of the heart in responding to Christ's knock with the notion of the soul as the bride of Christ and has related the two themes to his cruel suffering. The poem opens with the appeal:

> Vndo thi dore, my spuse dere,
> Allas! wy stond i loken out here?
> Fre am I thi make.
>
> Loke mi lokkes & ek myn heued
> & al my bodi with blod be-weued
> For thi sake. [21]

[19] Mead, *The Squyr of Lowe Degre*, p. 71, n. 534; Laura A. Hibbard, *Mediaeval Romance in England: A Study of the Sources and Analogues of the Non-Cyclic Metrical Romances* (New York: Oxford University Press, 1924), p. 264; K. S. Kiernan, "Undo Your Door" and the Order of Chivalry," *SP* 70 (1973), 345. As will be obvious, I disagree entirely with Kiernan's suggestion that the author intended *The Squyr* to be a burlesque of the romance genre. The stress which he notes hero and heroine place on money and property seems to me to be there for quite other purposes.

[20] Mead, *The Squyr of Lowe Degre*, pp. xi, 2 and 46.

[21] *Religious Lyrics of the XIVth Century*, ed. Carleton Brown, 2nd ed., rev. G. V.

In response the sinner recognizes,

> Allas! allas! heuel haue i sped,
> For senne iesu is fro me fled,
> Mi trewe fere.
>
> With-outen my gate he stant alone,
> Sorfuliche he maket his mone
> On his manere.

Like this sinner whose love for his Lord is not strong enough to cause him to throw open his heart to admit Him, the King's Daughter delays opening the door to her beloved Squire. At first she fails to recognize that the man outside her door is her Squire. Even when reassured on this point she delays, and later admits with regret,

> "Alas, . . . and weale away!
> For all to long now have I lay."
> (*Squyr*, ll. 675-76)

However, the passage, "Behold I stand at the door, and knock: if any man hear my voice, and open the door, I will come in to him" (Rev. 3:20) is reminiscent of another voice that knocks at a door, that of the bridegroom in the Song of Solomon. There the beloved, having heard the knocking voice, stops to worry about material matters until her lover is from her fled:

> I have put off my coat; how shall I put it on? I have washed my feet; how shall I defile them? My beloved put in his hand by the hole of the door, and my bowels were moved for him. I rose up to open to my beloved; and my hands dropped with myrrh, and my fingers with sweet smelling myrrh, upon the handles of the lock. I opened to my beloved; but my beloved had withdrawn himself, and was gone: my soul failed when he spake: I sought him, but I could not find him; I called him, but he gave me no answer. (S. of S. 5:3-6)

Having failed to respond promptly because of her concern for mundane matters, the Bride must endure the rough treatment of the keepers of the city, and must undertake a weary search for her beloved. This, although her delay was only momentary. The Church of the Laodiceans, on the other hand, has not ceased to delay as the words addressed to it by the "Amen" show:

> I know thy works, that thou art neither cold nor hot: I would thou wert cold or hot. So then because thou art lukewarm, and neither cold not hot, I will spue thee out of my mouth. Because thou sayest, I am rich, and increased with goods, and have need of nothing; and knowest not that thou art wretched, and miserable, and poor, and blind, and naked: I counsel thee to buy of me gold tried in the fire,

Smithers (Oxford: Clarendon Press, 1965), p. 86. Archaic characters have been modernized.

that thou mayest be rich; and white raiment, that thou mayest be clothed, and that the shame of thy nakedness do not appear; and anoint thine eyes with eye-salve, that thou mayest see. As many as I love, I rebuke and chasten: be zealous therefore, and repent. Behold, I stand at the door, and knock: if any man hear my voice, and open the door, I will come in to him, and will sup with him, and he with me. To him that overcometh will I grant to sit with me in my throne, even as I also overcame, and am set down with my Father in his throne. (Rev. 3:15-21)

In its trust in material wealth and in its own powers, the lukewarm Church of the Laodiceans is not very different from the outright harlotry of the whore of Babylon, and the speech of the Princess as she delays opening the door to the Squire reflects many of the same attitudes. She has not correctly understood her Father's character and as a result fears the consequences (for the Squire, to be sure) if he asks for her hand. She is, after all, "the kynges doughter of Hungre" (l. 579). He must earn a higher rank, but in her worldly wisdom she sees that this presents difficulties:

> I wote well it is lyghtly sayd,
> 'Go forth, and be nothyng afrayde.'
> A man of worshyp may not do so,
> He must have what neds him unto;
> He must have gold, he must have fe,
> Strength of men and royalte.
> (*Squyr*, ll. 595-600)

Unaware that the King has already equipped her Squire, she proffers him gold and fee as one who says, "I am rich and increased in goods, . . . and know[s] not that [she] is . . . poor." Although her concern is for the Squire rather than for herself, she trusts in worldly wealth rather than in the gold tried in the fire, wealth she will "buy" through her later suffering. When she sees the disguised corpse on her doorsill her eyes are so blinded by material considerations that she is unable to perceive the deception.[22] Hence, too, her father who loves her permits her to be chastened by grief until she has overcome this dependence on external appearances.[23] The completion of this change in her is signalled when the corpse she has cherished so lovingly for seven years has fallen into powder small, and she can no longer hold it (ll. 930-32).

The possibility that she would reform was suggested in the scene in which she delays opening the door, and was forced on our notice by the

---

[22] This does not contradict the previously suggested interpretation that the unrecognizable face represents the Princess's own marred identity because it is reliance on material wealth that inhibits her true identity from being realized.

[23] The King plays, of course, the role of God, and so the chastening he allows the Princess to undergo is evidence of his love rather than behaviour hard to reconcile with it as Mead (p. lxxx) and Hibbard (p. 264) think it.

contradiction involved. Although she throws a "mantell of gold" about
her on hearing the disturbance, when she opens the door some one
hundred lines later, she is "also naked as she was borne" (l. 673). Her
initial reaction signifies that she is more conscious of physical than of
spiritual nakedness, but her condition when she finally flings open the
door reflects both her concern for her beloved and a shift in her values.
Anxious about the Squire, she has forgotten propriety. The golden
mantle, symbolic of material wealth, has fallen from her as she recognizes true wealth, the life of her beloved.

 This marks a real change in the King's Daughter for, although she
now has no desire to console herself with the luxuries her Father can
provide, there was a time when she flirted with other ways of life than
the austere one she adopts following the "death" of her Squire. The
King contrasts her present mourning "cheer" with her previous way of
life in words that call to mind the luxuries enjoyed by Babylon:

> Ye ware both golde and good veluet,
> Clothe of damaske with saphyres set;
> Ye ware the pery on your head,
> With stones full oryent, whyte and read;
> Ye ware coronalles of golde,
> With diamoundes set many a foulde.
>
> (*Squyr*, ll. 717-22)

At that time the Squire feared to court her because "Ye are so ryche in
youre aray" (l. 119) and was ready to journey to a remote land and
become a hermit there for her sake (ll. 135-42). As her seven years of
mourning draw to a close, the King overhears his daughter bid farewell
to all luxuries and resolve to take "the mantell and the rynge, / And
become an ancresse in my lyvynge" (ll. 954-55). Her love has now
matched the Squire's love for her.

 It seems that she was, like the Church of the Laodiceans, lukewarm
in her devotion to the Squire. Her window is closed and carefully
secured:

> Every wyndowe by and by,
> On eche syde had there a gynne,
> Sperde with many a dyvers pynne.
>
> (*Squyr*, ll. 96-97)

At the sound of the Squire's love complaint,

> Anone that lady, fayre and fre,
> Undyd a pynne of yvere,
> And wyd the windowes she open set,
> The sunne shone in at her closet.
>
> (*Squyr*, ll. 99-102)

She will undo the window, but not the door, and she proceeds to play
hard to get when the Squire tells her openly of his love. She begins her
relationship with the Squire with a St. Peter-like avowal,

> Though I for thee should be slayne
> Squyer, I shall the love agayne.
> (*Squyr*, ll. 153-54)[24]

However, she then stipulates that, if he is to win her love, "with chyvalry [he] must begynne" (l. 172) and must continue in it for seven years. For the Squire these demands are good because it would never do if he who has the capacity to become a king should remain a "gentleman usher." Nevertheless, because she is not ready to abandon her high position for him, the Princess does not know the true depths of her love. Only when events have shown her that the Squire has already won her love, and that nothing else will satisfy her, is she ready to receive him as her bridegroom.

By thus exploiting the features which the Church of the Laodiceans and the whore of Babylon have in common, and the motif of the unanswered door which the Laodiceans share with the Bride of the Song of Solomon, the author of *The Squyr* is able to change the static figures of the harlot and the mourning bride into a character capable of development.

In a sense, of course, the harlot and the mourning bride are themselves developments. Una and Duessa began life under circumstances that bore a marked resemblance to one another. Una is the daughter.

> Of ancient kinges and queenes, that had of yore
> Their scepters stretcht from east to westerne shore,
> And all the world in their subjection held,
> (*F.Q.* I, i, 5)

and we may reasonably infer that Duessa, too, has the same august ancestry and that it is part of her malady that she prefers to call herself the daughter of a mere emperor of the west and is too proud to claim her true inheritance by acknowledging herself the daughter of Adam and Eve. There is even the suggestion that Fidessa did for a time exist and that it was not until she was overtaken by faithlessness (Sansfoy) that her resemblance to Una ceased and she turned from mourning bride to harlot.

Gregory[25] and the fifteenth-century writer Osbern Bokenham[26] (no doubt in imitation of Gregory) attribute to Mary Magdalene the most excellent of all good works, perseverance, and consider that it was because she remained at the tomb seeking that the Magdalene should have had the special grace of seeing the risen Lord first.[27] In the same

---

[24] The allusion seems to be to Matt. 26:35, "Though I should die with thee, yet will I not deny thee."

[25] *P.L.*, 76, 1189.

[26] Osbern Bokenham, *Legends of Hooly Wummen*, ed. Mary S. Serjeantson, EETS OS 206 (London: Oxford University Press, 1938), p. 156.

[27] Ibid.

way, Una, although she rides as one that inly mourns, rides to find a knight errant to free her parents from the dragon that has dispossessed them, and to find him a second time when he has deserted her. Her mourning manner is like that of Speranza who "not all so chearefull seemed" as her sister Fidelia, though the cause of her melancholy is not altogether clear (*F.Q.* I, x, 14).

The mourning bride must, it seems, be aware that she has no apparent grounds for hope, yet she must not despair for in despairing she becomes the harlot. It is in fulfillment of this requirement that the King's Daughter seemingly unaccountably waits out seven years of grief before resolving to become an anchoress. Though a desire for symmetry may have dictated that both the Princess and the Squire should serve a Jacob-like seven years for each other, the Princess's delay in defiance of logic is required to give her the attribute which makes her like Una rather than like Fidessa. She mourns the death of her beloved, yet she fulfills the promise she had given him to wait his return for seven years. She has no reason to hope, yet she behaves as though she had.

Finally, it should be noted that both poets conform to the Revelation pattern (5:8-9, 14:3-4, 19:7-17) in bringing back music and revelry for the marriage at the end. Una throws away her "widow-like sad wimple" (*F.Q.* I, xii, 22) and, after the Archimago interruption, the assembled multitude celebrates her betrothal to the Red Cross Knight with wine, incense, music and feasting. Similarly, when, by her rejection of all the luxuries he has offered her as consolation, the King is satisfied that there is no truer lover than his Daughter, he brings forth the Squire with all kinds of music (ll. 1063-79) and summons all the neighbouring chivalry to a wedding celebration that, "with myrth and game and muche playe" (l. 1107), lasts for forty days. Once the couple do not put them first, the pleasures of life may safely be enjoyed.

Through this examination of the tradition of the harlot and the mourning bride, we have found, I think, that the románce writers worked, as did the Old English poets, in units larger than words. Although words were chosen with considerable precision, the significance of the choice is only apparent to the reader who is familiar with the traditional use of the larger features and so can appreciate the variations an author is making in relating and combining them, or in evoking the archetypes. These authors, it seems, created their works out of conventional platelets, prefabricated through centuries of use until they had become the surest means of directing the reader's attention away from the illusion of merely surface reality to the inner reality of everyday life. To complain that in such a work character and plot are not convincing, or that speeches do not engage the reader in the emotions of the speakers[28] is like complaining that a mosaic lacks interesting brush

---

[28] As does, for example, Lillian Herlands Hornstein, "Miscellaneous Romances," *A*

strokes. The character as a person does not exist; the incident is not taking place. The illusion, therefore, of characters and actions must be kept transparent if the reader is to see what the opaqueness of external reality hides.

If the plot were believable readers might think that the outcome was the purpose of the work. If the characters developed convincingly, they might think that the author's intention was to introduce them to these people and to tell the story of their lives. His purpose is, rather, to set up a model of internal reality and by externalizing it to draw to his readers' attention realities which daily life tends to hide.

The stylized speeches are not exchanged by the characters and overheard by the reader, but addressed frankly to the reader who must respond to the implications of the speeches with an understanding made precise by a recognition of an archetypal situation.

Because the archetype already existed in the reader's mind, the writer had only to present his material with a sufficiently unnatural surface to provoke a recognition that he was defining the spiritual condition of his characters in traditional terms. Far from desiring to provide an "escape from reality or an idealization of it,"[29] the romance writer was bluntly calling a spade a spade. What the minutiae of daily life might obscure, the conventions of romance revealed in all its startling improbability. The reader was not expected to identify with hero or heroine but to recognize in their blunders and follies his own way of life presented in a different key. This the author of *The Squyr of Lowe Degre* does when, under the image of a girl who chatters on while her boy friend is being killed, he pictures Everyman's daily sacrifice of his deepest convictions to comfort, expediency or petty advantage.

A later appearance of the harlot and the mourning bride will remind us that, when applied to fact rather than to fiction, the clear signals of romance cannot be trusted nearly as implicitly. The two figures come together again in Donne's "Show me, dear Christ, Thy spouse so bright and clear." Romance permits an author to draw his characters in a way that makes their moral status quickly identifiable by the reader. Duessa is in disguise when we meet her and shows nothing of the ugly old hag revealed later. Yet from the outset the reader has no doubt that her arrival spells trouble for the Red Cross Knight. Her resemblance to the whore of Babylon makes clear to the reader all that is hidden from the Knight. Donne, however, is concerned, not with the characters in a story, but with the characteristics of institutions as they are encountered in life. Therefore, outward appearance is less helpful. The "She, which on

Manual of the Writings in Middle English, 1050-1500, gen. ed. J. Burke Severs (New Haven: Connecticut Academy of Arts and Sciences, 1967), I, 157.

[29] Margaret Schlauch, *English Medieval Literature and its Social Foundations* (Warsaw, 1956), p. 191.

the other shore / Goes richly painted''[30] is not thereby ruled out as the real bride of Christ. Nor does the fact that the other ''rob'd and tore / Laments and mournes in Germany and here'' identify her as the true spouse. One thing alone betrays the true Bride and that is that she plays the harlot. Christ's ''mild Dove''

> . . . is most trew, and pleasing to thee, then
> When she is embrac'd and open to most men.

[30] *The Poems of John Donne,* ed. Herbert J. C. Grierson, 2 vols. (Oxford: Clarendon Press, 1912, rpt. 1966), I, 330.

"Restlesse anguish and unquiet paine": Spenser and the Complaint, 1579-1590

HUGH MACLEAN

I

That Spenser was from the outset of his career much attracted to the genre of complaint is clear enough. The poet's wide-ranging employment of that genre in his earlier poetry has been remarked by many critics; and virtually every study of *The Faerie Queene* has at least paused over one or another of the numerous plaints and laments that occur throughout the great poem.[1] No critic, however, so far as I am aware, has undertaken to explore Spenser's employment of complaint in the earlier poetry and also in the first three Books of *The Faerie Queene*, with a view to demonstrating the poet's developing control of the genre.

[1] For the purposes of this article, the work of such scholars as, e.g., Harold Stein, *Studies in Spenser's Complaints* (New York, 1934), W. L. Renwick, ed., *Complaints* (New York, 1928), and William Nelson, *The Poetry of Edmund Spenser* (New York, 1963) on Spenser's earlier poetry is collectively less to the immediate point than are the remarks on pastoral and love complaint made by Hallett Smith, *Elizabethan Poetry* (Cambridge, Mass., 1952), pp. 19-23, 103-26; see also Smith's essay, "The Use of Conventions in Spenser's Minor Poems," in *Form and Convention in the Poetry of Edmund Spenser*, ed. William Nelson (New York, 1961), pp. 122-45. Among studies of *The Faerie Queene* that allow the complaints in the poem more than a glance, the following are especially incisive: Thomas P. Roche, Jr., *The Kindly Flame: A Study of the Third and Fourth Books of Spenser's Faerie Queene* (Princeton, N.J., 1964); Kathleen Williams, *Spenser's World of Glass: A Reading of The Faerie Queene* (Berkeley, California, 1966); Paul Alpers, *The Poetry of The Faerie Queene* (Princeton, N.J., 1967); Roger Sale, *Reading Spenser: An Introduction to The Faerie Queene* (New York, 1968); Rosemary Freeman, *The Faerie Queene: A Companion for Readers* (London, 1970); and Isabel G. MacCaffrey, *Spenser's Allegory: The Anatomy of Imagination* (Princeton, N.J., 1976). J. S. Weld's article, "The Complaint of Britomart," *PMLA* 66 (1951), 548-51, remains a uniquely valuable essay. Citations from Spenser's works in the present essay refer to *The Works of Edmund Spenser, A Variorum Edition*, ed. E. Greenlaw, C. G. Osgood, F. H. Padelford, et al., 9 vols. (Baltimore, Md., 1932-1949).

That is not very surprising, of course, given the difficulty of assigning precise dates to poems in the *Complaints* volume or to the materials that make up Books I-III of Spenser's epic; not to mention the great variety of plaintive passages that must be taken into account by a truly definitive study. Yet, as Touchstone says, "one must adventure." If that larger study is still to seek, the present essay will suggest, in a preliminary way, that Spenser's use of the complaint in the period 1579-1590 reflects his awakening recognition of the functionally sophisticated role that complaint might play in larger poetic structures, effectively culminating in Book III of *The Faerie Queene*, with the complaints of Britomart (iv. 8-10), Cymoent (iv. 36-39), Arthur (iv. 55-60), Timias (v. 45-47), and Scudamour (xi. 9-11).

It may be noted that in this essay the term "complaint" refers not merely to "a sub-category of reprobative literature during the Middle Ages and the Renaissance," but generally to plaintive poems, or plaintive passages within larger poems, expressing grief or lamentation for any of a variety of causes: unrequited love, the speaker's affairs, or the sorrows of the human condition. As Smith observes, "a revival of the complaint form, with new emphasis and character, took place late in the [sixteenth] century, . . . the *Mirror* tradition has interesting connections with the pastoral convention, with the Petrarchan love tradition, and with Ovidian-mythological poetry."[2] And it is in terms of this extended context that Spenser's use of complaint has particular interest for the student of his art.

To speak generally, it appears that in his earliest work, Spenser rather briefly explored the potential of complaint as distinctive entity: a free-standing, relatively lengthy, and formally elaborate lament, conforming as a rule to one or another of the conventional contexts (pastoral, Petrarchan, or "reprobative") that made part of his literary heritage. Yet he was also experimenting with the genre in the minor poems of this period, exploring ways in which plaintive elements might be made variously contributory to larger structures. Even in the *Calender* the individual plaintive eclogues, of course, contribute to a greater totality, taking their place within the framework of idea that informs the whole poem; and the "October" eclogue, though described by "E.K." as "moral," might also be said to reflect the poet's desire to infuse his work with dramatic force by the interplay of plaintive and (refutative) moral elements. *Mother Hubberds Tale* and *Muiopotmos* also, generically satiric and mock-heroic rather than plaintive, incorporate relatively

---

[2] Smith, *Elizabethan Poetry*, p. 103. The definitive study of "complaint" in its narrower, "reprobative," sense is that by John Peter, *Complaint and Satire in Early English Literature* (Oxford, 1956). See also *The Princeton Encyclopedia of Poetry and Poetics*, ed. Alex Preminger, F. J. Warnke and O. B. Hardison, Jr. (Princeton, N.J., 1965), "Complaint," p. 148.

brief plaintive elements that are more or less successfully combined with the total pattern of each poem. And, if *Daphnaida* is "not the happiest of [Spenser's] experiments," one can agree with Nelson that "Spenser strove hard to vary the traditional form [of pastoral elegy]," while noting too that the purpose of this "sevenfold passion of luxuriant rhetoric" was to intensify the element of complaint by raising it to a higher power.[3] Finally, the first three Books of *The Faerie Queene* contain a great variety of plaintive elements; but if Spenser is still in some degree concerned to demonstrate his command of the complaint as elaborately distinctive entity, he is much more interested in its potential for the illumination of character and (especially) informing idea. And the complaints in Book III—taking into account their placement, structure, and imagery—epitomize the supple control of the genre that Spenser, over ten years of wide-ranging experiment in this kind, at length achieved.

By the time Spenser published the *Calender,* the literary complaint had become the focus of a rich and varied tradition, developed most elaborately in Italy and France (and, for English poetry, by Chaucer), while everywhere recalling the pervasive influence of classical models, particularly Ovid. Looking about, Spenser might choose among a considerable range of context, occasion, and form.[4] The poet's interest in complaint might, for instance, be expressed in the context of pastoral romance (lamenting a lost Golden Age, or the consequences of the Judgment of Paris); or in that of the *dits amoureux* (on the model of Machaut's *Dit de la Fonteinne amoreuse,* or its Chaucerian derivative, *The Book of the Duchess*); or in the related context of Petrarchanism (with its substantively Neoplatonic and formally Ovidian overtones); or in that of the literature centring on the Fall of Princes (e.g., *A Mirror for Magistrates,* especially the lament of "Shore's wife" composed by Churchyard).[5]

The complaint might usually be occasioned by the unresponsiveness of a mistress, to whom the lover vainly appeals for relief. But the poet's unhappy state might equally occasion complaints addressed to a higher power (as in Chaucer's "Complaint unto Pity"), or poems that, initially plaintive, find relief in the acceptance of disenchantment itself (e.g., Wyatt's "Farewell, love, and all thy laws for ever"). Or a complaint might lament the poet's low estate or evil circumstance, indepen-

---

[3] Nelson, *Poetry of Edmund Spenser,* p. 69.

[4] The views expressed in this and the following paragraph reflect my considerable debt to James Wimsatt, *Chaucer and the French Love Poets: the Literary Background of the Book of the Duchess* (New York, 1972), and to Rossell Hope Robbins, "The Structure of Longer Middle English Court Poems," forthcoming. Professor Robbins' essay was originally read at English 2 ("Middle English"), on 29 December, 1972, at the meeting of the Modern Language Association in New York City, and later expanded into its present form.

[5] Cf. Smith, *Elizabethan Poetry,* pp. 19-23, 102-03.

dently of his fortune in love: Chaucer's "Complaint to his Purse" provides a light instance of the kind. And yet again, the poet (or a character in his poem), initially stirred to complaint by the hard heart of a mistress or by the buffetings of fortune, might press past lament to question those higher forces presumed to control his world: justice, destiny, Providence itself—as Troilus, "fallen in despeir," plunges into that thickety meditation on free will, necessity, and divine prescience.

Finally, with regard to form and structure, several alternative possibilities were available to the poet anxious to display his command of the genre. A complaint, evidently, might stand by itself; but from an early date, French poets in particular had combined complaint with larger narrative in various ways. As Robbins observes, "the majority of the *dits amoureux* or long love ditties are structured about a complaint"; he instances the *Supplicacio Amantis, The Temple of Glas,* and *The Assembly of Ladies*. The *Temple of Glas*, in particular, "introduces quasi-narrative themes and digressions to turn what promises to be a simple extended dramatic complaint into a *dit amoureux* of promised fulfillment."[6] Again, complaints might be incorporated into a narrative: whether the rhyme-scheme of these complaints differed from that of the larger poem (as in Chaucer's *Book of the Duchess*), or conformed to it (as in the *Roman de la Rose*), the relationship of complaints to narrative was by no means everywhere identical. Complaints might serve as decorative punctuation within a narrative considered by the poet to be of primary importance (as, generally, in de Lorris' portion of the *Roman de la Rose*); conversely, decorative complaints might themselves be of greater interest to the poet than the narrative containing them (as in *The Flower of Courtesy* and *The Complaint of the Black Knight*).[7] Or the complaint might be employed as a functional, perhaps even a motivating, force in the narrative. Wimsatt instances "the complaint of Amant ... near the beginning of Jean de Meun's continuation [of the *Roman de la Rose*] (ll. 4059-4220), for there the lament calls forth Raison to answer at considerable length."[8] He draws attention also to "the complaint-and-comfort plot of Machaut's *Remede de Fortune*," which "dominates and unifies the work."[9] However that may be, it is clear enough that the complaints in Chaucer's *Troilus and Criseyde* are often dramatic, and that at the very least they "heighten the narrative."[10] In fact, they are essential elements in the larger narrative and thematic patterns that inform Chaucer's poem.

For the special purposes of this paper, Chaucer's extensive use of complaint, especially in its formal aspects, is of much interest. The

[6] Robbins, "Structure."
[7] Wimsatt, *Chaucer and the French Love Poets*, p. 105; Robbins, "Structure."
[8] Wimsatt, *Chaucer and the French Love Poets*, p. 108.
[9] Ibid.
[10] Robbins, "Structure."

initial attraction of the lover's complaint as independent poem (evidenced by the presumably early "Complaint unto Pity" and "Complaint to his Lady") did not last; only the curious "Complaint of Venus" (not properly a complaint at all) otherwise exemplifies this kind before the frankly parodic "Complaint to his Purse" of 1399—for the "Complaint of Mars" combines complaint proper with a larger narrative element to which the complaint refers. As early as 1368-1370, in *The Book of the Duchess*, Chaucer is combining independently-rhymed eleven-line "complaynte" (ll. 475-486) and extended lament, integrated into the couplets (ll. 560-709), within the containing structure of his poem. To be sure, it appears that the greater number of the independent tragedies later used for the Monk's Tale were composed in the "transitional" period of 1372-1380; still, to "biwaille, in manere of tragedie, / The harm of hem that stoode in heigh degree, / And fillen so that ther nas no remedie / To brynge hem out of hir adversitee . . . ," is to abandon the contexts and occasions of lovers' complaints in favour of those appropriate to verse lamenting the Fall of Princes. In any event, these "tragedies" were, after all, reserved for the larger framework of the *Tales*. As for plaintive elements in other poems of these years, the complaint that centres and dominates *Anelida and Arcite* is certainly more elaborately complex than any of Chaucer's earlier efforts in this vein; yet a narrative structure, however "ill-developed," does contain the lyric, and it is arguable that the poet intended to continue and complete the poem with "the passage of the Teseida which at another time he made the basis of the description of the temple in the *Palemon and Arcite*."[11] Then, too, as Shannon observes, this complaint (unlike conventionally stereotyped examples of the genre) "is based upon a distinctive situation, and is full of a spirit of reality and genuine feeling which places it quite outside this type."[12]

Dido's "compleynt" in *The House of Fame* (ll. 300-10, 315-59) is of special interest. Chaucer explicitly directs the reader to "Virgile in Eneydos / Or the Epistle of Ovyde" (378-79) as his chief sources for Dido's history; and if her plea in Chaucer's poem "has no exact parallel in the *Aeneid*," it remains true that "most of the circumstances are from Virgil," while "Chaucer's conception of the character and spirit of Dido had evidently already been formed from the *Heroides* [vii]."[13] Having indulged in "some reflections on the folly of women in trusting to the goodly appearance and fair words of men,"[14] Chaucer assigns primary stress in the first part of Dido's lament (ll. 300-44) to her passionate

---

[11] *The Works of Geoffrey Chaucer*, ed. F. N. Robinson, 2nd ed. (Boston, 1957), p. 303.

[12] Edgar F. Shannon, *Chaucer and the Roman Poets* (Cambridge, Mass., 1929), p. 29.

[13] Robinson, *Works*, p. 781; Shannon, *Chaucer and the Roman Poets*, pp. 57, 59.

[14] Shannon, *Chaucer and the Roman Poets*, p. 56.

distress in sharing the universal plight of "wrechched wymmen" deceived by their lovers. This essentially Ovidian note continues to sound in the last fifteen lines of the complaint, but the context is effectively altered by the Vergilian apostrophe to Fame that (glancing back to ll. 305-06) centres the concluding section:

> O wikke Fame! for ther nys
> Nothing so swift, lo, as she is!
> O, soth ys, every thing ys wyst,
> Though hit be kevered with the myst.
>
> (349-52)

In short, Chaucer manages his plaintive materials so as to illustrate and dramatically heighten his immediate narrative concern (Dido's passionate response to her lover's unfaithfulness); but the complaint draws attention also to the poignant bearing of a natural and universal principle on the experience and knowledge of individual men and women.

To turn to *Troilus and Criseyde* is to observe the full range of Chaucer's mastery. Given that the greater number of these plaintive passages look to *Il Filostrato* for their placement and expression, it was Chaucer, after all, in whom Spenser took special delight:

> . . . through infusion sweete
> Of thine owne spirit, which doth in me survive,
> I follow here the footing of thy feete. . . .
>
> (*F.Q.* IV.ii.34)

Several of the complaints in Chaucer's poem serve chiefly as decorative punctuation of the narrative: one thinks of the Petrarchan "song" and the directly sequent "pitous" appeal to Cupid in Book I (400-20, 422-34), together with the lovers' complaints to night and to the dawn in Book III (1422-42, 1450-70), as well as Troilus' "song" and complaint to the moon in Book V (638-44, 650-58). The "compleynte" in which Criseyde laments her impending departure from Troy (IV. 743-98), and that of "woful Troilus" on the first night after Criseyde's departure (V. 218-45) are in some sense a matched pair in the context of characterization: each mourns for the other, but Chaucer contrives that Criseyde's "heigh compleynte" shall conclude (as the Boccaccian original does not) on a note of sacrifice—"So ye wel fare, I recche naught to deye" (798)—while effectively retaining the pervasive note of self-pity that is dominant in Boccaccio's version of Troilus' "lungo pianto" (*Filostrato*, V. 23). In these laments, mutual self-absorption leaves no room for an appeal to whatever higher powers may control the natural realm; other complaints in the poem, however, find Troilus appealing for relief to Fortune (IV. 260-336), to "blisful lord Cupide" (V. 581-602), and at length to "God . . . that oughtest taken heyde / To furtheren trouthe, and wronges to punyce" (V. 1906-07), whose failure to "don a vengeaunce

of this vice" Troilus questions with the same despair and dismay that
mark the end of this passage:

> But trewely, Criseyde, swete may,
> Whom I have ay with al my myght yserved,
> That ye thus doon, I have it nat deserved.
>
> (1720-22)

Boccaccio provided a source for all these complaints, however
much Chaucer re-pointed their accents and emphases; there remains the
soliloquy on predestination derived from Boethius, inserted at IV.
960-1082. To describe the passage as merely another variety of the
complaint is evidently wrong-headed. Still, Troilus' musings spring
from deep emotional depression: "He was so fallen in despeir that day, /
That outrely he shop hym for to deye" (954-55). As Patch says, the
speech-soliloquy "expresses not Chaucer's moral, but Troilus' emotional reaction, and it is therefore completely relevant."[15] Yet (to quote
Robinson) "at the same time it is to be observed that more than once in
the *Troilus* the reader is made to feel a deep sense of overruling
Destiny."[16] The lines that conclude the passage in question combine
these elements.

> Thanne seyde he thus: "Almyghty Jove in trone,
> That woost of al this thyng the sothfastnesse,
> Rewe on my sorwe, and do me deyen sone,
> Or bryng Criseyde and me fro this destresse!"
>
> (1079-82)

Opening on a note of particularized despair, then, the passage traces
Troilus' extended effort to pierce the veil of enshrouding larger principle; at length the baffled lover leaves it all—the knowledge and (perhaps)
the pity—to God. The shadowy outlines of complaint remain dimly in
presence; but the genre has been transcended. The experience of love,
its joy and its sorrow, impels Troilus to thrust beyond conventional
forms and expressions into the mazy realm of philosophical discourse,
searching out as he can (if "to ben lorn, it is [his] destinee") the role of
human life within the fearful complex of "necessitee" and "divine
purveyaunce."

II

If a measure of obscurity still hangs about the precise chronology of
Chaucer's works, one can at least with some degree of confidence assign
individual poems to generally delimited periods in the poet's career, as,
for example, Robinson so assigns them.[17] With Spenser, the problem of

---

[15] Robinson, *Works*, p. 830; cf. H. R. Patch, "Troilus on Predestination," *JEGP* 17
(1918), 399-423; and "Troilus on Determinism," *Speculum* 6 (1931), 225-43.
[16] Robinson, *Works*, p. 830.
[17] Ibid., p. xxix.

chronology is rather more challenging. While it seems probable that the poet, soon after the publication of the *Calender* in 1579, turned to the task that would chiefly occupy him for the rest of his life—the composition and arrangement of *The Faerie Queene*—one has to recognize that the pieces drawn together for the *Complaints* volume of 1591 effectively represent, not a clearly intermediate stage in Spenser's poetical development, but rather the variety and range of his concern with modes other than pastoral and epic, composed over a period including the *Calender* and some considerable part of the great epic. Further, one cannot of course assume that the final form and substance of Book I necessarily antedate those of Books II and III, or even that the materials comprising later Books do not include elements originally given shape well before 1590. It is therefore not feasible, in this matter of Spenser's use of the complaint, to advance a simplistic argument that the poet's progressively more sophisticated manipulation of the genre closely reflects or matches Chaucer's example; or even to demonstrate that chronology generally determines the scope and reach of Spenser's art in this respect.

What the available evidence does suggest is that Spenser, initially regarding the complaint somewhat as Christmas-tree ornament, a suitable vehicle for elaborately decorative art, soon turned to more challenging modes: the incorporation of complaint within larger structures, notably the more or less sophisticated articulation of plaintive elements within an encompassing framework of idea. The early *Teares of the Muses*,[18] a precisely arranged garland of nine matched laments prefaced by nine introductory stanzas, represents an employment of the genre not typical of other poems in the *Complaints* volume. Structurally, *The Ruines of Time* and *Mother Hubberds Tale* may be faulted on several counts; but each reflects the poet's concern to draw plaintive elements together with other materials so as to enhance dramatic effect (as in *The Ruines of Time*) or heighten the emotive force and immediacy of traditionally-based satire (as in the passage on "suters state" added in 1590 to *Mother Hubberds Tale*), combinedly glancing on to the harmonious achievement of *Daphnaida*. And if no formal "complaint" makes part of *Muiopotmos*, the gloomy reminder in mid-poem that

> ... thousand perills lie in close awaite
> About us daylie, to worke our decay ... ,

together with the acknowledgement of human helplessness in respect of divine will, represents Spenser's most economically telling use in these

---

[18] I follow Dodge, Renwick, and Stirling in preferring to assign the poem to 1579-1580: cf. *Works*, "The Minor Poems," Vol. 2 (Baltimore, Md., 1947), pp. 533-40. But I do not argue that Spenser's progressively developing command of complaint can be precisely and chronologically matched with particular poems in the *Complaints* volume.

minor poems of plaintive materials to illuminate the idea informing a larger narrative structure.

It is only when one turns to the *Calender*, however, that the poet's care for the *combination* of complaint with other elements may properly be described as a concern for structural *articulation*; and, in the context of the minor poems, only here that Spenser's desire to exhibit his wide-ranging control of a literary genre must make room for the awakening recognition that complaint may usefully illuminate character and bring informing idea into high relief. "E. K." 's general encomium, in the "Epistle," of "this our new poete, as a bird . . . that in time shall be hable to keepe wing with the best" is reinforced by the glossator's commendation of Spenser's art and technique, chiefly in the "plaintive" eclogues: "a pretie allegory" ("December"), a "staffe . . . full of verie poetical invention" ("June"), "a prety epanorthosis . . . , and withall a paranomasia or playing with the word" ("January"); not to mention the bold claim, in the Argument to "November," that "this Aeglogue is made in imitation of Marot his song . . . but farre passing his reache. . . ." The young poet, after all, evidently regarded the *Calender* as something of a display case for the spectrum of his talent. That "E. K." should explicitly draw attention to particular facets of Spenser's commanding art was appropriate enough. Yet the plaintive eclogues are, of course, much more than compelling instances of technical expertise. Placed at beginning, middle, and end, they effectively control the structure of the *Calender*; as well, together with their accompanying apparatus, they shed a various light on character and theme. Colin's "carefull case," initially "sore travelled" by a love that breeds "both joy and pain," while it derides and baffles art, goes from bad to worse: by midsummer Colin has renounced "all comfort, and hope of goodnesse to come," and the Argument to "December" introduces a figure quite checked and overwhelmed by a seasonal decay that brings learning, love, and art at last equally to nothing.

> Of all the seede, that in my youth was sowne,
> Was nought but brakes and brambles to be mowne.
>   (101-02)

The position is sufficiently familiar in plaintive tradition, if not many of Spenser's predecessors could match the sensitive variety with which he maintains the account of a dejected shepherd against the cycle of the turning year.

But "November," the most admired of these plaintive pieces, is a complaint with a difference; for the dirge, given all its elaborate craft, is no more than an extended prelude to the joyful stanzas proclaiming Dido's release from death, time, and the natural cycle. To move from these verses and from "E. K." 's account of the Emblem concluding "November" to Colin's despairing complaint, as "he proportioneth his

life to the foure seasons of the yeare," is to recognize how utterly
Colin—together with those "that swincke and sweate for nought, / And
shooting wide, doe misse the marked scope"—has passed by "(as
Chaucer sayth) the grene path way to life." We are invited, in fact,
essentially by virtue of the positioning and consequent interplay of
plaintive elements, to smile gently at this shepherd's woe, and implicitly
also to recognize that Colin is a more substantial and intriguing creation
than the typical sad shepherd of traditional complaint.

Throughout the *Calender*, finally, allusions to Chaucer regularly
appear in close conjunction with the plaintive eclogues. "The name of
Tityrus," in the gloss to "January," must needs recall "E. K."'s
graceful compliment in the "Epistle" to "the olde famous Poete
Chaucer... [that] Loadestarre of our Language"; in the gloss to "June"
and in "E. K."'s commentary on the "November" Emblem, Chaucer
is "the God of Poetes," whose art keeps company with Christian conviction; at last, in the Envoi, his inimitable style is singled out for praise.
Language, style, poetry, and faith: it is as if Spenser calls up the old
artificer's enduring example in the genre of complaint to underscore the
power of an art irradiated by Christian faith to triumph over time. If art
and human love are often, as for Colin, destructively at odds, the most
gifted makers form their poems (complaint or satire, ode or epic) in the
spirit of a higher love that resolves every discordance. Through and past
Colin's blindness, as it were, we see with Spenser "that all thinges
perish and come to theyr last end, but workes of learned wits and
monuments of poetry abide for ever."

III

Spenser's achievement in the *Calender*, then, owes much to the
poet's subtle manipulation of plaintive materials; yet to turn from that
early undertaking to *The Faerie Queene* is (in the context of complaint)
to pass from crystal set to full-colour television. This is not to say that
the picture is all at once or everywhere clear. One has rather the
impression that the rich and various use of plaintive elements in Books I
and II is somewhat experimental, as the poet finds his way toward
effective integration of complaint with larger narrative structures. It
appears that Spenser employs the genre in these first two Books chiefly
in three ways: (a) relatively formal narrative flashback, assigned indifferently to figures central or peripheral, false or true; (b) relatively
informal parody, typically assigned to deceitful characters, but also to
the deluded or misled; (c) rather brief, even fragmentary, but intensely
emotional expressions of perturbation or dismay, assigned to Una and to
Prince Arthur. A prime instance of the first category is Fradubio's
lament (I.ii.31-43); others include the dying Amavia's account of her
"huge misfortune" (II.i.49-56) and the complaint of Phedon, "thral of

wretchednesse" (II.iv.17-33), not to mention "the storie sad" with which Una responds to Arthur's concern for her "cause of griefe" (I.vii.43-51). Examples of the second group are for the most part given to Duessa, notably in the lament with which she enervates the "stout heroicke heart" of Redcrosse (I.ii.22-26); but the exaggeratedly alliterative lament of the false Una, "wringing her hands in wemens pitteous wise," as she beguiles Redcrosse (I.i.51-54), and, in a slightly different way, Amavia's first speech in Book II (xxxvi-xxxvii), also make part of this category. Especially interesting examples of the third variety are the interrupted plaints of Una in I.vii (22-25, 39-42), and Arthur's account of the love that has "mated" him (I.ix.8-15).

It might be argued that these three varieties of complaint respectively reflect Spenser's concern to display his command of the genre as elaborately distinctive entity, to employ complaint in the service of characterization, and to make play with its potential for the illumination of informing idea. But this is too simplistic a reckoning. It is true that the extended lamentations of Fradubio, Amavia, Phedon (and even of Una, in so far as the passage at I.vii.43-51 has its own independent interest, apart from the maiden's conversations with Arthur that introduce and conclude the account of her travail) find Spenser happily laying himself out to elaborate each detail of "set-piece" narrative; also that Duessa's plaints give lively expression to the bland hypocrisy, eager malice, and invincible self-absorption that combinedly define her character. Still, *The Faerie Queene* is an allegorical poem: every character and episode ordinarily shadows forth one or another aspect of the larger idea with which the poet is in a given Book chiefly concerned. In the "Legend . . . of Holinesse," it is appropriate that Fradubio's account should lead at length to that "living well" by which alone his bonds may be dissolved. Just so, in Book II, Guyon establishes the context of Phedon's lament:

> Squire, sore have ye beene diseasd;
> But all your hurts may soone through temperance be easd.
>
> (II.iv.33)

Again, the posturings of Duessa, together with her weakness for the infelicitous phrase, signal her incapacity to comprehend the meaning of holiness. "O but I feare the fickle freakes (quoth 'shee) / Of fortune false"—that Fortune which, she fancies, first reduced her to the status of "virgin widow," then "betraide" her to the power of Redcrosse (I.iv.50; ii.22-24). The "goodly golden chaine" that links virtue and true nobility within the controlling purview of "heavenly grace" Duessa and Night can figure only as "the chayne of strong necessitee, / Which fast is tyde to *Joves* eternall seat" (I.ix.1; viii.1; v.25). Informing idea peers through each kind or level of complaint in these Books.

Yet there is after all a distinction to be made. The longer, "set-piece" complaints invite multilevelled allegorical interpretation, to be sure, but they do not significantly interweave character and idea. By consequence of their narrative emphasis on event, they make their effects, so to speak, extensively rather than intensively. For the most part, a reader derives from them not much sense of the full emotional range that the genre of complaint in its subtler forms can encompass and express. Somewhat similarly, while Duessa's plaints aptly match her nature and intent, they indicate also the limits that forever bound and pervert the outlook of that "wicked witch." The speech of such "flat characters" can never be other than two-dimensional. For Una and Arthur, on the other hand, faith in higher laws is recurrently challenged by doubt; the convictions of Christian humanism are interlaced with agonizing questions, in a way that speaks to all and each of Spenser's readers, taps his and their common experience. The *mixed* character of human nature, one might say, speaks through their plaining expression. Even as Una, glancing wildly at the "cruell fates" that dispart her "life and love," sinks toward despair, she tells a deeper truth in the allusion to "lightsome day, the lampe of highest *Jove*, / First made by him, mens wandring wayes to guyde" (I.vii.22-23): the impact of bitterly heartfelt experience on persistent "intellectual" conviction stirs in the reader an instinctive recognition and response. So too when Arthur appears, fulfilling the earlier hint at vi.7:

> His goodly reason, and well guided speach
> So deepe did settle in her gratious thought,
> That her perswaded to disclose the breach,
> Which love and fortune in her heart had wrought....
>
> (I.vii.42)[19]

And in fact the extended narrative complaint that follows, for all its doleful emphasis, provides some hints of Una's continuing faith:

> Be judge ye heavens, that all things right esteeme,
> How I him lov'd, and love with all my might,
> So thought I eke of him, and thinke I thought aright.
>
> (I.vii.49)

Arthur's account of the "secret wound" that "grieve[s] the gentlest hart on ground" (I.ix.6-16) also reflects a doubt more than merely personal: "Nothing is sure, that growes on earthly ground" (st. 11). But, as his words had revived Una's spirit, on this later occasion it is Una who

---

[19] Cf. Thomas Wilson, *The Arte of Rhetorique* (London, 1553), ed. R. H. Bowers (Gainesville, Florida, 1962): "where as man through reason might have used order, manne throughe follye fell into erroure.... Even nowe when man was thus paste all hope of amendemente, God still tendering his owne workemanship, stirred up his faythfull and elect, to perswade with reason, all men to societye. And gave his appoynted ministers knowledge bothe to se the natures of men, and also graunted them the gift of utteraunce, that they myghte wyth ease wynne folke at their will, and frame theim by reason to all good order" (10).

quietly reminds the Prince, "True Loves are often sown, but seldom grow on ground" (st. 16). Her words recall his own steadfast, if troubled, expression of faith in divine purpose:

> Full hard it is (quoth he) to read aright
> The course of heavenly cause, or understand
> The secret meaning of th'eternall night,
> That rules mens wayes, and rules the thoughts of living wight.
>
> (I.ix.6)[20]

Still, it is true that the particular effectiveness of these plaintive expressions, their "psychological realism," is in some measure dependent on those dramatic exchanges between Una and Arthur that preface, even annotate, the actual complaints themselves. Complaint as such, that is, here takes its place as one (admittedly central) component within a dramatic episode, depending for its full effect on elements extrinsic to complaint proper. Clearly, the subtle interpenetration of diverse materials must always make part of full achieved structural unity. It remains true that the complaints of Una and Arthur are finally effective by virtue of overtly dramatic reinforcement; the autonomy of complaint, so to speak, is not in these instances secure. It is only in Book III that the poet demonstrates a confident command of formal complaints that are virtually self-contained, matching decorative figure to psychological insight and care for larger idea within an organically disciplined structure.

IV

Critical response to the formal complaints of Britomart, Cymoent, Arthur, Timias, and Scudamour, in Book III of *The Faerie Queene*, is remarkably disparate in character. Understandably, scholars of the poem are apt to single out for attention those two or three complaints that reflect each individual's critical position, and to ignore or quickly dismiss other complaints in Book III. Still, the variety of response to these passages is remarkable. Only one scholar, so far as I am aware, has even briefly considered the five complaints as a related group. More typically, one encounters such contrasting views as (for example) those of Rosemary Freeman and Isabel MacCaffrey on the complaints of Britomart and Arthur. To Freeman, Britomart's complaint "creates little emotional effect because it depends too obviously upon well-worn analogies"; the two laments "possess slight poetic merit—all they do is to hold up the narrative while the feelings of the thinker are expressed."[21] But for MacCaffrey, if Britomart employs "one of the

---

[20] See also II.ii.1-11: Guyon, at first "right hard amated" by the apparently remediless misery of human life, eventually (having "harkned to his reason") perceives that Ruddymane's bloody hand is in fact "a sacred symbole . . . for all chaste dames an endlesse moniment").

[21] Freeman, *The Faerie Queene: A Companion for Readers*, pp. 195-96.

hoariest images of Elizabethan love poetry," she is nevertheless "observing her own emotions and objectifying them": the complaint "shows a degree of self-knowledge in the heroine."[22] This critic notices too, with regard to Arthur's complaint, that "Error dwells in this Stygian deep [i.e., of Night and the oblivion it connotes], and something of its menace has already been experienced by Prince Arthur, the very paradigm of virtue."[23] Kathleen Williams also responds to Britomart's recognition of "secret laws which control our experience even when we do not know them"; but she is not much moved by Arthur's complaint ("a grumpy night outdoors"). Yet her response to Cymoent's lament, scarcely noticed by MacCaffrey, is sensitive: that nymph's "endeavour to control fate only makes her its instrument."[24] So it goes. Neither Williams nor MacCaffrey has much to say of the laments assigned to Timias and Scudamour; some others (notably Freeman and Roche) contribute a penetrating phrase or so. It is left for Roger Sale to perceive that Timias' "lyric choice to love his saviour silently and fatally... turn[s] the plaintive loneliness of Britomart, Cymoent, and Arthur into a kind of heroic virtue."[25]

This observation indicates the unrealized potential of the matter at hand. Sale recognizes that these complaints are somehow thematically as well as generically related; but he gets no farther, chiefly (I believe) because he fails to identify the organizing idea of Book III, the "informing principle" to which each component part of the Book is mutually related. For Sale, "the subject of Book III is not marriage but union —human, natural, and divine coming together."[26] Yet there is more to be said. It is Book III, after all, that in *The Faerie Queene* first conjoins and emphasizes, as even Books I and II had not, the elements of "romance": love, adventure, especially magic and the magician's power. And it is Merlin who gives direction, not for Britomart alone, but in a larger sense for all the persons in Book III. Responding to Britomart's appeal, "Pitty our plaint, and yield us meet reliefe," Merlin reassuringly emphasizes the role of painful challenge to heart and mind that makes part of the divine plan:

> For so must all things excellent begin,
> And eke enrooted deepe must be that Tree,
> Whose big embodied braunches shall not lin,
> Till they to heavens hight forth stretched bee.
> (iii.22)

[22] MacCaffrey, *Spenser's Allegory: The Anatomy of Imagination*, pp. 291-92.
[23] Ibid., p. 296.
[24] Williams, *Spenser's World of Glass*, pp. 91, 115, 119.
[25] Sale, *Reading Spenser*, p. 93.
[26] Ibid., p. 146.

Equally, he affirms

> ... the streight course of heavenly destiny,
> Led with eternall providence, that has
> Guided thy glaunce, to bring his will to pas:
>
> (st. 24)

and he lays particular stress on the mysterious interplay of impulses human and divine.

> Indeede the fates are firme,
> And may not shrinck, though all the world do shake:
> Yet ought mens good endevours them confirme,
> And guyde the heavenly causes to their constant terme.
>
> (st. 25)

Through the pains and pleasures of love to recognize the meaning of chastity, to come to terms with the limits and potential of one's being, and to acknowledge one's role in the divinely-directed stream of time: that is the "organizing principle," the contextual idea that gives meaning to the formal complaints of Book III (as to everything else in the Book). Each is a distinctive artistic entity; each is crafted to accord with and shed light on the psychological posture of the speaker; each enables a reader rather precisely to position that speaker in the context of larger idea that informs Book III.

Britomart is young and troubled; thinking to "beguile her grievous smart" with "selfe-pleasing thoughts" of Arthegall, she thereby intensifies that pain, somewhat as young Redcrosse at the outset of his quest acts in ways reflecting his inexperience. But the "silly mayd" is a "royall infant" too: "trained up in warlike stowre," she is always alert to the forms and demands of a traditional courtesy. It is therefore perfectly proper that her complaint should be couched in familiar terms: her youth and her inbred regard for established forms combinedly account for the choice of just this image. We smile, yet we also respect the decorum of it all. And, as MacCaffrey observes, the poet smilingly reinforces his effect by placing Britomart on the seashore: "Spenser no doubt enjoyed playing these games, but the games have also a serious thematic point."[27] If her complaint contains interrogative and prayerful moods, its tone is essentially declarative; it is not profound, but it is a thoughtful and reasoned effort to confront and account for emotional turbulence, so as in some measure to bring that turbulence within the compass of rational control. The three stanzas constitute an organically interrelated entity. Britomart first attends to the emotional impact of that "strife" in her being, moving from the conventional figure of a stormy sea to the felt agony that "in these troubled bowels raignes, and rageth rife." The second stanza is intellectual in character. Britomart acknowledges the combined power of restless Love and uncertain For-

---

[27] MacCaffrey, *Spenser's Allegory*, p. 292.

tune to disturb the psyche; but that they should "saile withouten starres, gainst tide and wind" evidently implies a reckless disregard for that larger control exercised through natural laws; and this is confirmed by the coolly amused rhetorical question, "How can they other do, sith both are bold and blind?" Finally, having in some degree mastered her unrest by subjecting it to thoughtful analysis, Britomart in the third stanza turns to faith, calmly confiding in that higher power which "may" bring her quest to a happy issue, and vowing to respond with appropriate piety. John Weld has perceptively observed that Britomart's "hoped haven of relief is on one level the long-sought Artegall; on another it is the tranquillity of soul which only the rule of right reason can restore . . .";[28] so far he is surely correct. To add that "on still another it is the final haven of which earthly tranquillity is an imperfect shadow," and that "Britomart's vow implies her need of grace," is, I believe (even granting the force of the double meaning in the second line of stanza 10), to press matters too hard. If Britomart's is not a strictly Christian humanist stance, the complaint is nonetheless perfectly appropriate for this heroine, in this Book of *The Faerie Queene:* its conventional simplicity and its ordered progression of emphasis are just and right for this chaste yet troubled "noble virgin."

    The lament of Cymoent, for Roger Sale, is "equally [with Britomart's] the complaint of one buffeted by an unavoidable fate."[29] But of course it is altogether in contrast with Britomart's complaint: exclamatory in mood, structurally erratic and diffuse, Cymoent's complaint everywhere reflects her perverse and misguided point of view. Even so, the lament does not altogether lack form: Cymoent's love for Marinell speaks through her opening words, and again, movingly, at the close. Those touching final lines (together with the half-line that precedes them) somewhat obscure and mitigate the recurrent self-pity of Cymoent's plaint.[30] Yet the deep despair from which her words spring is in control throughout. Reason is quite overwhelmed by a wildly extravagant sorrow that can make room only (in stanza 38) for a grovelling logic utterly subservient to the speaker's frantic terror and dismay. Addressed variously to Marinall, Proteus, and herself, Cymoent's lament is equally random in its effort to assign blame: by turns she accuses Nereus, Proteus, herself, "accursed fate," and "the heavens." Glancing quickly past the momentary recognition of her own part in Marinell's fall, she prefers to luxuriate in thoughts of a self-destruction that (by her narrow logic) aptly responds to the envious malice of divine will. Both complaints recall Merlin's words in the previous Canto: Britomart's

---

    [28] Weld, "The Complaint of Britomart," p. 551.
    [29] Sale, *Reading Spenser*, p. 81.
    [30] Cf. the first 6 lines of st. 39 with Lady Capulet's reaction to the news of Juliet's (apparent) death: *Romeo and Juliet*, IV.v.43-48.

plaint effectively illustrates her recognition that a life of steady endeavour, subject to heaven's will, leads on to fulfillment divine and human. But Cymoent's lament, struck through with wild passion and ungoverned wilfulness, reflects a fearful neglect of reason and faith alike. As Roche says, Cymoent "understands only the surface and not the reality of Proteus's prophecy."[31] And the truth that "mens good endevours . . . guyde the heavenly causes to their constant terme" is still for Cymoent hidden and unknown.

Arthur's complaint is different again: superbly so, and in ways that match his heroic role. It is important to see that, as he begins his plaint, the Prince is uneasy, and beset by confusing "fancies"; also that his demeanour on the day following is not at all cheerful:

> So forth he went,
> With heavie looke and lumpish pace, that plaine
> In him bewraid great grudge and maltalent.
>
> (st. 61)

Arthur's complaint recalls that of Britomart in that each figure may be said generally to "think through" a mazeful problem. But Arthur's thought is pitched at a higher level than is that of the "noble virgin": discursive, intellectual, even philosophical in character, it quests eagerly after truth, and must be impatient with less. This complaint is searching and explorative. The speaker quickly thrusts past those initially obtrusive "semblants vaine," and as the dawn breaks he remains unsatisfied. Yet the complaint remarkably illustrates the capacity of Arthur, pressed down by circumstance, to find his way up to light. The first four stanzas are addressed directly to Night. A careful outline of her ancestry leads to the central question: What need had God of Night? In turn, this suggests a more profoundly troubling inquiry: Whence and to what end evil? In the fifth stanza, direct address gives way to the meditative third person: stanza 50 does not in fact account for the existence of evil, certainly, but it does affirm the ultimate dominance of Truth, and the rest of "Dayes dearest children," over "darknesse" and the evils associated with that figure. The revision of 1596 introduces the important suggestion that love, at last, enables day's triumph over the dark, life over death. The final stanza once again employs direct address, but now to the sun: and the concluding allusion to day's capacity for good governance balances the opening stanza's reminder that night was, after all, "begot in heaven." The total effect suggests a monstrous and threatening upheaval of all things chaotic and obscure, checked and finally controlled (if not annihilated) by "right reason." Night "yeeld[s] her roome to day"; but even an Arthur's eager spirit can be shaken by the night's "restlesse anguish and unquiet paine," which still haunts the

[31] Roche, *The Kindly Flame*, p. 205.

Prince as he rides out before the dawn. This complaint, so organically decorous in terms of character and idea, must surely stand as Spenser's signal achievement in that kind.

It remains to consider the complaints of Timias, in Canto v, and Scudamour, in Canto xi. While the two laments are widely separated, nor are they directly connected with those of Canto iv, they are certainly related to each other, in form and idea. Further, if these complaints are rather more narrowly motivated than are those of Arthur and Britomart (even of Cymoent), the counsels of Merlin continue distantly to sound through them, helping a reader to distinguish between the deeply contrasting viewpoints of the two youths. Their plaints are broadly parallel, of course: each speaker suffers the pangs of love, more or less deliberately attempts to account for and master these pangs, at length remains effectively baffled. But the immediate motivation of each passage is distinctive: Scudamour complains of his inability to be united with Amoret, Timias (more subtly) of the complex demands made by love's service. And the argumentative modes are quite opposed too. Scudamour, occupied chiefly with justice and injustice, proceeds logically down the chain of being: an implicit challenge to divine justice is supported by the fact of Amoret's plight and Scudamour's inability to do anything about it. Disregarding Britomart's reminder that, if "life is wretchednesse," yet "vertues might, and values confidence" are, within a divinely-directed scheme, more than a match for "all the sorrow in the world," Scudamour at length abandons himself to despair. Given the actual success of "blacke Magicke . . . [w]hat boots it then to plaine that cannot be redrest?" Those initial doubts of heaven's justice have led him at length to acquiesce in the final power of earthly injustice.[32]

The complaint of Timias takes a course very nearly opposite to this. Striving "with reason dew the passion to subdew," the squire speaks first of honour and shame, preferring death to the "disloyalty" of desire. In a sense, that is a constant throughout his complaint: death before dishonour. Yet the terms are slightly altered in the second stanza: to die "rather . . . then ever from her service swerve." An element of sacrifice ("Thy life she gave, thy life she doth deserve") has, it appears, somewhat displaced the immediate demands of courtly honour. A code of courtesy, one might say, is giving way to virtuous principle. And the final stanza completes this movement: divine example best instructs lovers to partake of the "love and service" that draw together earth and heaven. "Dye rather, dye, then ever so faire love forsake." Where Scudamour's complaint sank gradually toward the bondage of earthly

---

[32] It may be granted that the dramatic exchange between Britomart and Scudamour that follows (in stanzas 13-24) the latter's complaint proper has some effect on Scudamour's resolve; yet the formal complaint itself clearly invites comparison with that earlier, relatively "free-standing" complaint of Timias in Canto v.

injustice, that of Timias rises steadily toward this vision of a freeing love that unites God and man. That must for Timias still be no more than a vision. But Merlin knew that a "hard begin" and "sharpe fits" must be endured if "mens good endevours" will reach "to heavens hight." Timias effectively acts out that counsel: "... never he his hart to her revealed, / But rather chose to dye for sorrow great, / Then with dishonorable termes her to entreat." And only by those ways will he be led at last "to the attainment of a love different from all the others in the poem."[33]

In later Books Spenser continued, of course, to employ the complaint, often with a graceful mastery that recalls the achievement of Book III. One thinks of Florimell's "carefull griefe" at IV.xii.6-11, or of the lament of Matilda (VI.iv.29-33); and the action of these later Books is now and again punctuated by briefer plaintive passages, e.g., Aldus' speech at VI.iii.4-5. And yet it is noticeable that the poet does not after all make much use of complaint in Books IV-VI. In fact, at those points in the action when one might reasonably expect such measures, Spenser often seems deliberately to disappoint that expectation. Radigund feels "heart-gnawing griefe" (V.iv.47), but she at once translates that pain into action, challenging Arthegall to single fight. Priscilla's "ruefull storie" (VI.ii.44) is briskly rendered in a single stanza of third-person narrative. As for Eirena, whose "right" Arthegall quests to restore, readers must be content with the briefest allusion to her "doleful spright" and "sorrowfull dismay" (V.xii.12). Spenser allows this silent princess neither complaint nor spoken expression of any kind over the course of Book V. Perhaps the poet was getting tired. No doubt also he was increasingly conscious of advancing age. It is tempting to think, too, that fictional complaint was steadily transmuted in these later Books to the poet's own expression of disenchantment with the times, the customs, his hopes. Certainly the Proems of Books V and VI, together with the stanzas that conclude the Legend of Calidore, sufficiently echo Spenser's frustration and dismay, in a world where all things "range, and doe at randon rove / Out of their proper places farre away . . ." (V, Proem, 6).

Be that as it may, the complaints of Book III collectively represent Spenser's best mastery of that genre. And that is, after all, quite appropriate. For the context of Book III, at once chaste and "courtly" in a manner not matched by that of other Books, is especially receptive to the full development of plaintive modes that at once recall mediaeval precedent and brilliantly illustrate this poet's complex art. In that Book, accordingly, Spenser more completely than elsewhere in the poem demonstrates his subtle management of the genre in its most controlled and yet most various forms.

[33] Roche, *The Kindly Flame*, p. 203.

Berkeley and Newtonianism:
the *Principles* (1710) and
the *Dialogues* (1713)

F. E. L. PRIESTLEY

When Berkeley published his *Principles of Human Knowledge* in 1710, he was not immediately concerned with Newtonianism. His primary purpose is, as might be expected, religious; the work is a continuation of the long series of attacks on "Hobbists, Atheists, Epicureans, and the like" mounted in the late seventeenth century by the Cambridge Platonists and their followers, including Newtonians like Bentley and Clarke, for example, and by more thorough-going Platonists like Berkeley's contemporary, Joseph Raphson, whose *Demonstratio de Deo* appeared in the same year as Berkeley's *Principles*. But Berkeley's attack, if not the most successful, is undoubtedly the most ingenious. He is not concerned, as a modern historian of philosophy is likely to suppose from the title, with problems of epistemology *per se* in the *Principles of Human Knowledge*, but with a large philosophical strategy by which to undermine materialists, atheists, and Manicheans through a denial of material substance. If there is no such thing as material substance, neither material monism nor Manichean dualism is tenable. As Berkeley points out, his *New Theory of Vision*, published the year before, had laid the groundwork for the comprehensive system of the *Principles*.

He begins his exposition of the system with an attack on Locke's doctrine of abstract general ideas. General ideas he will allow: "An Idea, which considered in itself is particular, becomes general, by being made to represent or stand for all other particular Ideas of the same sort." This sort of universal is admissible, in which a particular is generalized merely to represent its class: it is not thereby given a special ontological status. But abstract general ideas are formed by abstracting from the particular objects a simple quality, extension, colour, motion, and supposing that this quality can be conceived without any particularity—not only that colour can be conceived without extension, or motion without colour or extension, but colour without any particular colour, colour "which is neither red, nor blue, nor white, nor any other determinate colour." Abstract ideas of this sort are purely verbal, corresponding to nothing that can exist; they are useful in language, particularly when their proper status and function are remembered. For Berkeley's purposes, this attack on abstract ideas is a necessary preliminary; it is important for him to deny the ontological status of abstract terms (particularly of such terms as "corporeal substance") while preserving the ontological status of particular ideas. For in "vulgar opinion" and indeed in the opinion of all, those philosophers who had distinguished and separated the "primary" and "secondary" qualities, "reality" consisted of "substance" in which extension, figure and motion *actually subsist* as the real cause of the merely mental sensible qualities, which are consequently termed "secondary."

As Berkeley recognizes, the kind of dualism thus established between the external world of physical "objects," possessed of qualities inaccessible to sense, and the internal world of mental "objects" made up of the sensible qualities, led inevitably to Locke's scepticism, to an unknowable reality whose correspondence with the world as humanly perceived might be assumed, but could not be shown or understood. Locke, despite his attacks on the doctrine of substance, and his assertion of its unknowability, nevertheless seems always tacitly to assume a correspondence, some sort of valid causal relation between primary and secondary qualities. But since we cannot know the "real essences" of things, we cannot know the nature of this relation, or, ultimately, know that there is one. Berkeley boldly cuts the Gordian knot. There can be no correspondence, no resemblance of any sort between an idea and what is not an idea. "An Idea can be like nothing but an Idea." Those philosophers who distinguish between primary and secondary qualities acknowledge that our ideas of the secondary qualities do not resemble anything outside the mind, but will insist that our ideas of the primary qualities are "patterns or images" of things which exist outside the mind in what they call matter. But if these are ideas of extension, figure and motion, they are just as much ideas in the mind as ideas of colour, sound, or taste—they are mental events, perceptions, and can neither exist except in a perceiving mind, nor resemble anything not mental. An idea is something *perceived,* its *esse* is *percipi,* in Berkeley's most famous phrase; it can exist only in a mind and nowhere else. The so-called primary qualities, moreover, are inconceivable apart from ideas of the secondary qualities; we can conceive no idea of motion, figure, or extension abstracted from all other qualities. These are not qualities of material bodies but relations, which are agreed to be mental. They belong in the same category as terms like "number" and "unity," and are abstract terms, not ideas.

For Locke, the "objects" of perception, the objects the mind concerns itself with when thinking, are ideas—ideas of sensation and of reflection. Outside the mind there is the other "real" world of objects, horses, tables, stars, made of material atoms, endowed with the primary qualities of size, shape, and movement, and with some sort of ability to act upon our organs of sense so as to produce in us sensations of the secondary qualities. This cosmic dualism, of mind or spirit and of matter, of mental objects and of material objects, Berkeley sweeps away. The hypothesis of an external material world is superfluous; it explains nothing, and creates more problems than it solves. What he puts in its place is a world in which the dualism is not that of two kinds of substance, but of active and passive functions of a single kind of substance. All existence is mental, made up of minds whose essence is actively to perceive, and ideas whose essence is passively to be perceived. Berkeley thus preserves what was, for his religious purposes, valuable in the other dualism, the reservation of active power to mind, soul, or spirit, and the denial of it to "things."

"Things" are, in this system, things as perceived: the clusters of sensations (of colour, texture, hardness, temperature, taste, smell, contour, etc.) to which we give names like "table," "horse," and so on—"various Sensations or Ideas imprinted on the Sense, however Blended or Combined together (that is, whatever Objects they compose)," "the several Combinations of sensible Qualities, which are called *Things*." (As Berkeley points out, he prefers the term "idea" to "thing," because "thing" is "generally supposed to denote somewhat existing without the mind," and because "thing" includes thinking things as well.) To these ideas Berkeley ascribes the inertness others ascribe to matter. "All our Ideas, Sensations, Notions, or the things which we perceive . . . are visibly Inactive; there is nothing of Power or Agency included in them. . . . The very Being of an Idea implies Passiveness and Inertness in it, insomuch that it is impossible for an Idea to do anything, or, strictly speaking, to be the Cause of anything; Neither can it be the Resemblance or Pattern of any active Being. . . ." "*Thing* or *Being* is the most general Name of all: it comprehends under it two Kinds entirely distinct and heterogeneous, and which have nothing common but the Name, to wit, *Spirits* and *Ideas*. The former are *Active, Indivisible, Incorruptible Substances*: the latter are *Inert, Fleeting, Perishable Passions*, or *Dependent Beings*, which subsist not by themselves, but are supported by, or Exist in Minds or Spiritual Substances." (He is of course using the term *passions* here as the noun of *passive*, not in the modern sense of strong emotions.) The existence of the passive *ideas* is contingent upon the active *spirit* which perceives them; Berkeley thus removes, as it were, the ontological autonomy of the world of "objects." He also removes the problem of the relation of phenomena to noumena, of appearance to reality; the world as perceived is the real world—in fact the only world. His system depends on the assertion of the real validity of sensation: its reality consists in its being a sensation, a perception.

Mental events are not, of course, confined to perception. The mind links perceptions by various kinds of relations, noticing sequences and resemblances; it stores memories of sensations; it imagines and dreams. These various kinds of activity Berkeley groups as ideas of sensation and of reflection or memory, using terms reminiscent of Locke's but with different significance. He faces the same problem as other philosophers in defining the difference between sensation and memory, waking and dreaming, perception and imagination. In a correspondence theory such as Locke's, the problem of how we know which of our ideas "correspond" to an external "reality" and which do not is precisely parallel. Berkeley's criterion is much the same as the usual one: ideas of memory and imagination are, at least to some extent, responsive to our will; ideas of sensation are not. "When in broad Daylight I open my Eyes, 'tis not in my Power to chuse whether I shall See or no, or to determine what particular Objects shall present themselves to my View; and so likewise as to the Hearing and other Senses, the Ideas imprinted on them are not creatures of my Will." Moreover, the ideas of sense are more "strong, lively, and distinct than those of the Imagination; they have likewise a Steadiness, Order, and Coherence, and are not excited at Random, . . . but in a regular Train or Series. . . ."

Knowledge cannot, of course, for Berkeley be limited to ideas. "Whoever shall attend to his Ideas, whether of Sense or Reflexion, will not perceive in them any Power or Activity: there is, therefore, no such thing contained in them." And since an idea can resemble nothing but an idea, "there can be no Idea formed of a Soul or Spirit," that is, of active substance. "The Words *Will, Understanding, Mind, Soul, Spirit*, do not stand for different Ideas, or in truth, for any Idea at all, but for Something which is very different from Ideas, and which being an Agent cannot be like unto, or represented by, any Idea whatsoever." This does not mean that for Berkeley spirit or active substance is unknowable: it is merely not perceived in sensation. (Later, in the edition of 1734, he admits that "we have some notion of soul, spirit, and the operations of the mind, . . . inasmuch as we know or understand the meaning of these words." His choice of the term *notion*, the usual translation of *notitia*, emphasizes the cognitive, and suggests a mode of immediate cognition. The addition presumably indicates no change in Berkeley's theory, merely a clarification.) "I can as well doubt of my own Being," he writes, "as of the Being of those things which I actually perceive by Sense:" we have an immediate consciousness of ourselves as perceiving beings, as of things as perceived beings.

It is in the source of the ideas of sense that Berkeley finds not only the explanation of their objective reality, the independent existence of the "things" we perceive, but also of their perceived order and patterns of recurrence. Since they are not creatures of the individual human will, "there is therefore some other Will or Spirit that produces them." Since again they have a "Steadiness, Order, and Coherence," forming "a regular Train or Series," recurring by "set Rules or established Methods," which by experience we learn and call "the *Laws of Nature*," and derive thus "a sort of Foresight which enables us to regulate our Actions for the benefit of Life," it is obvious that their cause is a spirit (an incorporeal active substance) far transcending the limits of the human spirit. This spirit is the author of Nature, God, "the Intelligence that sustains and rules the ordinary course of Things." The permanence of the world given to us in perception, the world of ideas, lies, since the essence of ideas is to be perceived, in the fact that the ideas are permanently perceived by the divine mind. "When I shut my Eyes, the things I saw may still Exist, but it must be in another Mind." This is an extremely important element—perhaps the most important in Berkeley's system, but it is one often ignored. It is ignored in the popular limerick about the tree "which ceases to be when no-one is here in the quad." This embodies a total misconception of Berkeley's view, and was properly corrected by the further limerick attributed, I believe, to Ronald Knox.

There is, in Berkeley's system, just as much of a permanent, external, objective reality as in any rival system: all that is gone is the hypothetical "material substance," or "matter," to which no real meaning or function can be assigned. "In short, tho' there were External Bodies, it is impossible we should ever come to know it; and if there were not, we shou'd have the very same Reasons to think there were that we have now." Since the world as we know it is made up of ideas and active minds or spirits, there is no need to invent a third kind of entity incapable of real function. The problem of how matter could affect or operate on mind had led on the one hand to Locke's scepticism, and on the other to Occasionalism. In this latter doctrine, the impossibility of a causal connection between matter and mind, of matter acting upon mind, is accepted, and events in the material world are made not the cause, but the "occasion" of events in our mental world. As Berkeley puts it,

> [Matter] neither acts, nor perceives, nor is perceived: For this is all that is meant by saying it is an Inert, Senseless, Unknown Substance: which is a Definition entirely made up of Negatives, excepting only the relative Notion of its standing under or Supporting [i.e. the term *substance*]: but then it must be observed, that it *Supports* nothing at all: and how nearly this comes to the description of a *nonentity*, I desire may be considered. But, say you, it is the

unknown occasion, at the presence of which Ideas are Excited in us
by the will of God. . . . The words *to be present*, when thus applied,
must needs be taken in some abstract and strange Meaning, and
which I am not able to comprehend.

Again, let us examine what is meant by *Occasion*: so far as I
can gather from the common Use of Language, that Word signifies,
either the Agent which produces any effect, or else something that is
observed to accompany, or go before it, in the ordinary course of
things. But . . . Matter is said to be Passive and Inert, and so cannot
be an Agent or Efficient Cause. It is also unperceivable, as being
devoid of all Sensible Qualities, and so cannot be the Occasion of
our Perceptions in the latter Sense. . . .

You will perhaps say that Matter, though it be not perceived by
us, is nevertheless perceived by God, to whom it is the Occasion of
Exciting Ideas in our Minds. . . . That is to say, that there are certain
permanent and distinct parcels of Matter, corresponding to our
Ideas, which, though they do not excite them in our Minds, or any
wise immediately affect us, . . . they are nevertheless to God, by
whom they are Perceived, as it were so many Occasions, to remind
him when and what Ideas to imprint on our Minds: that so things
may go on in a constant, uniform manner. [Note the implications
behind Berkeley's precise "permanent and distinct parcels," and
"corresponding to our ideas."]

This, says Berkeley, is to conceive of God as needing a sort of
cosmic score, like that a musician uses to help him produce "that
harmonious train and composition of Sound, which is called a *Tune*:
though they who Hear the Music do not Perceive the Notes, and may be
intirely ignorant of them." This neat and devastating analogy prepares
for the final question of the need for the "occasions": "On the part of an
All-sufficient Spirit, what can there be that should make us believe, or
even suspect, he is *directed* by an inert Occasion to excite Ideas in our
Minds?"

Berkeley by no means underestimates his task of exposition, nor
the force of prejudice in favour of matter. He is attacking a very long
tradition, of ideas as images or reflections of an outer "real" world of
matter. He knows that to many he will seem to be denying the existence
of a real world and reducing all to fantasy or illusion. And this, to be
sure, is the popular misconception. And one must assume that the great
majority dismissed his system on hearsay, and without inspecting his
argument. Dr. Johnson, after all, may not have been a skilled metaphysi-
cian, but he was far from stupid: it is hard to believe that he could have
made his famous "refutation" of Berkeley by kicking a stone if he had
actually read the *Principles* or the *Dialogues between Hylas and
Philonous* (1713) in which Berkeley reaffirmed his doctrines. To kick a
stone is to affirm the reality of sensation, and this Berkeley equally
affirms:

It will be objected that by the foregoing Principles, all that is real and
substantial in Nature is banished out of the World: And instead

thereof a Chimerical Scheme of Ideas takes place.... What there-
fore becomes of the Sun, Moon, and Stars? What must we think of
Houses, Rivers, Mountains, Trees, Stones; nay, even of our own
Bodies? Are all these but so many Chimeras and Illusions on the
Fancy? To all which... I Answer, that by the Principles premised,
we are not deprived of any one thing in Nature. Whatever we See,
Feel, Hear, or any wise Conceive or Understand, remains as secure
as ever, and is as real as ever. There is a *rerum natura*, and the
Distinction between Realities and Chimeras retains its full force.

But again, in the popular mind, the whole conception of science is
intimately linked with that of "material substance," with atoms or
corpuscles in motion. Is not Berkeley's system a rejection or destruction
of science? To this important question Berkeley turns more than once in
the *Principles:*

> You will say there have been a great many things explained by
> Matter and Motion: take away these, and you destroy the whole
> Corpuscular Philosophy, and undermine those Mechanical Princi-
> ples which have been applied with so much success to account for
> the *Phenomena.*

It will be noted that this is a Cartesian, rather than a Newtonian objection: Newton's principles are very deliberately *mathematical,* not
mechanical. Berkeley's response to the objection is thoroughly conso-
nant with orthodox Newtonianism. He points out first that the very
phrase account for, or explain, the *phenomena,* that is, the appearances, is identical in meaning with showing "why upon such and such
occasions we are affected with such and such ideas." But since no
corpuscular philosopher even pretends to explain how matter can operate on a spirit, or produce any idea in it, such a philosopher is obviously
not offering a corpuscular or material explanation of the *phenomena,*
which are ideas. He is not using matter as his explanation. The natural
philosophers, in fact, who do attempt to account for things, do it "by
figure, motion, and other qualities" which are in truth themselves ideas.
Further, a good many modern philosophers, like some of the school-
men, although they allow matter to exist, yet they "will have God alone
to be the immediate efficient cause of all things." These are the
philosophers who, like the orthodox Newtonians, insist on the inertness
of matter.

Matter, then, neither offers nor can offer an explanation of the
phenomena. This does not mean an end to the investigation. What we
mean by natural philosophy, or science, is the explanation of the *rerum
natura,* of the *laws of nature.* But what are these laws? They are
regularities and uniformities of *phenomena* (that is, of our ideas) discovered by observation, "reasonably collected from the phenomena."
They serve to furnish us with "sure and well-grounded Predictions,
concerning the Ideas we shall be affected with, pursuant to a great Train

of Actions, and [enable us] to pass a right Judgment of what would have appeared to us, in case we were placed in Circumstances very different from those we are in at present.'' In other words, science is a set of rules, gathered from sense experience and ordered by reason, by which we predict the possibility of sense experience. This rather modern-sounding definition of science is, of course, full of implications. It would, however, be misleading to take it out of the context of Berkeley's system, within which its implications are severely limited.

The argument from design, the favourite teleological demonstration of God through his works, favourite with orthodox astro-theologists and physico-theologists and with Deists alike, is not, Berkeley argues, affected by a denial of material substance. Using the familiar analogy of God as the watch-maker, he presents the objection that ''if it be a Spirit that immediately produces every Effect by a *fiat*, or Act of his Will, we must think all that is fine and artificial in the Works, whether of Man or Nature, to be made in vain.''

> By this doctrine, though an Artist hath made the Spring and Wheels, and every Movement of a Watch, and adjusted them in such a manner as he knew would produce the Motions he designed; yet he must think all this done to no purpose, and that it is an Intelligence which directs the Index, and points to the Hour of the Day. If so, why may not the intelligence do it, without his being at the pains of making the Movements, and putting them together? Why does not an empty Case serve as well as another? And how comes it to pass, that whenever there is any Fault in the going of a Watch, there is some corresponding Disorder to be found in the Movements, which being mended by a skilful Hand, all is right again? The like may be said of all the Clock-work of Nature....

To this objection Berkeley makes several replies. In the first place, the objectors themselves would admit that God could achieve all effects simply ''by the mere command of his Will, without all that *apparatus,*'' which is not only an equal problem with a material apparatus, but a greater, since they acknowledge that matter has no ''activity or efficacy'' in it, and hence is not even an apparatus for producing the effects we call the *phenomena* of nature. Why God should choose to ''take those roundabout Methods of effecting things by Instruments and Machines,'' instead of directly, is an equal problem with either system. What Berkeley suggests is that though the use of instruments, the ''Fabrication of all those Parts and Organs,'' is not absolutely necessary, yet it is ''necessary to the producing of things in a constant, regular way, according to the Laws of Nature.'' God chooses, in other words, to ''act agreeably to the rules of mechanism.'' It will be recognized that in using the term ''mechanism'' Berkeley is not conceding the existence of material substance—he very shortly defines his meaning: ''Ideas are formed into Machines, that is, artificial and regular Combinations.'' The reason for this is "the same with that for combining Letters into Words."

What we call the laws of nature, or the laws of mechanism, or science, or principles of natural philosophy, is the connections of ideas. These connections do not imply the relation of cause and effect, "but only of a Mark or *Sign* with the Thing *signified*." Just as letters combine into words, and words into sentences and even volumes, so we may construct (or rather *learn the structure of*, Berkeley would say) the book of Nature:

> It is the searching after, and endeavouring to understand this Language, (if I may so call it) of the Author of Nature, that ought to be the Employment of the Natural Philosopher, and not the pretending to explain Things by Corporeal Causes; which Doctrine seems to have too much estranged the Minds of Men from that active Principle, that supreme and wise Spirit, '*in whom we Live, Move, and have our Being.*' . . . The steady, consistent Methods of Nature may not unfitly be Styled the Language of its Author, whereby he discovers his Attributes to our View, and directs us how to act for the Convenience and Felicity of Life. And to me, those Men who frame General Rules from the *Phaenomena,* and afterwards derive the *Phaenomena* from those Rules, seem to be Grammarians, and their Art the Grammar of Nature. . . . The best Grammar of the kind we are speaking of, will be easily acknowledged to be a Treatise of Mechanics, demonstrated and applied to Nature, by a Philosopher of a Neighbouring Nation, whom all the World Admire.

(The "neighbouring nation" is of course England, and the philosopher Newton.) There is here not only a tribute to Newton, but a deliberate echo of his own pronouncements: Omnis enim Philosophiae difficultas in eo versari videtur, ut a Phaenomenis motuum investigemus vires Naturae, deinde ab his viribus demonstremus phaenomena reliqua. (For the whole burden of philosophy seems to consist in this, that from the phaenomena of motions we seek to discover the forces of Nature, and then from these forces demonstrate the remaining phaenomena.) . . . Ex Phaenomenis Naturae, duo vel tria derivare generalia Motus Principia; et deinde explicare quemadmodum proprietates et actiones rerum corporearum omnium ex Principiis istis consequantur; id vero magnus esset factus in Philosophia progressus, etiamsi Principiorum istorum Causae nondum essent cognitae. (From the phaenomena of Nature, to derive two or three general principles of motion, and then to explain how the properties and actions of all corporeal things follow from these principles: that truly would be a great step forward made in philosophy, even if the causes of those principles were not yet known.)

And again,

> Quemadmodum in Mathematica, ita etiam in Physica, investigatio rerum difficilium ea Methodo, quae vocatur *Analytica*, semper antecedere debet eam quae appellatur *Synthetica*. Methodus

Analytica est, experimenta capere, phaenomena observare; in-
deque ex rebus compositis, ratiocinatione colligere simplices; ex
Motibus, vires moventes; et in universum, ex effectis, causas; ex
causisque particularibus, generales; donec ad generalissimas tan-
dem sit deventum. Methodus *Synthetica* est, causas investigatas et
comprobatas assumere pro Principiis, eorumque ope explicare
Phaenomena ex iisdem orta, istasque explicationes comprobare.
(As in mathematics, so also in physics, the research into difficult
matters by the method called analytic ought always to precede that
which is named synthetic. The analytic method is to choose experiments, to observe phaenomena; and then, from the composite facts,
by exercise of reason to gather the simple—from motions, the
moving forces; and in general, from effects, causes; from particular
causes, general ones; until finally the most general has been arrived
at. The synthetic method is to assume the discovered and established causes as principles, and by their help to explain the
phaenomena which owe their origin to them, and to confirm these
explanations.)

In his view of science, and of the function of science, "to recreate
and exalt the Mind, with a prospect of the Beauty, Order, Extent, and
Variety of Natural Things: Hence, by proper Inferences, to enlarge our
Notions of the Grandeur, Wisdom, and Beneficence of the *Creator*: And
lastly, to make the several Parts of the Creation, so far as in us lies,
subservient to the Ends they were designed for, God's Glory, and the
Sustentation and Comfort of our Selves and Fellow-Creatures," Berkeley is of course in general agreement with the Newtonians, and indeed
with the prevailing notions of his time. He is also in general agreement
with the Newtonians on such matters as the ascription of energy and
activity solely to spirit, the unknowability of causation, and the fond-
ness for the text from Acts 17:28, "in whom we live, and move, and have
our being." The text, to be sure, gives him no special alliance with the
Newtonians, although his application of it does; it must surely be one of
the most-quoted texts of the age, used to support a variety of doctrines,
including those of Spinoza and Malebranche. It is susceptible of a fair
range of exegetic flexibility.

There are several important matters, however, in which Berkeley is
critical of Newton. In the first of these he is probably aiming, not at
Newton, but at mechanistic Newtonians; for he is essentially at one with
Newton himself, at least with the Newton of the *Principia*. He raises
first a general objection to "the current Opinion that every thing includes within itself the Cause of its Properties." The Peripatetics "pretend to account for Appearances" by Occult Qualities; the more recent
fashion is for mechanical causes, like the Cartesian figure, motion,
weight, and so on of insensible particles. This is all, in Berkeleyan
terms, to assign one *idea* for the cause of another, "whereas in truth
there is no other Agent or Efficient Cause than *Spirit*." Then he continues:

> The great Mechanical Principle now in Vogue, is *Attraction*. That a
> Stone falls to the Earth, or the Sea swells towards the Moon, may to
> some appear sufficiently explained thereby. But how are we Enlight-
> ened by being told this is done by Attraction? Is it that the Word
> signifies the manner of the Tendency, and that it is by the mutual
> drawing of Bodies instead of their being impelled or protruded
> towards each other? But nothing is determined of the Manner or
> Action, and it may as truly (for ought we know) be termed *Impulse*,
> or *Protrusion*, as *Attraction*.

This is, of course, pointing out what Newton had shown himself to be
aware of: that the choice of term constitutes, or seems to constitute, a
description of the cause. Whether it would have been possible to select a
term that was causally non-committal is hard to say—something like
adgression might have signified a tendency for bodies to approach each
other without suggesting how the tendency originated or operated,
perhaps—but there is still the question which Berkeley is here raising, of
why Newton chose *attraction*.

"Again," Berkeley continues, "the Parts of Steel we see cohere
firmly together, and this also is accounted for by Attraction; but in this,
as in the other Instances, I do not perceive that any thing is signified
besides the Effect itself: for as to the Manner of the Action whereby it is
produced, or the Cause which produces it, these are not so much as
aimed at." He deliberately chooses phaenomena, gravitation and cohesion, which seem to him (and did also to Newton) to involve different
principles, and by bringing both under the same term of attraction (as
indeed many writers did) tries to suggest the emptiness of the term.

He wishes to make two points. The first is that naming gets con-
fused with explaining; the second is that the natural philosopher, in
seeking an order in nature, works by generalization and by analogy, and
is not always alert to the dangers of his method.

"In the Falling of a Stone to the Ground, in the Rising of the Sea
towards the Moon, in Cohesion, Crystallization, &c.; There is something alike, namely, an Union or Mutual Approach of Bodies. So that
any one of these or the like *Phaenomena*, may not seem Strange or
Surprising, to a Man who has nicely observed and compared the Effects
of Nature. . . . That Bodies should tend towards the Centre of the Earth,
is not thought strange, because it is what we perceive every Moment of
our Lives. But that they should have a like Gravitation towards the
Centre of the Moon, may seem odd and unaccountable to most Men,
because it is discerned only in the Tides. But a Philosopher, whose
Thoughts take in a larger compass of Nature, having observed a certain
similitude of Appearances, as well in the Heavens as the Earth, that
argue innumerable Bodies to have a mutual Tendency towards each
other, which he denotes by the general Name *Attraction*, whatever can
be reduced to that, he thinks justly accounted for."

The difference between the natural philosopher (that is, the scientist) and other men, says Berkeley, is not that they have a more exact knowledge of the *efficient cause* of the phenomena of nature, since the efficient cause can be no other than the *will of a spirit*. But the philosopher has "a greater Largeness of Comprehension whereby Analogies, Harmonies, and Agreements are discovered in the Works of Nature, and the particular Effects explained, i.e. reduced to general Rules. . . ." This special quality of mind brings a danger: "We are apt to lay too great a Stress on Analogies, and . . . humour that Eagerness of the Mind, whereby it is carried to extend its Knowledge into general Theorems." Attraction furnishes an example of this over-enthusiasm:

> In the business of Gravitation, or mutual Attraction, because it appears in many Instances, some are straightway for pronouncing it *Universal*; and that to *Attract, and be Attracted by every other Body is an Essential Quality, inherent in all Bodies whatsoever.*

As his phrasing makes clear, Berkeley at this point is attacking not only the tendency to universalize an analogy, but the quite separate tendency of certain readers of Newton and of Locke to ascribe to matter active powers as essential and inherent qualities—something which Newton himself may appear to do, but apparently does not intend. Having combined two attacks in the one sentence, Berkeley continues each in turn. As to the assertion of universality, it is evident the fixed stars have no such tendency towards each other, "and so far is that Gravitation from being *Essential* to Bodies, that in some Instances a quite contrary Principle seems to shew itself; as in the Perpendicular Growth of Plants, and the Elasticity of the Air." The problem of the elasticity of gases, the powerful force by which they resist compression, apparently operating in a contrary sense to the force of attraction, was, like the emission of light particles despite the gravitational attraction of the sun, recognized also by Newton as something of a paradox. And again, Berkeley's position is not incompatible with Newton's own:

> There is nothing Necessary or Essential in the Case, but it depends intirely on the Will of the *Governing Spirit*, who causes certain Bodies to cleave together, or tend towards each other, according to various Laws, while he keeps others at a fixed Distance; and to some he gives a quite contrary Tendency to fly asunder, just as he sees convenient.

This is very like Newton's recognition of various "active principles," each affecting different phenomena, and each the result of divine ordinance.

Berkeley's real disagreement with Newton is over absolute motion and absolute space. It will be evident from what has been said of Berkeley's system that for him motion and space (or extension) are ideas of relation, and Newton's treatment of them exhibits the same ontological error attacked in the first part of Berkeley's *Principles* (and prepared for in the *New Theory of Vision*.) He sums up the deep underlying objection he has to this sort of thinking when he refers to

> that dangerous *Dilemma*, to which several who have imployed their Thoughts on that Subject imagine themselves reduced, *viz.*, of thinking either that Real Space is God, or else that there is something beside God which is Eternal, Uncreated, Infinite, Indivisible, Immutable, &*c*. . . . And some of late have set themselves particularly to show the incommunicable Attributes of God agree to it.

A note in Berkeley's *Philosophical Commentaries* makes it clear that he has in mind the doctrines of Locke, More, and Raphson. One would judge that at this time Berkeley had not read the 1706 *Opticks,* or in this context some comment on the "sensorium" passage would be expected. His recent editor, Jessop, sees in the mention of the fixed stars as not gravitating (quoted above from section CVI of the *Principles*) a reference to the 1706 *Opticks*. This would be to Query 20 (later 28), but the relevant phrase comes only a few sentences before the first "sensorium" passage, and it seems incredible that Berkeley would pass that over in silence. And at an earlier point in the *Principles* he has complained about philosophers who

> vulgarly hold, the Sensible Qualities do Exist in an Inert, Extended, Unperceiving Substance, which they call *Matter*, to which they attribute a Natural Subsistence, exterior to all Thinking Beings, or distinct from being perceived by any Mind whatsoever, even the Eternal Mind of the *Creator*, wherein they suppose only Ideas of the corporeal Substances created by him: if indeed they allow them to be at all Created.

Now, it is one of the main points Newton makes in the "sensorium" passage that God perceives, not the ideas or images of things, but the things themselves "immediately and thoroughly." If Berkeley had known the passage, he could hardly have ignored it here.

All the direct references to Newton in the *Principles* are to the *Principia*, and it is Newton's treatment in that work of absolute motion and space, and his mathematical use of infinitesimals in the fluxions, that Berkeley specifically attacks. "Absolute motion exclusive of all external relation is incomprehensible," he asserts, and as to the experiment with the revolving bucket of water by which Newton sought to demonstrate absolute motion (in the Scholium after Defintion VIII at the beginning of the *Principia*) it demonstrates nothing of the kind—"for the Water in the Vessel, at that time wherein it is said to have the greatest Relative Circular Motion, has, I think, no Motion at all." Apart from the objection based upon his dislike of abstract general ideas, and the habit of thinking "every noun substantive stands for a distinct idea," that is, a real entity, Berkeley also recognizes that Newton's system is essentially a system of relations:

> For to denominate a Body *Moved*, it is requisite, First, that it
> change its Distance or Situation with regard to some other Body:
> and Secondly, that the Force occasioning that Change be impressed
> on it. If either of these be wanting, I do not think that agreeably to
> the Sense of Mankind, or the Propriety of Language, a Body can be
> said to be in Motion.

His most detailed attack is upon the conception of finite extension as
infinitely divisible. This gives raise to the paradoxes which alternately
entertained and infuriated the orderly eighteenth-century mind, all
based upon treating infinity as a real number. Many of the mathematical
doctrines to which Berkeley is objecting were still being taught in
schools in this century: a number divided by zero equals infinity; any
finite line contains an infinite number of points, so a two-inch line
contains the same number of points as a one-inch one, and so on. The
paradox was not relieved by treating a finite linear dimension as "made
up" of an infinite number of points of no dimension. For Berkeley, these
are all examples of prepossession by the doctrine of abstract general
ideas. Given Berkeley's doctrine of universals, the paradoxes disap-
pear. In a geometrical diagram, the particular lines and figures are
supposed to stand for innumerable others of different sizes. The geome-
ter "abstracts" them from their magnitude, "which does not imply that
he forms an Abstract Idea, but only that he cares not what the particular
Magnitude is, . . . but looks on that as a thing indifferent to the Demonstration." Hence, "a Line in the Scheme, but an Inch long, must be
spoken of as though it contained ten thousand Parts, since it is regarded, not in itself, but as it is universal; and it is universal only in its
Signification, whereby it represents innumerable Lines greater than
itself, in which may be distinguished ten thousand Parts or more, though
there may not in it." The inch line, in other words, "is said to contain
Parts more than any assignable Number," and we must "speak of the
Lines described on Paper, as though they contained Parts which really
they do not." "When we say a Line is *infinitely Divisible*, we must mean
a line which is *infinitely Great*."

　　His objection to the fluxions, or calculus, which he was to elaborate
later in pamphlets, is put in a single paragraph:

> Some there are of great Note, who, not content with holding that
> Finite Lines may be divided into an Infinite number of Parts, do yet
> farther maintain, that each of those Infinitesimals is itself sub-
> divisible into an infinity of other Parts, or Infinitesimals of a second
> Order, and so on *ad infinitum*. These, I say, assert there are In-
> finitesimals of Infinitesimals of Infinitesimals &c., without ever
> coming to an end. . . . Others there be who hold all orders of In-
> finitesimals below the first to be nothing at all, thinking it with good
> reason Absurd, to imagine there is any positive Quantity or Part of
> Extension, which though multiplied Infinitely, can never equal the
> smallest given Extension. And yet on the other hand, it seems no

less Absurd, to think the Square, Cube, or other Power of a positive real Root, should itself be nothing at all; which they who hold Infinitesimals of the first Order, denying all of the subsequent Orders, are obliged to maintain. . . .

If it be said that several Theorems undoubtedly true, are discovered by methods in which Infinitesimals are made use of, which could never have been, if their Existence included a contradiction in it, I answer, that upon a thorough Examination it will not be found, that in any Instance it is necessary to make use of or conceive Infinitesimal Parts of finite Lines, or even Quantities less than the *Minimum Sensible*. . . . And whatever Mathematicians may think of *Fluxions* or the *Differential Calculus* and the like, a little Reflection will show them, that in working by those Methods, they do not conceive or imagine Lines or Surfaces less than what are perceivable to Sense. They may, indeed, call those little and almost Insensible Quantities *Infinitesimals* or *Infinitesimals of Infinitesimals*, if they please: but at Bottom this is all, they being in truth Finite, nor does the Solution of Problems require the supposing any other.

Berkeley's objections are, as we have noted, in part his general attack on abstract general ideas. In part they are directed against confusing the infinite with the indefinite, and recall Cudworth's similar objections. And in part they are an attack on what seem to him the illogical foundations of the calculus. Modern mathematical historians have agreed with Berkeley that while the calculus produced results, in the eighteenth century its theoretical basis was by no means coherent. Given the eighteenth-century view of mathematics as the most certain of the sciences, based on self-evident truths and incontestable deductions, Berkeley's suggestion that the calculus, though based on fiction or convention, could nevertheless be used to discover "theorems undoubtedly true," made little sense. He seemed rather to be denying the whole validity of this new branch of mathematics, and found himself engaged in a minor pamphlet war. It is unlikely that the general public, or even the general reading public, took much notice of this aspect of his work. Nor, to be sure, did they of his main argument. As A. C. Fraser has said, "His governing conception was unintelligible to his contemporaries, and to generations of his successors."

It must be remembered that his contemporaries could not see Berkeley in the perspectives we are accustomed to; we tend to think of him as an empirical epistemologist belonging in some sort of linear progression from Locke to Kant, or as some variety of idealist to be ranged in comparison and contrast with, say, Fichte, Schelling, and Hegel. None of these contexts were available to his age, nor, I think, this kind of technical and historical approach to philosophy. To his contemporaries, and doubtless to Berkeley himself, the most important of his concerns is with the doctrine of substance, not simply as a metaphysical problem, but as a metaphysical problem with most important religious implications: he is interested in the questions of epistemology in so far as he wishes to attack the "scepticism" of Locke, not because he finds them interesting philosophical questions. The irony of Berkeley's situation is that his denial of material substance seemed to his contemporaries a much more sceptical position than Locke's; wedded as they were to a dualist doctrine of substance, and a conviction that the material world was the "real" one, they felt that Berkeley was trying to cut them off from the reality to which Locke had at least left a link of correspondence. The ordinary response to the *Principles* is to be clearly seen in the *Three Dialogues between Hylas and Philonous,* which Berkeley published in 1713. Hylas, as his name denotes, is the spokesman for the believers in material substance; Philonous the spokesman for Berkeley. "Can anything be more fantastical," exclaims Hylas, "more repugnant to common Sense, or a more manifest Piece of Scepticism, than to believe there is no such thing as *Matter*?"

About all Berkeley can do is, like Browning's St. John, patiently to re-state his case and let it work, and he uses the dialogue form very skilfully to present objections, elaborate his own arguments, and try to clear up misconceptions. Some of the elaborations are important. He develops an interesting theory of Creation, for which he claims complete orthodoxy:

> All objects are eternally known by God, or, which is the same thing, have an eternal Existence in his Mind; but when Things before imperceptible to Creatures, are by a decree of God, made perceptible to them; then are they said to begin a relative Existence with respect to created Minds. Upon reading therefore the *Mosaic* Account of the Creation, I understand that the several Parts of the World became gradually perceivable to finite Spirits, endowed with proper Faculties.... [I acknowledge] a twofold State of Things, the one Ectypal or Natural, the other Archetypal and Eternal. The former was created in Time; the latter existed from Everlasting in the Mind of God.

For the believer in matter, creation was "not the creation of things sensible, ... but of certain unknown natures," but *"Moses* tells us of a Creation. A Creation of what? of unknown Quiddities, of Occasions, or *Substratums?* No, certainly; but of Things obvious to the Senses." This insistence on the reality of perception, of "things sensible," of the world of ideas, is what seemed to his contemporaries the novelty and the paradox. In the Platonic tradition, the world of things sensible was derivative from the world of Ideas or Forms: it corresponded to or imitated, or reflected, or participated in the reality of the world of Forms, but it was not itself the real world. Similarly, in the tradition of the new science of matter, the world of sensation derived from, and in some way corresponded to the real world of matter, of the "primary qualities," but was not itself the real world. But to Berkeley, these latter doctrines contain the paradox, not his:

It is none of my business to plead for Novelties and Paradoxes. That the Qualities we perceive are not in the Objects: that we must not believe our Senses: that we know nothing of the real Nature of Things, and can never be assured even of their Existence: that real Colours and Sounds are nothing but certain unknown Figures and Motions: that Motions are, in themselves, neither swift nor slow: that there are in Bodies absolute Extensions, without any particular Magnitude or Figure: that a Thing stupid, thoughtless, and inactive [matter] operates on a Spirit: that the least Particle of a Body contains innumerable extended Parts. These are the Novelties, these are the strange Notions which shock the genuine uncorrupted Judgment of all Mankind. . . . And it is against these and the like Innovations, I endeavour to vindicate common Sense.

In an echo of Newton, Philonous rejects the doctrine of material substance as "an hypothesis, and a false and groundless one," and asserts, "I do not pretend to frame any hypothesis at all. I am of a vulgar cast, simple enough to believe my Senses, and leave things as I find them." The hypothesis of matter has led only to problems and obscurities:

In Natural Philosophy, what Intricacies, what Obscurities, what Contradictions, has the Belief of Matter led Man into! To say nothing of the numberless Disputes about its Extent, Continuity, Homogeneity, Gravity, Divisibility, *etc.*, do they not pretend to explain all things by Bodies operating on Bodies, according to the Laws of Motion? and yet, are they able to comprehend how any one Body should move another? . . . Have they been able to reach the mechanical Production of any one Animal or Vegetable Body? Can they account by the Laws of Motion, for Sounds, Tastes, Smells, or Colours, or for the regular Course of Things? . . . Then in *Metaphysics*; what Difficulties concerning Entity in Abstract, Substantial Forms, Hylarchic Principles, Plastic Natures, Subjects and Adjuncts, Principle of Individuation, Possibility of Matter's thinking, Origin of Ideas, the Manner how two independent Substances, so widely different as *Spirit* and *Matter*, should mutually operate on each other? Even the *Mathematics* themselves, if we take away the absolute Existence of extended Things, become much more clear and easy. . . .

It is still possible, of course, within Berkeley's system, to speak of the body, and of corporeal motions. Indeed, in comparing God and man, and their modes of perception, it is necessary. (And again, as Berkeley considers this topic, one would expect a reference to Newton's *sensorium* passage, if he had read it.)

We who are limited and dependent Spirits, are liable to Impressions of Sense, the Effects of an external Agent, which, being produced against our Wills, are sometimes painful and uneasy. But God, whom no external Being can affect, who perceives nothing by Sense as we do, whose Will is absolute, and independent, causing all things, and liable to be thwarted or resisted by nothing; it is evident, such a Being as this can suffer nothing, nor be affected with any painful Sensation, or indeed any Sensation at all. We are chained to

a Body, that is to say, our Perceptions are connected with corporeal
Motions. By the Laws of our Nature we are affected upon every
Alteration in the nervous Parts of our sensible Body. . . .

At this point the reader might think himself suddenly back on familiar
ground, with corporeal motions of atoms in the body producing mental
sensations in the soul or mind, but Berkeley smoothly continues

. . . which sensible Body, rightly considered, is nothing but a Com-
plexion of such Qualities, or Ideas, as have no Existence distinct
from being perceived by a Mind; so that this Connexion of Sensations with corporeal Motions, means no more than a Correspondence in the Order of Nature between two Sets of Ideas, or Things
immediately perceivable.

The relation of body and mind, or physical events and mental, so acute a
problem as long as body and mind are thought of as distinct substances
with no common qualities, and physical and mental events as belonging
to quite different orders, becomes in Berkeley's system merely a part of
the general order of nature. Both body and the sensations of the mind
belong to the same order. What we call "physical events" are events we
perceive, that is, patterns of related ideas, as are all the "things" the
mind constructs from sensations. The connection between the sets of
ideas we call "corporeal motions" and those we call "perceptions"
contains no unbridgeable gap; all together form a unity of relations
which we call "the order of nature."

Berkeley sees his own system as offering a more powerful proof of
the existence of God than the usual argument from design. The wonders
of creation, as wonders, remain precisely what they are: the celestial
system, "Innumerable Worlds revolving round the central Fires," exhibit "the Energy of an all-perfect Mind displayed in endless Forms,"
and "all the vast Bodies that compose this mighty Frame, how distant
and remote soever, are by some secret Mechanism, some divine Art and
Force, linked in a mutual Dependence and Intercourse with each
other. . . . Is not the whole System immense, beautiful, glorious beyond
Expression and beyond Thought?" But for Berkeley, not only the order
and beauty, but the very existence and permanence of the system
depend upon their perception by God. Other philosophers, he points
out, "acknowledge all corporeal Beings to be perceived by God, yet
they attribute to them an absolute Subsistence distinct from their being
perceived by any Mind whatever, which I do not." Where others say,
"There is a God, therefore he perceives all things," Berkeley says,
"*Sensible things do really exist; and if they really exist, they are necessarily perceived by an infinite mind: therefore there is an infinite Mind,
or God.* This furnishes you with a direct and immediate Demonstration,
from a most evident Principle, of the *Being of a God.*"

It was perhaps natural for those who read Berkeley without strict attention to jump to the conclusion that he was a follower of Malebranche, whose doctrines had recently been attacked in the posthumously published volume of Locke's work (*An Examination of Malebranche's Opinion of seeing all Things in God*, published, with other writings and letters, in 1706). In a work to be published later (1720) Locke singled out John Norris as an English Malebranchian. Norris, as a mystic, shows a number of influences, including not only that of Malebranche, but also of Henry More and earlier traditions of Platonic mysticism. Berkeley makes it evident in the *Dialogues* that he has been placed by some readers in the same category as Norris. He has Hylas put the blunt question: "Do you not think it [your doctrine] very like a notion entertained by some eminent moderns, of *seeing all things in God?*" When Philonous asks for details of this "notion," Hylas elaborates

> They conceive that the soul, being immaterial, is incapable of being united with material Things, so as to perceive them in themselves, but that she perceives them by her Union with the Substance of God, which being spiritual, is therefore purely intelligible, or capable of being the immediate Object of a Spirit's Thought. Besides, the Divine Essence contains in it Perfections correspondent to each created Being: and which are, for that Reason, proper to exhibit or represent them to the Mind.

This is indeed so far from Berkeley's own doctrine that merely putting it so compactly emphasizes the differences, but Philonous goes on to point out rapidly that Berkeley's *ideas*, being inert and passive, cannot be any part of the essence or substance of God, and that the doctrine Hylas has presented is also open to all the other objections he has raised to matter, since it too has a created world of material things existing independent of any mind. But, says Hylas, "are not you too of opinion that we see all things in God?" blandly ignoring these differences. I agree, replies Philonous-Berkeley, in accepting the text from Acts, "in God we live, and move, and have our being," but not in their interpretation of it. For Berkeley rejects the theory that "we see things in His essence." The ideas or things we perceive exist, to be sure, in the mind of God, and owe their permanent existence to being perceived by Him, their *esse* being *percipi*. But they are not more part of the active being of God than, indeed, they are part of the active being of the human soul—they are the passive objects of perception. They are "known by the Understanding, and produced by the Will of an infinite Spirit," they are not part of his infinite active substance, nor do we perceive them as part of that substance, or in Malebranche's terms, "by perceiving that which represents them in the intelligible substance of God." "This," says Berkeley, "I do not understand."

One final point of special interest in the *Dialogues* is of direct relevance to Newtonianism. This is the introduction of a new argument in connection with the laws of motion. Hylas, still speaking for the supporters of material substance, asks what effect Berkeley's theories will have upon the concept of mass as the quantity of matter in equations dealing with momentum and forces affecting motion.

> I lay it down for a Principle, he says, that the Moments, or Quantities of Motion in Bodies, are in a direct, compounded Reason [i.e. ratio] of the Velocities and Quantities of Matter contained in them. Hence, where the Velocities are equal, it follows, the Moments are directly, as the Quantity of Matter in each. But it is found by Experience, that all Bodies (bating the small Inequalities arising from the Resistance of the Air) descend with an equal Velocity; the Motion therefore of descending Bodies, and consequently their Gravity, which is the Cause or Principle of that Motion, is proportional to the Quantity of Matter.

"But," objects Philonous, "is not this arguing in a circle?" The principle that momentum is proportional to mass times velocity is laid down as an axiom, and used to prove a proposition "from which the existence of matter is inferred." Even if one allows that "the motion is proportional to the velocity, jointly with the extension and solidity,"

> yet it will not thence follow, that Gravity is proportional to *Matter,* in your Philosophic Sense of the Word; except you take it for granted, that unknown *Substratum*, or whatever else you call it, is proportional to those sensible Qualities: which to suppose is plainly begging the Question.

It is of course Berkeley's steady questioning of the validity of the hypothesis of material substance that brings him to see the circularity of the Newtonian equations. He presents the same objection as Ernst Mach was to present towards the end of the next century, but though the two agree in seeing the circularity, and in objecting to the introduction of unobservables, they have proceeded towards the common destination by very different roads, conveyed by very different vehicles.

Yet they do meet, and thus serve to remind us once more of how the context of ideas shifts the implications of doctrines. There are in Berkeley's system, or perhaps rather in parts of it, areas of implication which can emerge in a different context, or when the parts are divorced from the total system. One of these is actually touched on by Berkeley himself. When an attack on dualist doctrines of substance has been completed, and the existence of a single substance argued, the terms appropriate to distinguishing the two substances tend to lose their meaning and it may not seem impossible to ask why one term rather than another should be applied. If there is only one substance, why not call it *matter* just as readily as *spirit?* At the very end of the *Dialogues*, Berkeley almost brings up this point. "What think you," asks Hylas, "of retaining the name *Matter*, and applying it to sensible Things?" "With all my heart," replies Philonous, "retain the word *Matter*, and apply it to the Objects of Sense, if you please, provided you do not attribute to them any Subsistence distinct from their being perceived." Hylas continues with his request to use the term: "I freely own there is no other Substance in a strict sense, than *Spirit*. But I have been so long accustomed to the Term *Matter*, that I know not how to part with it." Berkeley is perhaps here doing no more than grant Hylas the right "to think with the learned, and speak with the vulgar," a practice he had recommended in the *Principles*. Hylas (and the reader) may be allowed to apply the terms of the traditional dualism of substance to the new dualism of active perceiver and passive perceived, as long as he is not deceived himself by the terms. In 1713 this is perhaps not a dangerous concession. But Berkeley has nevertheless given to his passive ideas, or "things," a number of the qualities traditionally ascribed to "matter," and thus blurred for some, at any rate, who do not grasp or accept his whole theory, the distinction between the two. It is significant of what this can come to mean in a changed context of ideas that when, half a century later, the Jesuit Roger Boscovich put forward his system of immateriality, Joseph Priestley turned it into a material system, on the ground that it was as reasonable to call the single substance "matter" as "spirit." Obviously, of course, much had happened to the concepts of "substance" in the intervening years.

A similar development of implication is possible, and takes place, as a result of Berkeley's definition of a "thing" as a collection of *sensa*, or ideas of sensation. It will be remembered that Locke had suggested that since substance is unknowable, the essential qualities are also unknowable. He tends to reduce "essential" qualities to those sensible qualities which seem to be inseparable, which always accompany the object. This is a different thing from his other (and more usual) criterion of conceptual inseparability. He also suggests that there may be other essential qualities than those we are ordinarily aware of. The shift in the notion of "essential" from a conceptual to a sensible basis, from "that without which the thing would be other than it is" to "that which we always find in the thing in ordinary sense experience" is a shift of far-reaching importance, a shift from a rational approach to an empirical one. It will be easily understood that Berkeley's definition of "thing," especially when separated from other elements of his system, can favour the latter. But most of these developments were, as has been indicated, to be in the future.

As we noted at the outset of this discussion of Berkeley, his relation to Newtonian doctrines and his agreement or disagreement with them is not a primary concern in these works. The Newtonians are clearly not among the "Hobbists, Epicureans and the like" he is attacking. Much of his system, indeed, is not irreconcilable with the orthodox Newtonian-ism based on the *Principia*, and some of the implications or apparent implications he does attack would also be rejected by the orthodox Newtonians. He ought, presumably, to have found more to attack in the 1706 *Opticks*, if he had read it; not only the "sensorium" passage, but the description of how matter was created by God, and the passages which seem to ascribe positive forces to matter would surely have called forth some comment. His treatment of space is perhaps more directed against Raphson and More than Newton, although Newton was soon to express much the same doctrine—it is really implicit in the "sensorium" passages. His most direct attacks are important, if limited. More impor-tant, perhaps, are the indirect implications. It is possible, I think, to view the orthodox Newtonianism as poised between a roughly Platonic animism and a roughly Epicurean atomism. It seems to me reasonably accurate to say that Berkeley isolates in his system the element which can be called "animist." The poise is a delicate one, easily destroyed; the balance can tip heavily on either side. Berkeley, by tipping it in one direction, destroys the balance as effectively as if he had tipped it in the other, and perhaps invites further tipping.

Wagner in *The Waste Land*

WILLIAM BLISSETT

I

At the beginning of Richard Wagner's music-drama *Tristan und Isolde,* a young sailor sings a song of high spirits and plain daylight that rouses in Isolde, an Irish girl herself, being carried by the fresh wind away from home to marriage with the King of Cornwall, a storm of passionate resentment that is to issue in passionate love for Tristan, her captor. In the middle of the drama the lovers first sing their love duet on a bank of flowers and then, being parted, sing a night song of longing and death. Through most of the last act, the wounded Tristan awaits the appearance of the ship carrying Isolde, but the watchman can report only that the sea is waste and empty.

Near the opening of *The Waste Land,* T. S. Eliot quotes the lines of the sailor and the watchman and implies the intermediate action:

> *Frisch weht der Wind*
> *Der Heimat zu:*
> *Mein Irisch Kind,*
> *Wo weilest du?*
> 'You gave me hyacinths first a year ago;
> 'They called me the hyacinth girl.'
> —Yet when we came back, late, from the Hyacinth garden,
> Your arms full, and your hair wet, I could not
> Speak, and my eyes failed, I was neither
> Living nor dead, and I knew nothing,
> Looking into the heart of light, the silence.
> *Oed' und leer das Meer.*[1]

Wagner's immense trilogy, *Der Ring des Nibelungen,* is introduced by an extended dramatic prelude, *Das Rheingold.* In it, from a single E

---

[1] I follow the text of the first edition as included in Mrs. Valerie Eliot's invaluable *The Waste Land: A Facsimile and Transcript* (London: Faber, 1971). Here I have corrected the Wagner citations by inserting the colon after *zu* and the umlaut in *Oed'.* Eliot's small scribal errors argue a close and over-confident familiarity with Wagner's text:

flat major chord is derived a torrent of sound expressive of the river, within which appear three nymphs, the Rhine-daughters, embodying primitive vitality and celebrating as symbol at once of love, of their integrity of soul, and of the goodness of creation, a cache of refulgent gold. Their song is initially one of joy but becomes a lament on later occasions when they recall how the gold was seized by the dwarf Alberich, made resolute by a renunciation of love. It is this wordless lament that Eliot quotes near the end of the third section of *The Waste Land,* and his three despoiled Thames-maidens balance the three Rhine-daughters.

It is certainly unusual for a poet to quote from the texts of two Wagner music-dramas; one is encouraged to search for other relevant evidence of Wagnerian interests. In *The Egoist* (1918) Eliot writes that "England puts her Great Writers securely in a Safe Deposit Vault, and curls to sleep like Fafner," and in the essay on John Ford (1932) he alludes briefly and casually to the love-potion in *Tristan.* The "Dialogue on Dramatic Poetry" is not friendly to the idea of stage-consecrating music-drama, and in it one of the speakers says to another (the church-going one): "I have also heard you railing at Wagner as 'pernicious.' But you would not willingly resign your experience of Wagner either." As editor of *The Criterion* Eliot accepted two essays on "The Legend of Tristram and Isolt in English poetry," by Sturge Moore, one of which appeared in the very first issue, along with *The Waste Land.* However, he never found it necessary to discuss Wagner at any length in his prose, and this fact seems to indicate that the music-drama never became problematical for him or a part of the programme of promotion and demolition necessary to clear the way for his kind of poetry and drama. On the other hand, the appropriate and direct quotation in *The Waste Land* is presumptive evidence of first-hand knowledge and more than casual concern, and the misquotation in the manuscript indicates that he was quoting from memory, that is "by heart." There is one highly important, yet maddeningly brief, item of corroborative evidence. When Igor Stravinsky and Eliot finally met, near the end of Eliot's life, "we managed to talk that afternoon, nevertheless," Stravinsky writes, "and though I hardly recall the topics, I remember that Wagner was one; Eliot's Wagner nostalgia was apparent and I think that *Tristan* must have been one of the most passionate experiences of his life."[2]

see Bernard Harris, "'This Music Crept by Me': Shakespeare and Wagner," in A. D. Moody, ed., *The Waste Land in Different Voices* (London: Edward Arnold, 1974), p. 110.

   [2] "Observations," by T. S. Apteryx, *The Egoist* 5 (1918), 69; *Selected Essays* (London: Faber, 1932), pp. 198, 48, 54; Igor Stravinsky and Robert Craft, *Themes and Episodes* (New York: Knopf, 1966), p. 125. In "The Possibility of a Poetic Drama," *The Dial* 69 (1920), 445, Eliot speaks disapprovingly of "the mixture of *genres* in which our age delights." His London Letter of July, 1921 (*The Dial* 71 [1921], 213-17) begins by mention-

The Wagner references in *The Waste Land* are by no means exhausted in those few direct quotations, emphatic though they are. The poet's early reference to winter sports and to happy times by the Starnbergersee near Munich echoes a passage in a letter by Rupert Brooke in which he reports the thoughts of a friend in Cornwall on hearing of the outbreak of war: "In answer to the word 'Germany,' a train of vague thoughts dragged across his brain. The pompous middle-class vulgarity of Berlin; the wide and restful beauty of Munich; the taste of beer; innumerable quiet, glittering *cafés*; the *Ring*; the swish of evening air in the face, as one skis down past the pines; a certain angle of eyes in the face; long nights of drinking, and singing and laughter; the admirable beauty of German wives and mothers; certain friends; some tunes; the quiet length of evening over the Starnbergersee." It was in the Starnbergersee that Wagner's friend and patron, Ludwig II of Bavaria, the quintessential Fisher King, met death by water. The Countess Marie Larisch, who as a young girl had mistaken Wagner for the tailor, who sang Elsa's music for King Ludwig, who played a role in the love-tragedy at Meyerling, who felt free in the mountains and went south in the winter, met the young poet before the composition of *The Waste Land*. One likes to think that they talked about Wagner and Wagnerites.[3]

Again, the line quoted from Paul Verlaine, "Et O ses voix d'enfants, chantant dans la coupole!" is the concluding line of his sonnet "Parsifal," first published in a group of sonnets by various poets, all on Wagnerian themes, in the *Revue Wagnerienne*. The poets Gérard de Nerval and Charles Baudelaire are also quoted in *The Waste Land*; one wrote a review of a performance of *Lohengrin* at Weimar, the other (as his longest and richest critical essay) an article on Richard Wagner and

---

ing the "fine hot rainless spring" but complains before the end of the first paragraph of a new form of influenza "which leaves extreme dryness and a bitter taste in the mouth." He continues (this is only a few months before the composition of *The Waste Land*) with the true Grail King's groan: "What is spring without the Opera? Drury Lane and Covent Garden mourn; the singers have flocked, we are told, to New York, where such luxuries can be maintained. They have forgotten thee, O Sion. Opera was one of the last reminders of a former excellence of life, a sustaining symbol even for those who seldom went" (213).

[3] Rupert Brooke, *Letters from America* (London: Sidgwick & Jackson, 1947), pp. 173-74; Countess Marie Larisch, *My Past* (London: Eveleigh Nash, 1913). See also George L. K. Morris, "Marie, Marie, Hold on Tight," *Partisan Review* 21 (1954), 231-33. Mrs. Eliot, *Facsimile*, pp. 125-26, discloses Eliot's acquaintanceship with the Countess. The Larisch parallel and related topics are explored by Herbert Knust in *Wagner, the King and 'The Waste Land'* (Pennsylvania State University Press, 1967): he proceeds on the assumption that Eliot—probably during his stay in Germany—came to know intimately both Wagner's literary works and the life and haunts of Ludwig II. On this it would be useful to have more information, as it would also be interesting to know whether he was likely to have read or seen a performance of Strindberg's *Ghost Sonata* in German: the presence of a "hyacinth girl" alerts one to many parallels of tone and technique.

Tannhäuser at Paris. Elsewhere, Eliot shows strong attachment to Laforgue, Mallarmé, and Valéry, each in his way a Wagnerite of that peculiar French symbolist cast that we shall need to consider in due time.[4]

Along with Sir James Frazer's *Golden Bough,* Eliot singles out Jessie L. Weston's *From Ritual to Romance* as a major source of the structure of poetic ideas in the poem. Miss Weston's first book had been on the *Legends of the Wagner Dramas*; she later wrote a ballad version of *Lohengrin*; and she recalls frequent conversations with a German scholar "during the Bayreuth Festival of 1911" as having led to the writing of *From Ritual to Romance,* a study that applies the anthropological methods of Frazer, Jane Ellen Harrison, Gilbert Murray and F. M. Cornford to mediaeval material, especially the legend of the Fisher King and the Waste Land, the Quester and the Grail-maiden—the material that Wagner had collected, selected, and used as the mythical basis of his *Parsifal.*

And yet, on the face of it, how unlikely it is that there should be any deep affinity between the voluble, amorous, opinionated, cultural and political adventurer who established an astonishing empire of the arts at Bayreuth, and Mr. Eliot,

> With his features of clerical cut,
> And his brow so grim
> And his mouth so prim
> And his conversation so nicely
> Restricted to what Precisely
> And If and Perhaps and But.

Though the longest poem in the English language, in Ezra Pound's phrase, *The Waste Land* in its 433 lines does not have quite the duration of a Wagner music-drama. The poem is all empty spaces, the music-drama all continuous plasma. *The Waste Land* is all styles, the music-drama one style. The poem is replete with quotations from and allusions to other writers in many languages, whereas Wagner (hiding what he stole) supplied all the words and all the music and oversaw the architecture and scenery and the details even of the costumes and acting, all with despotic energy. In *The Waste Land* one sees crowds of people walking round in a ring; complex though the word-tone-art of Wagner is, his action is simplicity itself and his characters are few. *Parsifal* may end, like *The Waste Land,* on the note of Shanti, Shanti, Shanti, but it would be absurd for a voice speaking for Wagner to say, "These fragments I have shored against my ruins."

---

[4] On French literary Wagnerism, see Kurt Jäckel, *Richard Wagner in der Französischen Literatur* (Breslau, 1931-32), and Léon Guichard, *La Musique et les lettres en France au temps de Wagnèrisme* (Paris, 1963). Not concerned with Wagnerism but otherwise most useful is E. J. H. Greene, *T. S. Eliot et la France* (Paris, 1951).

II

In order to arrive at a perspective from which the details of affinity here collected may make sense, I propose a long detour that should prove nevertheless the shortest way home. This will involve mention of Edgar Allan Poe, or rather that elegant French writer, Edgar Poe (sometimes Edgard, sometimes Poë), and the French response to his challenge from the time of Baudelaire a century before, to T. S. Eliot, who wrote on "Mallarmé et Poe" in 1926 and "From Poe to Valéry" in 1948. Baudelaire translated most of Poe's best prose and Mallarmé some of his poems: what concern us are the critical writings, especially one sentence from one of them, the dictum that there is no such thing as a long poem, a long poem is a contradiction in terms.[5]

By asserting that a poem must be single in its effect and that effect unalloyed by anything not purely poetic, Poe not only precludes the possibility of extended narrative and epic poetry (not a serious deprivation for the French), he also forbids the sort of connective tissue and stiffening the French are renowned for—argument, eloquence. It was in obedience to Poe's strictures (which had precedence also in August von Schlegel and in certain French critics of the eighteenth century) that Verlaine exclaimed, "We must take eloquence and wring its neck." The sort of poem resultant upon this self-denying ordinance is presentational not discursive, a gem-poem not a tree-poem, timeless and spaceless and, if the poet is not careful, vague and formless. It is no accident that the spoof collection of the tiny imaginary symbolist poet, Adoré Floupette, was named *Les Déliquescences*.

We should keep that challenge and that rather unsatisfactory response in mind for a moment while we bring to mind another challenge, another response, in another art.

Richard Wagner, though far from being either a clear thinker or a good writer, was the first thoroughgoing intellectual, in the modern sense, among the great composers. He could not live without an ideology, and for some years at the height of his powers he could not write music at all until he had solved the problem of the relation of music to drama, to his satisfaction. It is indeed a formidable problem: if all the words of a play are made song, the work becomes impossibly slow and protracted; if the dramatic and emotional high points are given full lyric expression and the rest of the play is rattled off in dry recitative or spoken prose, the work loses unity and becomes a string of "numbers" and "effects," musically unworthy of the great tradition of the Bee-

[5] Edgar Allan Poe, "The Poetic Principle" (1850) in James A. Harrison, ed., *Complete Works* (New York: AMS Press, 1965), XIV, 266. See Patrick F. Quinn, *The French Face of Edgar Poe* (Carbondale: Southern Illinois University Press, 1957), especially pp. 36-37.

thoven symphonies, those dramas without words that at the end found words indispensable. What was needed was a way to give opera symphonic structure, continuity as music, coherence as drama and poem, and an intellectual and moral seriousness worthy of comparison with Greek drama—which Wagner believed to have been musical. It is the problem of coherence that is the point of analogy between Wagner and the poets. Few words, strong dramatic situations, endless melody without arias: these went some distance in solving the problem of coherence, but two important new devices were added by Wagner. Both of these were inexorably borne in upon anyone who, like so many of the French intellectuals of the past century, subjected themselves to the animated world of Wagnerian discussion and immersed themselves for hours (often round a piano) in his despotic art. No one can listen to a Wagner music-drama without being changed by it; no one can go on a pilgrimage to Bayreuth without being marked for life.[6]

The first of these devices was to use legendary, mythical material, strong, simple, appealing at a deep level of awareness and avoiding all superficial complications of plot or "intrigue." The second was to impose upon the endless stream of musical sonority patterns of repetition reaching out beyond the music, by the assignment of a particular musical phrase, or leitmotif, to certain persons or objects or actions or passions or ideas, whenever they appear in the unfolding experience of the music-drama.

Baudelaire himself never heard the mature music-dramas, but he was acute enough to hail Wagner's use of legend as a signal contribution to the arts. "Their general aspect is definitely legendary: *Tannhäuser*, legend; *Lohengrin*, legend; *The Flying Dutchman*, a legend. And it is not merely an inclination natural to every poetic mind that led Wagner to this apparent specialty: it is a formal, deliberate decision determined by the study of the conditions most favorable to lyric drama." He goes on to quote Wagner's critical prose with approval, observing later that "the drama of *Lohengrin*, like that of *Tannhäuser*, possesses the sacred, mysterious and yet universally intelligible character of legend," and after commenting on the appearance of leitmotifs (in their earlier, not rigorously systematic form), shows his preoccupation with the state of poetry and Wagner's possible bearing upon it by remarking, "Indeed, without poetry, Wagner's music would still be a poetic work, endowed as it is with all the qualities that constitute well-made poetry; self-explanatory in that all of its elements are so well combined, united,

---

[6] From the time of the visit of Catulle Mendès, Judith Gautier and Villiers de l'Isle-Adam to Wagner and Cosima at Tribschen in 1869, French spoke of themselves as "pilgrims." See for example Lavignac's *vade mecum*, the popular and much-reprinted *Le Voyage artistique à Bayreuth*.

adapted to one another, and—if one may use a barbarism to express a superlative quality—scrupulously concatenated."[7]

Suddenly, twenty years after Baudelaire's impassioned defence of *Tannhäuser* against the whistling jocks at the Paris Opéra, Wagner and Wagnerism crop up everywhere. In a half-dozen literary periodicals appear translations of the prose and the dramas, commentaries and reviews of performances, critical expositions of Wagner's ideas, poems and fiction on Wagnerian subjects—everywhere excited reverie, everywhere an aspiration to the condition of music, which in the context means the condition of Wagnerian music-drama. Two small but pointed samples may be given of Wagnerian vogue in intellectual circles, one concentrated in time, the other extended. A symbolist journal (perhaps the leading one) was actually called *La Revue Wagnérienne*: it included in its pages poems on Wagnerian subjects by René Ghil, Stuart Merrill, Stéphane Mallarmé, Paul Verlaine and others, reprints of Wagner commentary by Franz Liszt and Gérard de Nerval, Mallarmé's essay on Wagner, and pieces by Villiers de l'Isle-Adam and its editor, Edouard Dujardin, whom Joyce was to hail years later as the originator of the stream-of-consciousness technique—all this in the space of the three years from 1885 to 1887. The name given to the Paul Verlaine figure in Camille Mauclaire's novel *Le Soleil des Morts* is Tristan Saumaize; whether for Wagnerian or Breton reasons, Edouard-Joachim Corbière renamed himself Tristan Corbière; Léon Leclère, a poet and painter of the turn of the century, invented the supreme pseudonym of Tristan Klingsor, outdoing Sami Rosenstock, the surrealist poet who first uttered the magic word Dada and called himself Tristan Tzara. I pour this information in rich profusion so that the cauldron of Wagnerism will sing all about our ears, for it was from this cauldron that Eliot plucked out his poem.

Interest, excitement, high intellectual fashion, soon pass and their literary reflection can fade rapidly if they are unaccompanied by a probing exercise of the critical intelligence and imagination. This exercise we find in Mallarmé and Valéry. Mallarmé, in an oracular pronouncement, explainable on a more leisurely occasion but not now, asserted that "since Wagner appeared, Music and Verse have combined to form Poetry," and, in apparent contradiction: "Oh strange defiance hurled at poets by him who has usurped their duty with the most open and splendid audacity: Richard Wagner!" I believe this to embody, among many other suggestions, Mallarmé's conviction that the experience and example of Wagner have taught poets, shamed poets, to do everything that he has done, without reverting to rhetoric or narrative. If so, it belongs with the famous dictum of Valéry (with whom he used to

[7] *Baudelaire as a Literary Critic*, ed. and trans. Lois Boe Hyslop and Francis E. Hyslop, Jr. (Pennsylvania State University Press, 1964), pp. 206, 213, 218-19.

go to "vespers"—Wagner concerts): "What was baptized *symbolism* may be very simply described as the common intention of several groups of poets (otherwise mutually inimical) to 'reclaim their own from Music' "—that is to say, from music in the sense of Wagner's composite, total art, organized by leitmotif and symbol into a tight and self-contained unity of immense implication. The foundations of symbolism could not have been laid without Wagner; they were in fact laid by the end of the nineteenth century, but the great works to be built on them did not arise for another generation, so long did it take the most adventurous minds to ready themselves for attempting *A la Recherche du temps perdu, Ulysses, The Magic Mountain, The Waves, A Passage to India, The Waste Land.* From this list of works in the symbolist mode, each one demonstably written to a significant degree under Wagnerian influence, it is clear that the long poem can again be achieved: ironically, the addition of Wagner to Poe has made possible the very thing that Poe was at pains to declare impossible.[8]

III

"... Any obscurity of the poem, on first reading, is due to the suppression of 'links in the chain,' of explanatory and connecting matter, and not to incoherence, or to the love of cryptogram." This observation was made not about *The Waste Land* but about the *Anabase* of St.-John Perse, by its translator, T. S. Eliot,[9] but it has clear application to the poem under discussion. Here, too, connective and explanatory material has been (from its earliest inception) suppressed, leaving only thematic matter, there being no part of the poem without poetic density in itself and unlinked with other parts. Leitmotifs run through it. The discernment of leitmotifs, the recognition of thematic material as forming somehow the "real structure" of works of literature, is so much a commonplace of modern criticism that it is hard for us to think of a time when this was not the case. There was such a time, the time before Wagner and literary Wagnerism. Though poets and musicians have always used the technique to some degree, it remained for Wagner to use it to the fullest degree and to make the whole world permanently aware of its resources.

The analogy of literature with music must always be more suggestive than exact, but I think it will be most helpful to apply the word *leitmotif* not to unchanging small elements but to recurring thematic

[8] Stéphane Mallarmé, *Selected Prose Poems, Essays & Letters*, trans. Bradford Cook (Baltimore: Johns Hopkins University Press, 1956), pp. 39, 73; Paul Valèry, *The Art of Poetry*, trans. Denise Folliot (New York: Random House, 1958), p. 42. In his introduction to the latter, Eliot discusses the musicality of symbolist poetry but makes no mention of Wagner. See also Joseph Chiari, *Symbolisme from Poe to Valèry* (London: Rockliff, 1956), p. 54, and Eliot's introduction.

[9] St.-John Perse, *Anabase*, trans. T. S. Eliot (1931; rpt. London: Faber, 1959), p. 9.

material, abbreviated or expanded and no matter how disguised. For instance, "I do not see / The hanged man" sounds the same motif as "Le prince d'Aquitaine à la tour abolie" because the dark disconsolate poet of that line, Gérard de Nerval, hanged himself. The motifs of Eliot are never trivial but possess strength, coherence, and interest in themselves, like those of Wagner, of which Bernard Shaw wrote, "on all occasions he insists on the need for sensuous apprehension to give reality to abstract comprehension, maintaining, in fact, that reality has no other meaning." This is, by the way, remarkably similar, even in phrasing, to Eliot's "direct sensuous apprehension of thought."[10]

By eschewing narrative connection and relying on leitmotifs, Eliot is enabled to obey the strictures of Edgar Poe and his French champions; he is enabled by the same means to avoid any use of rhetoric as stiffener—rhetoric, that is to say, in the sense of continuous argument, and rhetoric in its other sense of eloquence, of speaking out consistently (perhaps factitiously) in a high style.

It would have been quite possible, while retaining the use of recurrent symbols as motifs, to have drilled and directed them to work in one way, to march in one direction. If Eliot's fire-symbols had all been destructive, his poem would have been, literally, a Fire-Sermon. But destructive fire is balanced by "the heart of light" and "inexplicable splendour of Ionian white and gold"; so too, water both revives and drowns; so too, the past is ranged against the present, to judge it, certainly, but also to stand under the same judgment. The ambivalence of the symbolism cancels any argument detachable from the poem as a whole. I am not one of those commentators who seem to think it to be a sermon on the text "Be fruitful and multiply"—and that to be the whole of the law.

To demonstrate how leitmotifs may be used, for coherence, for amplification of meaning and reverberation without bulk, and (after their full establishment) for tolling reminiscent bells, so that these fragments form an ideal order, let us consider one major leitmotif in *The Waste Land,* the water-motif, in its two main aspects, the sea (including Tristan's sea) and the river (including the Rhine-maidens' river).

Fragments of the motif appear very early in "spring rain," "forgetful snow," "a shower of rain," "no sound of water"; then follows the full statement already quoted—the sailor's song associating the sea with love and anticipation, the happy moment glimpsed and lost, gleaming with moisture, and at the end the sea as empty and waste as the land. Cryptic, oracular pre-introductions of motifs resume: "the drowned Phoenician sailor," "fear death by water," even "crowds of people walking round in a ring," are all later subsumed in the whirlpool that

[10] *The Perfect Wagnerite* (1898) in *Major Critical Essays* (London: Constable, 1931), p. 220.

claims the body of Phlebas. The first sounding of the river motif is likewise oblique:

> A crowd flowed over London Bridge, so many,
> I had not thought death had undone so many.

The second section, "A Game of Chess," is a scene of unrelieved aridity. The opening allusion turns Cleopatra's barge into a chair and sets it upon marble; what is "poured" is the glitter of her jewels, and it is perfume that "drowns" the sense. The reference to "sea-wood" in the fireplace ironically removes us far from the sea, as the carved dolphin in this sad light removes us farther from Antony's delights than would be the case had it never been mentioned. Waste and empty this marble sea, with no promise of change in "The hot water at ten. / And if it rains, a closed car at four."

"The Fire Sermon" opens with a description of the river in winter, in which the water is defiled in the very act of describing it as undefiled. Three still shots from the moving picture of the poem touch on the water theme: "By the waters of Leman I sat down and wept"; "While I was fishing in the dull canal"; "They wash their feet in soda water"—the last being perhaps a parodic allusion to Kundry and Parsifal. The section concludes with the second explicitly Wagnerian passage of the poem, quoting this time not *Tristan* but *Die Götterdämmerung*. The Thames is evoked, as it is and as it was, in two styles, which may be called imagistic and symbolist, the latter being altogether in line with the post-Wagnerian aesthetic of French symbolism: after each, the wordless song of the Rhine-daughters is heard:

> The river sweats
> Oil and tar
> The barges drift
> With the turning tide
> Red sails
> Wide
> To leeward, swing on the heavy spar.
> The barges wash
> Drifting logs
> Down Greenwich reach
> Past the Isle of Dogs.
>   Weialala leia
>   Wallala leialala
>
> Elizabeth and Leicester
> Beating oars
> The stern was formed
> A gilded shell
> Red and gold
> The brisk swell
> Rippled both shores
> Southwest wind

Carried down stream
The peal of bells
White towers
 Weialala leia
 Wallala leialala

The poet's note identifies the next speakers as three Thames-maidens. They sing their songs of spoliation beside river and sea. The concluding four lines of the section, by adding fire to the water-song of the maidens, will recall the destructive cleansing of the halls of men and gods by the combined action of river and fire at the end of *The Ring*. I am encouraged in this reading by the presence in the poem of a strong motif of "falling towers."

'Trams and dusty trees.
Highbury bore me. Richmond and Kew
Undid me. By Richmond I raised my knees
Supine on the floor of a narrow canoe.'

'My feet are at Moorgate, and my heart
Under my feet. After the event
He wept. He promised "a new start."
I made no comment. What should I resent?'

'On Margate Sands.
I can connect
Nothing with nothing.
The broken fingernails of dirty hands.
My people humble people who expect
Nothing.'

 la la
To Carthage then I came
Burning burning burning burning
O Lord Thou pluckest me out
O Lord Thou pluckest

burning

In the fourth section, "Death by Water," the crowds of people walking round in a ring are concentrated in one, the drowned Phoenician sailor, entering the whirlpool. In the last, the motifs that we have been examining appear as fragments or in negative form, or in such complex combinations with other motifs as to preclude analysis here.

IV

The image-concept that gives its name to *The Waste Land* is in a sense a leitmotif like water or fire, like the hanged man or the drowned man; but it is more than that. More than any of the others it implies and demands a narrative, and a particular narrative of that momentous, simple, primitive, subliminal character we term mythical. The waste land is the ruined empire of the soul. The inner wound of the king and outward waste of the kingdom are one. He and his land await the deliverer, whose "overwhelming question" alone can lift the curse. The King himself can do nothing: long dwelling on the paradoxes and counterclaims of joy and pain, desire and disgust, attachment and detachment, have so annulled his will that "the refusal propagates a fear," and he can only wait and groan, his suffering alleviated from time to time by an elusive female figure, now a maiden, now a crone, whose ministrations bring the relief of momentary beauty and momentary wisdom, yet whose beauty and wisdom are tainted, she being the seductress through whom came the wound.

The main features of the Grail story are given by Jessie L. Weston as "the Waste Land, the Fisher King, the Hidden Castle with its solemn Feast, and mysterious Feeding Vessel, the Bleeding Lance and Cup." Though Eliot goes out of his way to state his indebtedness to Miss Weston, saying that her book "will elucidate the difficulties of the poem much better" than his notes can do,[11] it should be observed at once that what is apparently absent from the poem is the Grail itself. Of the hidden castle we catch only a glimpse in the line from Verlaine's "Parsifal" recalling the boys' voices in the dome singing in celebration of the feast; apart from that, we see only the Fisher King in the Waste Land, the Kundry figure with many names and natures—whether as Maiden (the hyacinth girl) or Harlot (Mrs. Porter) or crone (the Sibyl, Mme. Sosostris), and, apparently, the absence or failure of the Grail hero, who cannot speak, who drowns, who is hanged. A reference to Wagner's *Parsifal* will correct, I believe, some of the inadequacies of this reading.

Throughout, but especially in its last section, the poem stands closest in tone of feeling to the beginning of the last act of the music-drama. The curtain rises on an "open, pleasant, spring landscape in the Grail's domain," but the natural response of the audience to the vernal scene is held in check by the wintry lento of the music and by the sight of Guernemanz grown old and the sound of Kundry groaning. The enfeebled Guernemanz tells of the death of the old King Titurel and the approaching dissolution of the Grail Brotherhood because Amfortas is no longer willing to distribute the healing sustenance, racked as he is by the pain of his wound. The glow of the Grail for him is felt only as the fever of longing and remorse. April is the cruellest month. It is spring, and in good time, on the return of Parsifal the deliverer, we are to hear the Good Friday Spell, but the mood of the old man (Guernemanz

[11] Jessie L. Weston, *From Ritual to Romance* (1920; rpt. New York: Doubleday, 1957), p. 3. Eliot seemed to wish to create the impression that the notes were written by a person on business from Porlock, but D. F. Raube is surely right in his conclusion that "in Eliot's hands the humble note becomes a literary device of great potency and flexibility": "The Notes on *The Waste Land*," *E.L.N.* 7 (1970), 294.

merges with Tiresias) is heavy and sombre, and even Kundry, through lassitude, has lost the galvanic energy to serve or to seduce and is no longer racked by "the laceration of laughter at what ceases to amuse."[12]

The poem appears not really to move from that point, or if it moves, it moves in every direction, dread and regret cancelling each other out, desire and disgust in stalemate. And yet its final section, "What the Thunder Said," I think is best interpreted not in terms of the sufferer, Amfortas the Fisher King, but in terms of the quester—the Parsifal of the third act, who enters to Guernemanz and Kundry, at the end of endless wanderings, weary, depressed, not knowing that it is Good Friday, that Titurel has died, that the Grail-Knights are dying:[13]

> After the torchlight red on sweaty faces
> After the frosty silence in the gardens
> After the agony in stony places
> The shouting and the crying
> Prison and palace and reverberation
> Of thunder of spring over distant mountains
> He who was living is now dead
> We who were living are now dying
> With a little patience.

Since winning back the sacred Spear from the magician Klingsor and reducing the magic garden of corrupt imagination to the desert it really is, Parsifal has been travelling through the world looking for the way back to Montsalvat, the Grail Castle—a thirsty journey evoked in the poem by the great passage descriptive of a sandy road winding among the rocks. Inner trials match outer. The pilgrim is oppressed by the burden of time and mutability, sounded in the motif of the falling tower. He is also vexed by fantasies racing out of control in the strange surrealistic passage (I call it so because it has the same literary sources as the surrealists). The conscious fear and unconscious dread of death reach their full statement in the arrival at the Chapel Perilous, a place of

[12] Thomas Mann quotes Wagner (1859): "A bad business! Think of it, for God's sake: it has suddenly become frightfully plain to me that Amfortas is my Tristan of the third act, at his unthinkable culmination." *Essays of Three Decades,* trans. H. T. Lowe-Porter (New York: Knopf, 1947), p. 323. On the Kundry figure, see Grover Smith, *T. S. Eliot's Poetry and Plays* (University of Chicago Press, 1956), pp. 70, 74, 86; and Herbert Howarth, *Notes on Some Figures Behind T. S. Eliot* (Boston: Houghton Mifflin, 1964), pp. 237-38.

[13] The relation of the quester to the fisher-king in the poem has been variously interpreted. See Anne C. Bolgan, *What the Thunder Really Said* (Montreal: McGill-Queen's Press, 1973), pp. 14, 74; Robert Langbaum, "New Modes of Characterization in *The Waste Land,*" in A. Walton Litz, ed., *Eliot in his Time* (Princeton, 1973), p. 108; David Ward, *T. S. Eliot Between Two Worlds* (London: Routledge, 1973), p. 10; Helen Williams, *The Waste Land* (London: Arnold, 1973), p.30. For the appearance of the Quester before *The Waste Land*—and before *From Ritual to Romance*—see Thomas C. Rumble, "Some Grail Motifs in Eliot's Prufrock," *Studies in American Literature,* ed. Waldo McNeir and Leo B. Levy (Louisiana State University Press, 1960), pp. 95-103.

the mind at the end of the journey, at the centre of the Waste Land, but also (if we remember the legend and the music-drama) very near the Grail Castle. Then suddenly, cock-crow, a flash of lightning, rain, the equivalent in the poem of Parsifal's recognition of where he is, and what day it is, and what at last he can do.

The poet chooses to end the action of the Deliverer here. It may be argued that the deliverance is implicit in his endurance of the vigil in the Chapel; it may be argued on the contrary that the deliverance is arrested and that the Fisher King's resolution "at least" to "set his lands in order" is as dispiriting as anything in the poem. Resolution was impossible, but Eliot was Wagnerite enough "at least" to set all his motifs in order in the final lines. My own opinion is that by resolving the leitmotif system without unequivocally resolving the action the poet did what the poem itself required, but that his subsequent life as a poet was to demand the completion of what had been arrested. *The Waste Land* having permitted no Good Friday Spell, he wrote an Ash Wednesday Spell. The paradox of the pleasure-garden as desert, the wilderness as paradise, strongly present in *Parsifal,* Eliot returns to again and again. The innocent and the fallen garden in Eliot thus are given direction and imaginative force by Wagner's use of the Grail myth (*Parsifal* being *the* Legend as the Bible is *the* Book, according to Catulle Mendès),[14] but they are never exclusively or even predominantly Wagnerian, and later become so enriched from the main Christian tradition as to obscure their Wagnerian bearings altogether. In *Parsifal* the children's voices in the dome sing of the Bread and the Wine and of the healer, wise through compassion, "durch Mitleid wissend"; and the wound of the King is healed at the touch of the Questioner's lance. The distance is great but the journey continuous from this to the Good Friday lyric in *East Coker*:

> The wounded surgeon plies the steel
> That questions the distempered part;
> Beneath the bleeding hands we feel
> The sharp compassion of the healer's art
> Resolving the enigma of the fever-chart.

V

After *The Waste Land* the influence of Wagner and literary Wagnerism on Eliot does not perhaps end, but it becomes almost impossible to isolate. For one thing, the poet seems to have had no one to talk to, being, with Paul Valèry, one of the very few continuing Wagnerites in an anti-Wagnerian world. Writers and thinkers whom Eliot found congenial, Hulme and Pound and Wyndham Lewis, Maritain and Benda, and most of the contributors to the *Criterion,* were in full reaction against the

[14] Catulle Mendès, *Richard Wagner* (Paris, 1909), p. 64.

grandiose and heroic, the northern, the misty, the unformed, in a word, the Wagnerian.[15] Musicians of Debussy's generation and Stravinsky's were concerned above all with doing the non-Wagnerian thing; and of course in due time the contamination of Bayreuth and the cause of Wagner by the Nazis made the anti-Wagnerian undertow all the stronger.

Conceding all that, is there not in Eliot's long concern with the theatre and his idealization of the ideal illiterate audience something of Wagner's idea of a ritual theatre of the Folk?[16] And is it not possible that the psychiatrist Sir Henry Harcourt Reilly, in *The Cocktail Party,* who sings the song of "the one-eyed Riley," is really, among many other things, a manifestation of Wagner's Wotan, who sacrificed an eye for wisdom?[17] What Reilly *sees* is the substance of *The Cocktail Party,* and what Wotan *sees* is the substance of *The Ring,* just as what blind Tiresias *sees* is the substance of *The Waste Land.*

I conclude by noting a certain discrepancy between Eliot's art as a poet and the classical doctrines he professed so eloquently and long. Richard Wagner is a source of what is inward, profound, symbolical, mythical in modern literature. Not for him, or for his, the sunlit surface of life, the Mediterranean and classical concern for the definite and bounded, the central, the humane. For all its professed classicism, the art of T. S. Eliot is unmediterranean because, like D. H. Lawrence and Thomas Mann, like James Joyce and Marcel Proust, like Jules Laforgue and Stéphane Mallarmé, he owes no Roman obedience and remains liegeman to the great Despot from north of the Teutoberg Forest.

[15] Ezra Pound, a representative anti-Wagnerite, attacked the Wagnerian aesthetic in *The Criterion* 2 (1924), 321-22. About 1933, on the way back from a Pergolese concert, "Pound expatiated on the superiority of Pergolese over Wagner, and began to imitate Wagner with groans and grunts, whistles and catcalls, amid much gesturing and cavorting": Louis Zukofsky's account in Charles Norman, *Ezra Pound* (New York: Macmillan, 1960), p. 318. Such a context makes more remarkable the fact that at no time did Pound persuade or attempt to persuade Eliot to discard any of the Wagner allusions in *The Waste Land*: he clearly recognized their centrality.

[16] *The Use of Poetry and the Use of Criticism* (London: Faber, 1933), p. 152. See Howarth, *Notes on Some Figures,* pp. 213, 307, for Eliot's continuing interest in a ritual theatre.

[17] Herbert Knust argues so, with brio, not to say desperation: see "What's the Matter with One-Eyed Riley?" *Comparative Literature* 4 (1965), 289-98. See also Grover Smith, *Eliot's Poetry and Plays,* pp. 87, 218, 220.

The Third Eye: The Relationship Between D. H. Lawrence and Maurice Maeterlinck

MICHAEL BALLIN

Twentieth-century literature is marked by a tense confrontation with the occult. Writers as diverse as W. B. Yeats, J. C. Powys, Aldous Huxley and Malcolm Lowry draw their inspiration from the occult roots of Gnosticism, Druidism, Hermeticism and Alchemy. D. H. Lawrence, a very representative writer of the twentieth century, is no exception. His occult roots, like those of Yeats, go back into the nineteenth century. The influence of Madame Blavatsky is particularly strong and has been well established if not exhaustively investigated.[1]

Theosophy provided Lawrence with an alternate to two elements in European western culture which he saw to be equally inimical and destructive: the established versions of orthodox Christianity, on the one hand, and nineteenth-century scientific materialism on the other. Hence occultism provided him with his "third eye." The term is part of occult tradition itself and refers to a third mystic perception resident physically in the pineal gland. Lawrence reacted against the perception of the world which lay at the back of Christianity and Scientific Materialism. He thought that Christianity tended to degenerate man's physical and bodily energies, while scientific materialism exaggerated the role of logical reason, placed an artificial barrier of abstract mentalism between

---

[1] Lawrence mentions Madame Blavatsky in connection with Rider, the publisher of the *Occult Review*. Aldous Huxley, ed., *The Letters of D. H. Lawrence* (London: Heinemann, 1956), p. 476. The influence of Madame Blavatsky is explored tentatively, in relationship to *The Plumed Serpent,* by William York Tindall, *D. H. Lawrence and Susan His Cow* (New York: Columbia, 1939). There is a more recent discussion of the influence of occultism on the earlier Lawrence in Emile Delavenay, *D. H. Lawrence: The Man and His Work, 1885-1919* (Carbondale and Edwardsville: Southern Illinois University Press, 1972), pp. 450-94.

subject and object and reduced mental perception to the "Kodak Vision" of a mental camera which merely reflects and is not instrumental in creating its object. The third eye of occult vision perceives, in contrast, the spiritual reality resident in the material and utilizes man's physical sensations as well as his mental vision in creating a total image that comprehends all of reality.

Occultism is thus a symbolic vision which, in terms of literary history, has a significant association with the symbolist movement, particularly the French symbolists such as Baudelaire and Verlaine. Related essentially to Lawrence's occultism is his symbolism. Harry T. Moore has drawn attention to Lawrence's "symbolist" associations.[2] Lawrence explains in his letters the importance of the symbolic mode for the writer who wants to include the whole truth about reality in his novels and to explore the mental realities which exist beneath the conscious ego of the personality. The stress on the presentation of the whole spectrum of experience extensively and intensively is the essence of Lawrence's occultism. He stressed, in relation to the question of Clifford's paralysis in *Lady Chatterley's Lover* that "all art is *au fond* symbolic."[3] Elsewhere he explores the mediaeval symbolic mode exemplified by the cathedral and asserts that it allowed the individual ego to see itself as part of a cosmic whole.[4] The main function of the symbolic mode was to universalize the application of individual experience and to create out of the "small futile tragedy" of a novel like *The Trespasser* an impersonal tragic vision.[5] Lawrence's development as a fiction writer involves a change from the mode of autobiographical realism informed by the symbolic in *Sons and Lovers,* to a dramatic symbolic mode. Lawrence's art of symbolism is essential to understand in order to get to grips with the formal qualities of his writing and with the nature of his tragic vision.

The explication of Lawrence's specific symbolic devices is an essential part of any more general understanding of his symbolism. The recurrent use of the horse symbol calls especially for explication. Lawrence uses this symbol in various ways from the time of *The Rainbow* and *Women in Love* to his last work, *Apocalypse.* His climactic use of it is in the short novel *St. Mawr* where the horse is almost the hero of the novel and certainly at the core of its symbolic meaning. It is important to arrive

[2] "He [Lawrence] was one of the first to adapt the methods of the French symbolists to the novel. Probably he did not realize that he was making any such adaptation; the influence may have been entirely osmotic. For in his youth he had read Baudelaire and Verlaine in the original, and probably other modern French poets." H. T. Moore, "*The Rainbow,*" in Harry T. Moore and F. Hoffman, eds., *The Achievement of D. H. Lawrence* (Norman: University of Oklahoma Press, 1953), p. 148.

[3] Harry T. Moore, ed., *Collected Letters* (New York: Viking Press, 1962), p. 1194.

[4] Ibid., pp. 301-302.

[5] D. H. Lawrence, *The Trespasser* (1912; rpt. London: Heinemann, 1955), p. 66.

at a specific analysis of this symbol and to apprehend the nature of its sequential development throughout his works. An analogue to this symbol in Maurice Maeterlinck reveals its occult roots in Lawrence's thought.

Horses have existed as symbols in European tradition from the time of the Greek Centaurs. Swift, and in our own time Edwin Muir, Ted Hughes, and Peter Shaffer, have availed themselves of the tradition in various ways. Part of the significance of Maeterlinck's analogue lies in the theosophical undercurrents of his thought. Maurice Maeterlinck (1862-1949) was consistently concerned with the presentation of the mystery beneath the surface of life in his plays and essays. In *The Great Secret*⁶ Maeterlinck explores the history of occultism and esoteric doctrine. He writes about Astrology, the Kabbala, nineteenth-century theosophy and contemporary psychical research. Many of these occult themes and theosophical sources are also reflected in Lawrence. Maeterlinck stresses the theosophical writings of Madame Blavatsky and Rudolph Steiner and describes the invasion of Oriental religion into nineteenth- and twentieth-century consciousness as the most important event since Christianity. Maeterlinck includes the following in his list of theosophical elements that are of outstanding interest to modern man: the rediscovery of Egyptian sources, a sense of the common unity of religions and the concept of an Atlantean past from which Man has declined. Maeterlinck also stresses a humanist identification of God with man: "God can only be found within yourself. Do not seek him in the Infinite" (71). Maeterlinck proclaims that man is the key to the universe and tries to revive the old occult correspondence between microcosm and macrocosm. Maeterlinck mentions such Renaissance occult sources as Paracelsus and Boehme.

These major themes are all echoed in various places in Lawrence's writings.⁷ The following works of Maeterlinck are known to have been read by Lawrence: *Pelleas and Mellisande* in 1909 and the drama *The Sightless* in the same year. The *Treasure of the Humble* is alluded to in 1911.⁸ The analogue to the horse symbol occurs in *The Unknown Guest*,

⁶ Maurice Maeterlinck, *The Great Secret* (New York: New York University Books, 1921).

⁷ "I honestly think that the great pagan world of which Egypt and Greece were the last living terms, the great pagan world which preceded our own era once, had a vast and perhaps perfect science of its own, a science in terms of life." Lawrence, *Fantasia of the Unconscious* (London: Heinemann, 1961), p. 6. Lawrence goes on at this point to talk about the unity of all religions and the mystery of Atlantis. "The subtle thing is the relation between the microcosm and the macrocosm. Get that relation—the Zodiac man to me —and you've got a straight clue to Apocalypsis." Harry T. Moore, ed., *Collected Letters*, p. 744. Lawrence is speaking about the imagery of Apocalypse, and mentions Jacob Boehme in this letter.

⁸ Jessie Chambers, in J. D. Charles, ed., *D. H. Lawrence: A Personal Record* (London: Frank Cass, 1965), p. 122.

first written in 1913 when Maeterlinck visited England. I have failed to find specific mention of this work in Lawrence but I first found reference to its discussion of the Elberfeld horses in *The Occult Review*, a periodical Lawrence certainly consulted more than once.[9] In the issue for 1919 there is a curious article by Ethel C. Hargrave, "Psychic Significance of Horse and Dog" where, with reference to Maeterlinck's essay it is stated that "there is in the horse and hence most probably in everything that lives in this earth a psychic power similar to that which is hidden beneath the veil of our reason."[10] I believe Lawrence is mainly concerned to explore this psychic correspondence.

In *Apocalypse* Lawrence actually explicates the use of his symbol. The horse, as symbol, is placed "far back, far back in our dark soul."[11] Such a location suggests a Jungian archetype, an area of primitive experience, communally shared, which is found in the recesses of the unconscious. He is in the dark area of the soul because he is hidden from the light of our conscious reason and he is seen as "the beginning of our godhead in the flesh."

The first use of the horse symbol in Lawrence's creative fiction is in *The Rainbow* just at the time when he wished to focus more fully on the deeper layers of psychic experience beneath the veil of consciousness. He often uses non-human analogues in order to define man's relationship to the material world. A psychic continuum is thus established between material and immaterial and between animal and human which affirms the essentially spiritual nature of reality.

The first appearance of the horse symbol comes at a climactic point at the close of this major novel. The heroine Ursula has separated from her lover Skrebensky, is with child by him and has written a letter in which she yields to him all her self-assertion and independence. She yields to the temptation to revert to the role of dutiful womanhood within the context of childbearing and submission to male dominance. She goes out for a walk and encounters the horses. They burst upon her and she climbs an oak tree to escape them. They pursue her, however, and in encountering them she apprehends, instantaneously and intuitively, a new knowledge. She is aware of the horses as an opposing

---

[9] Ethel C. Hargrave, "The Psychic Significance of Horse and Dog," in Ralph Shirley, ed., *The Occult Review* 30 (1919), 45-49.

[10] Lawrence wrote to S. S. Koteliansky for a copy of this review. Aldous Huxley, ed., *Letters of D. H. Lawrence* (London: Heinemann, 1956), p. 476. Maurice Maeterlinck, *The Unknown Guest* (London: Methuen, 1914).

[11] "Far back, far back in our dark soul the horse prances. He is a dominant symbol, he gives us lordship: he links us, the first palpable and throbbing link with the ruddy-glowing Almighty of potence: he is the beginning of our godhead in the flesh. And as a symbol he roams the dark underworld meadows of the soul. He stamps and threshes in the dark fields of your soul and mine. The sons of God who came down and knew the daughters of men and begot the great Titans, they had 'the members of horses,' says Enoch." Lawrence, *Apocalypse* (London: Martin Secker, 1932), pp. 109-10.

power. They conquer her and she is left weak and helpless after her trauma. The horses, too, are reduced in power. What knowledge does Ursula gain from her trauma? Eventually she gains "a new knowledge of Eternity in the flux of Time."[12] She also has to be born anew to a knowledge of her own identity and to realize her independence of Skrebensky despite the growth of his child within her. The horses, in assuming a hostile and threatening appearance, act out in symbolic form a psychic process. A suppressed part of Ursula's deeper psyche has taken its revenge on her whole psyche. In this way a false order is broken up and there is a chance for a new order to assert itself. The vision which directs this order comes from an eternal life source, independent of the ego but psychically continuous with the stuff of life and creation. The horses are a testimony to the independent reality of an extra-personal life energy to which man's psyche is dynamically connected. The vision is indeed occult, based on a mystic correspondence between the eternal life process and the psyche of man. Eternity and Time are brought together and the eternal principle renewed. In *Apocalypse* Lawrence is to emphasize that the horse is a symbol of our godhead in the flesh. Ursula's apostasy has thus been to her true created origin for, in Lawrence's view, spirituality is born out of materiality. Lawrence stresses the same viewpoint in his ironic reversal of "the Word is made Flesh"[13] in his unpublished foreword to *Sons and Lovers*. Ursula has betrayed the eternal principle manifest as her own true created origin.

The next major appearance of the horse symbol is in Chapter IX of *Women in Love*, "Coal Dust." This episode of Gerald Crich's brutal subjugation of the horse presents a series of oppositions between man and nature; between industrialism and organicism and between rational and instinctual modes of control. Gerald is in opposition to the horse; Ursula is in opposition to Gerald (associated with the horses in the previous novel) and Gerald is even opposed to Gudrun.

Gerald seems to demonstrate a masterful control over the horse which he is riding. The mastery seems to proceed from sensitivity as well as wilful control over the animal consciousness. Lawrence describes how, "whilst the two girls waited, Gerald Crich trotted up on a Red Arab mare. He rode well and softly, pleased with the delicate quivering of the creature between his knees."[14] Then the Satanic force of mechanical energy enters in the form of the railway locomotive. Gerald forces the horse to confront it. Ursula cries out in horror but

---

[12] Lawrence, *The Rainbow* (London: Heinemann, 1968), p. 492. All subsequent references are to this edition.

[13] Huxley, ed., *Letters*, p. 96.

[14] Lawrence, *Women in Love* (London: Heinemann, 1966), pp. 102-106. All subsequent references are to this edition.

Gerald forces the mare round, "like a keen edge biting home" (104). Gerald wounds the horse in his dominance and even presses on the wound. Ursula regards Gerald's act as one of senseless bullying. The gate-keeper, as impersonal observer, admires Gerald's persistence and reveals another opposition between Gerald and Thomas Crich. The Christian charity of the father is opposed to the ruthless control of the son. In another opposition, Ursula's exaltation of the delicacy and sensitivity of the horse is contrasted with the indomitable quality which Gudrun isolates in Gerald. Lawrence describes "a sort of soft, white magnetic domination from the loins and thighs and calves, enclosing and encompassing the mare heavily into unutterable subordination, soft-blood subordination, terrible" (106).

These three major references to the horse symbol in Lawrence follow a climactic progression. An upsurging life force shattering the harmony of the psyche in *The Rainbow* is followed by the presentation of the brutal subjection of the life principle in man in *Women in Love.* In Lawrence's final work, *Apocalypse,* the horse makes a triumphant last appearance as a divine archetype within the soul.

Maurice Maeterlinck's *The Unknown Guest*[15] presents a series of analogues which cast some light on the themes Lawrence explores in this sequence and may explain his continued reversion to this symbol. The analogue also casts light on one central theme explored in the symbolic sequence: a simultaneous process of technological advance and spiritual regression.

Maeterlinck wrote this work at a time when he was severely censured by the Catholic church for his views (Maeterlinck thought, wrongly, that he had been excommunicated). His visit to England in 1913 may well have attracted attention. At this time he had become interested in psychic phenomena and in September 1913 he went to Germany and met Herr Krall (later proved to be a fake) in a small Rhineland town. The German had supposedly trained his four horses at Elberfeld to do simple mathematical calculations by hoof tapping. To Maeterlinck the rapidity of the horses' response suggested the operation of an intuitive knowledge. The experience of this encounter with the horses together with Maeterlinck's contact in the same year with London's Society for Psychical Research fed his anti-rationalist vein of thinking.

The horse, named Muhamed, in *The Unknown Guest* presents an opposition betweeen freedom and bondage which is parallel to Lawrence's opposition between technological advance and spiritual regression. Maeterlinck tells us that there is present in Muhamed an "indefinable vast anxiety, a tear-dimmed regret for the boundless stream-crossed plains where his sires sported at will before they knew

[15] *The Unknown Guest,* pp. 202ff.

man's yoke" (202). The state of the free and unconstrained psyche put "far back in the soul" in Lawrence's *Apocalypse* is close to Maeterlinck's conception. This is the state which had caused such upheaval in Ursula in *The Rainbow* when she decided to capitulate to the male will. The horses are said to represent "the unknown" to Ursula, later defined a little more closely as the presence of Eternity manifested in Time. In Maeterlinck too the horses represent the unknown and the mysterious. The occult knowledge of the horses forces in Maeterlinck a questioning of the origin of our "silent brothers." The result of this quest is to create a "blush at man's long injustice. You look around you for some sort of trace, obvious or subtle, of the mystery."

The horse in Lawrence's *Women in Love* is attacked by the brute force of mechanism with a physical savagery which, in its turn, is an image of the distortion and fundamental disharmony of man's psyche. Modern science also attacks the mystery of existence, the sense of wonder which had left Ursula in *The Rainbow*. Maeterlinck's words describe very well the effects of the horses upon her: "You have felt a breath from the abyss upon your face. You would not be more astonished if you suddenly heard the voice of the dead" (208-209). After Ursula has thus confronted the unknown or the principle of Eternity in Time, she is forced to consider again the fundamental question of ends and goals. The miracle of the speaking horses forces Maeterlinck to ask "whither we are tending and what lies ahead of us" (217-18). Ursula similarly has to face the task of discovering her own life progress and, since the life of the individual psyche is also bound up with the progress of the whole Utopian order, the emerging forms of early twentieth-century society.

On the personal level Ursula is shaken out of her mixture of depression and complacency by the horse trauma and her imperative duty is to be an impersonal agent of the life force pushing us on into the quest for the unknown. The chief function of the horse trauma was to create an engagement in this quest. Maeterlinck has an interesting parallel in his account of the Elberfeld horses. He says, ". . . we might even ask ourselves if we have not here, on two different planes, a tension, a parallel pressure, a new desire, a new attempt of the mysterious spiritual force which animates the universe and which seems to be incessantly seeking fresh outlets and fresh conducting-rods" (253).

Even the flash of inspiration which galvanizes the horses does not last, however. As Maeterlinck puts it, men "behave very much as the animals do: we promptly lapse into indifferent sleep which suffices also for our miserable ways. We ask no more of it, we do not follow the luminous trail that summons us to an unknown world, we go on turning in our dismal circle, like contented sleep-walkers, Isis' sistrum routes without respite to rouse the faithful" (253). Maeterlinck's words are an excellent gloss on the passage in *The Rainbow* and they isolate for us Ursula's double fault. First comes Ursula's drift into a passive state of submission marked by her letter to Skrebensky. Then she goes to the wood in Willey Water where the horse trauma occurs. Lawrence describes how "she flitted along, keeping an illusion that she was unnoticed. She felt like a bird that has flown in through the window of a hall where vast warriors sit at the board" (486).

E. L. Nicholes has drawn attention to the analogue to a passage from Bede alluded to in Wordsworth's "Ecclesiastical Sonnet."[16] The bird passing in and out of the hall is a symbol of the soul passing from the unknown to the unknown. It is, in the words of Maeterlinck's title, "an unknown guest."

Eternity is a drama played out within time: the *whole* life process is concerned with past, present and future. The function of Lawrence's symbolism is to stress this inclusive time-continuum present in the depths of the human soul. Phrases from Maeterlinck's *The Unknown Guest* reflect a closely similar concern. Maeterlinck in his introduction refers to "blows struck from without by an unknown" (8). The psychic power in the horse is said to be "similar to that which is hidden beneath the veil of our reason" and it also forces us to "recognise the genius of the universe itself." Maeterlinck even affirms that it is from the darkest corners of our ego "that the unconscious directs our life: it alone knows the long path that preceded our birth and the endless future that will follow our departure from this earth." Lawrence similarly brings out (mostly through Ursula and elsewhere in symbolic allusion in *The Rainbow*) the sense of a counterpoint between the life of the personal ego and the life which is the ultimate ground of all our being. The life force represents within the individual not only the species but that which preceded it and that which will follow it.

Maeterlinck's *Treasure of the Humble* is a work which Lawrence had certainly read. It represents a compendium of Maeterlinck's ideas collected together over a long period of time.[17] The work is concerned once again with the spiritual element "struggling far down in the depths of humanity" and Maeterlinck stresses that it is in the workaday lives of the humblest of men that spiritual phenomena manifest themselves. The lives of Anna or Ursula Brangwen would be included by Maeterlinck amongst those in which can come that sudden Joycean epiphany which proclaims the spiritual nature of the humdrum. Such an experience is truer for Lawrence's women than for Lawrence's men. Maeterlinck also proclaims, "Women are the nearest kin to the Infinite that are about us"

---

[16] E. L. Nicholes, "The Symbol of the Sparrow in *The Rainbow*," in Hoffman and Moore, eds., *The Achievement of D. H. Lawrence*.

[17] Maurice Maeterlinck, *The Treasure of the Humble* (1896; rpt. New York: Dodd, Mead, 1903).

and that there is in our lives a necessity for a perpetual revelation of the divine.

The revelation of spiritual reality through woman reflects one of the deepest concerns in Lawrence's fiction. Ursula's kinship to the Infinite is proclaimed through her experience with the horses. It is also implicit in the symbolism of her name, alluded to in the novel in the episode where Birkin and Ursula talk to the couple in the barge. The name symbolism involves a triple allusion. Ursula, as a character who moves in the world of the Brangwen family, establishes her surface ego. Then she is St. Ursula, the educational adventurer of the soul, who is martyred at the end of a lengthy spiritual quest. (The "martyrdom" is echoed in the horse trauma.) Thirdly, there is an Ursula who is a moon goddess, representing, in the novel, the pagan forces of womanhood and its separate isolation.

Ursula thus acts as an impersonal agent of the life force. By means of a single character Lawrence is able to present dual aspects of the self: the "surface ego" which is part of the rational personality and the deeper permanent ego which is the bedrock of the personality. The abnegation of the self encouraged by Christianity is linked with the first self and the pagan life of knowledge in the flesh with the other. The Christian persona acts as a spiritual superego. The world of social interaction and professional work creates another self which is Ursula rather than *St.* Ursula. The ancient goddess "Ursa" is the "third eye" of the self, linked with the horses who effect retribution upon the martyr self, Ursula's Christian spirituality. Ursula's three personae reflect three warring and unintegrated strands in early twentieth-century civilization.

It is profitable to see *The Rainbow* and *Women in Love* as parallel in their relationship to one another rather than in a sequential relationship. When Lawrence began writing *The Sisters,* the large project which eventually resulted in the two separate novels, he had just finished working through the personal trauma of *Sons and Lovers.* In the novels which preceded it Lawrence had dealt with a more restricted experience in narrative. He describes *The Trespasser* as "the small personal tragedy." In his letters he emphasizes the desirability of moving beyond this restrictive sphere to present the impersonal, cosmic forces which control life. This development involves a movement towards a distinctively Lawrencian mode of tragedy which the writings of Maeterlinck again help to illuminate. It is necessary to examine the relationship between Ursula Brangwen in *The Rainbow* and Gerald Crich in *Women in Love* in a parallel fashion in order that the tragic perspective can be revealed.

Maeterlinck's stress upon spiritual epiphany in the lives of the humble may well have been significant to Lawrence at the time when he was concerned to raise the context of "the small personal life" to the level of the Infinite. The drawing of man into relation with cosmic powers had been achieved appropriately by means of the horse symbol. The humble domestic aid of man is given the occult dignity of a primitive archetype. Lawrence tries to do the same for his human characters.

The unique tragic status of Ursula and Gerald in Lawrence's fiction is also illuminated by Maeterlinck's writing. In *Treasure of the Humble* Maeterlinck shows how "there comes to us a sudden revelation of life in its stupendous grandeur, in its submissiveness to the unknown powers, in its endless affinities, in its awe-inspiring mystery" (110). Here Maeterlinck is exploring thematically the mystery which he had embodied symbolically in the horse in *The Unknown Guest*. It is just such a revelation at the close of *The Rainbow* which gives the appropriate tragic dimension to the character of Ursula. An almost Greek sense of Fate accompanies Lawrence's characteristically occult apprehension of a life force which sweeps the soul along to realize its destiny. Ursula conforms to the figure of the female Prometheus at the point where she climbs the oak tree and indulges in a kind of crucifixion of her feminine identity.[18] The death principle lies within the self and the human individual is thus the instrument of his own destructive crucifixion or creative resurrection.

In *Women in Love* the death principle is symbolically apprehended in terms of mechanism in the personality of Gerald Crich. His suppression of the horse symbolizes the repression of his own instinctual self and, on a larger scale, of the unknown powers of the life mystery. At the close of the novel there occurs a similar crucifixion and destruction of the individual to the one which had overtaken Ursula in *The Rainbow*. The Life Force wreaks a crushing vengeance upon Gerald. He is destroyed because he embraces the mechanical principle and yet he has to act as the submissive agent of unknown powers. This tragic dilemma comprises the irony of his Fate. The very term "Fate" suggests a tragic perspective reminiscent of the works of Thomas Hardy (to whom Lawrence was greatly indebted) in which man is the ironic victim of capricious gods. A degree of pessimism creeps into *Women in Love,* a novel which presents a perspective close to that of Hardy's view of tragedy, for Lawrence suggests that man himself may eventually be replaced by another kind of creation in the evolutionary scale.[19] The sense of waste and the element of heroic fatalism which Lawrence builds into the character of Gerald produces an authentic tragic tone in this work. It is important to note, however, that Gerald's tragic fatalism is presented as being the product of his own narrower perceptions about the nature of the universe. Lawrence's use of the occult and theosophical tradition

[18] *The Rainbow,* pp. 314, 315.
[19] *Women in Love,* p. 489.

enables him to place man within the context of a larger spiritual process which is sweeping him on to the realization of his ultimate destiny. The individual who blocks that life process in fact destroys himself. Man, in other words, is not in Lawrence's view a plaything of the gods or a mere victim of inanimate nature but a consciousness whose responsibility it is to realize its ultimate destiny. Man moves towards an apocalyptic fulfillment of the self. Lawrence's difficulty in this novel was the task of reconciling the evolutionary perspective with the theosophic.

The symbol of the horse was Lawrence's expression of his conception of man's ultimate origin. In *St. Mawr* Lawrence proclaims in fictional form the theosophical mysticism expressed in his explication of the horse symbol in *Apocalypse*. The importance of *St. Mawr* lies in the fact that it re-asserts that man's spirit is the oldest in the universe, that the body of man precedes the creation but that his pattern eternally changes. This is a perspective which replaces rather than works within the evolutionary perspective of the nineteenth century but at the same time transcends it. The vision is mystic, alchemical and occult, for it uses a framework of cyclic recurrence which is at the same time progressive. Man must know again his own spiritual origin in order to develop. This anterior knowledge urges him on to further forms of psychic and personal development. The full elaboration of this perspective comes in *The Plumed Serpent,* but *St. Mawr* is an important preliminary stage. *St. Mawr* certainly marks a climax in the developing sequence of the horse symbol, for in this tale the horse is the major character if not the hero of the work.

"How far from merely sexual the significance of the stallion is" comments F. R. Leavis in his discussion of *St. Mawr*.[20] St. Mawr is an ambiguous hero and the appearance of the horse in Lawrence has suggested that St. Mawr is a logical culmination of the symbol. The forces of modern life frustrate the instinctual energies embodied in the horse and thus he often displays antagonism. Leavis summarizes St. Mawr's dual function. As well as standing for "the deep springs of life" he embodies "the warning perception of the vitally dangerous, the wrong path" (239). Leavis also agrees that the symbol is in need of further elaboration.

Fresh elements certainly enter into the presentation of the symbol. He combines, in a new way, the symbolic elements already presented in the two major novels, *The Rainbow* and *Women in Love*. He also embodies a more distinctly "occult" symbolic message which is reinforced by the more obviously occult context within the work. St. Mawr points the way to a spiritual quest which man can follow in order to defend himself from the inimical mechanical energies of the modern world. A major physical journey from England to Texas, from the Old to

[20] F. R. Leavis, *D. H. Lawrence Novelist* (New York: Alfred Knopf, 1956), p. 298.

the New Worlds, accompanies the spiritual quest. *St. Mawr* arises out of a conflicting set of experiences. Lawrence departed from Mexico in 1923 to return to England. He found England dreary except for a trip he made to Shropshire (part of the action of *St. Mawr* is set there) where he met Frederick Carter, author of *The Dragon of the Alchemist* and mystic English painter. Carter was deeply involved in theosophy. He invited Lawrence to provide a preface to his book which was concerned with the pagan basis of the imagery of *The Book of Revelation*. The preface was never written but the material for it became Lawrence's last prose work: *Apocalypse*. *Apocalypse* investigated *Revelation* and contains the final presentation of the symbol of the horse.

The passage of the action of the novel from Shropshire to Texas symbolically reflects Lawrence's pilgrimage from the Christian rational world of western civilization to more esoteric reaches of thought in the traditions of the occult and the theosophical. The true significance of *St. Mawr* is surely to be found in the latter tradition. The horse is the symbolic focus that links the characters and the shifting location together.

Lou Witt is the human heroine, rival in this respect to the horse. She is an American, displaced in Europe and unable to find her way in English society. In her lack of purpose and direction, she symbolizes the spiritual bewilderment of contemporary western consciousness. She has a suitor, the rather flamboyant dilettante artist, Rice. When Lou first sees the horse St. Mawr, she becomes aware of Rice's deficiencies. St. Mawr is an alien in the London world of fashion. His power and energy reveal that Rice can only be a representative of the intuitive consciousness gone wrong. St. Mawr is not built for the London world of fashion in Rotton Row. Eventually he throws Rice while he is riding him and Rice's mother threatens to emasculate the horse. Lou's fascination for the horse almost amounts to a love relationship which paradoxically draws her away from the world of sexuality. She recognizes, nevertheless, the qualities of hostility and unconscious repression in St. Mawr.

St. Mawr thus functions partly as a mirror for the psychic disturbance of modern man. His groom comments: "If he was a human being, you'd say something had gone wrong in his life."[21] St. Mawr represents the archetypal experience of man, our ultimate psychic ancestry, and demonstrates that something has gone wrong with the physical consciousness of man.

The horse also provides a model for a rival mode of consciousness. He succeeds in partially releasing Lou's emotional repression and mental control. The horse embodies the concept of spirit in the form of its unity with the physical body. Lawrence tells us that he looked at Lou

[21] Lawrence, *St. Mawr* (Harmondsworth: Penguin, 1950), p. 20. All subsequent references are to this edition.

"out of another world" (122). These symbolic elements in the presentation of the horse were present in *The Rainbow* and *Women in Love*. He
looks backwards to the past psychic life of man and points the way to an
alternative, non-rational vision for the future. He also demonstrates the
demonic power of energy which is blocked or frustrated and which can
then become evil or destructive.

Lawrence does not only recapitulate the symbolic values explored
in the earlier works, for he makes a further exploration in *St. Mawr*. He
expands the capacity of his symbol to point to the true nature of man and
to provide an alternative vision to the progressive and evolutionary one
of the earlier major novels. The horse becomes the mythic embodiment
of man's ultimate origin. Lawrence conjectures, "Perhaps the old Greek
horses had lived in St. Mawr's world" (27). Lawrence also recognizes
that to the Greek rationalist vision the Centaurs represented the values
of a barbaric world where "they moved in a prehistoric twilight where all
things loomed phantasmagoric."

For this reason emasculated twentieth-century English culture
reacts only with fear and mistrust to St. Mawr's challenge. The essence
of the horse's power is conveyed through allusive imagery. Lawrence
hints at a dark vitality, a wisdom within a dark fire. Rather like William
Blake's tiger, St. Mawr seems to represent revitalizing energy or Satanic
destruction, according to the way in which you relate to him. The
function of the symbol is again to attack and disturb the calm assump-
tions of western Christian culture and to present the elements in life and
nature which the Christian and/or rational tradition cannot encompass.

The horse operates as a touchstone, setting off the psychic sensitivity of all the major characters. As soon as Lou sees St. Mawr she cries
over him, "the wild, brilliant alert head of St. Mawr seemed to look at her
out of another world" (20). Once more the horse is presented as an
"unknown guest" who comes to trouble, disturb and reveal the deficiencies of man. The most momentous result of this visitation for Lou
Witt is her dislocation from the normal tracks of social life and marriage.
She now has to embark upon a solitary pilgrimage into the unknown.
Lou realizes that the question "where are we going?" is one of ultimate
importance to her. She is destined to engage in the onward struggle for
further creative life.

The blow St. Mawr strikes against the human characters is again
"from the unknown." St. Mawr may stand, as Leavis says, for the
forces of life but he stands also for a secondary visionary quality which
points the way to a mode of consciousness in direct antithesis to the
modern rationalistic one. This concept is revealed in Lou's experience:
"When he [St. Mawr] reared his head and neighed from his deep chest,
like deep wind bells resounding, she seemed to hear the echoes of
another darker, more spacious, more dangerous, more splendid world
than ours, that was beyond her" (34).

This more splendid world is defined symbolically in the two separate geographical locations of the novel: Shropshire, and New Mexico. First, all the characters move from London to Shropshire. Rural England is a foil to the modish life of London. The transition from the city is a step in the direction of rediscovery of a more natural image for man, and it helps to point the way to a more vital relationship between man and the universe. Dean Vyner is a new character in the tale who first appears in the Shropshire environment. It is he who makes St. Mawr's symbolic function quite clear for he indicates that the horse manifests an alternative religious mode of vision for twentieth-century man provided by the context of the occult. Lawrence tells us that Dean Vyner "studied esoteric matters like astrology and alchemy." The combination of these subjects is repeated significantly in Frederick Carter's *Dragon of the Alchemist*. Vyner mentions the vision of the third eye, an occult mode of vision whose reality is established within that tradition. In the course of a social conversation the subject of the great god Pan is raised rather awkwardly. The terms "goat Pan" and "god Pan" are interchanged whimsically. Pan was once a great God before he was transformed into a half human entity. Through the persona of Vyner, Lawrence appears to be searching for a pre-Hellenic vision, a quest which he had pursued in his researches into the *Book of Revelation*. Pan is an entity which transcends sex or any personal form of identity. He can be perceived symbolically as darkness by the spiritual eye which can perceive only what is hidden from the material eye. Lou and Mrs. Witt agree that the unfallen Pan is hidden from them all. But he is in St. Mawr who is neither satyr nor Centaur but a being who balances spiritual power with the energy of the physical body.

Lawrence reflects the one basic physical truth that man is a fallen creature who has departed from his true nature. He shares this much at least with orthodox Christian belief. Lawrence's view of man's salvation is presented in a more individual way and in terms of occultism rather than in any official religion. The record of the visit to the Devil's Chair in Shropshire first presents an image of the demonic as the reversal of energy. The earth is said to be inundated like the Old Atlantis with an engulfing flood of evil (76). St. Mawr is not evil himself: he represents man's crucifixion of the natural forces of life, for Lawrence perceives that "Life must destroy life in the unfolding of creation" (79). When St. Mawr overturns Rice he is kicking back at man's desertion of the vital life principles. St. Mawr is grieving for man's Judas-like desertion of him.

Lou and Mrs. Witt are urged onwards to reach out for more than England's rational, established Christian world. The object of their search is the creative spirit of life preserved in Nature, particularly in the horse and other aspects of animal creation. The mother and daughter are attracted by the occult traditions of Celtic peoples, introduced into the tale in the person of Lewis, St. Mawr's groom. It is important to note that a human character, associated in a vital way with the occult power of the horse, is himself an occultist who believes neither in the perspectives of modern science nor in the vision of Christianity. He uses the third eye of occult vision for he claims to be able to see "the moon people" who live forever, to be able to listen to the speech of trees and apparently to live in an animalistic world. Laura Ridley comments, "I shouldn't wonder if he [Lewis] had psychic powers... could *see* things—and hypnotic too" (130).

The occult folk tradition of England prepares for the final relocation of the action and of St. Mawr from England to Texas. The transference is not as haphazard or as inconsequential as it may seem. In New Mexico Lawrence was to find a fresh religious vision which showed how man's psyche could be reconnected with the universe. *St. Mawr* marks a change in Lawrence's perspective on the nature of twentieth-century man from that which he had dramatized in *The Rainbow* and *Women in Love*. In the earlier novels he had worked within a pessimistic tragic framework possibly derived from the novels of Thomas Hardy. The evolutionary perspective was harnessed to a tragic and destructive pessimism which presented an impersonal life force overtaking and destroying the human form of life and not hesitating to replace it with some other manifestation higher or lower on the evolutionary spiritual ladder. Lawrence asserts, through Birkin in *Women in Love*, the consoling power of this concept for "if humanity ran into a cul-de-sac, and expended itself, the timeless creative mystery would bring forth some other being, finer, more wonderful, some new, more lovely race, to carry on the embodiment of creation" (470). The theosophical tradition gave Lawrence an alternative with which to work. The symbol of the horse is employed in a more positive way in its latest manifestation in *St. Mawr*. The spiritualistic vision of *Apocalypse* informs the horse symbol as it is used in *St. Mawr* for the horse is rescued from the destructive forces which predominate in the earlier major novels. The symbol enables Lawrence to present Man not as a late evolutionary phenomenon in Nature, in accordance with the Darwinian perspective, but as the eternally changing pattern of the mind of the greater Man. Progress is ironically a matter of return to ultimate origins. If man defects from the responsibility for this return to origins he can destroy not only himself but all of universal order.

The clarification of Lawrence's symbolism is an important part of a full critical realization of the complexity of his fiction. The occult context of the symbolism, illuminated in the case of the horse symbol by the Maeterlinck analogue, helps to provide another layer of mythical meaning which complements the emotional level present in the psychological action. Lawrence strove to universalize the human action of his novels within a philosophical framework which could expand and make more sympathetic the Protestant Christian tradition within which he was nurtured.

Iris Murdoch and Vladimir Nabokov: An Essay in Literary Realism and Experimentalism

I

This commentator may be excused for repeating what he has stressed in his own books and lectures, namely that "offensive" is frequently but a synonym for "unusual"; and a great work of art is of course always original, and thus by its very nature should come as a more or less shocking surprise. I have no intention to glorify "H.H." No doubt he is horrible, he is abject, he is a shining example of moral leprosy, a mixture of ferocity and jocularity that betrays supreme misery perhaps, but is not conducive to attractiveness. He is ponderously capricious. Many of his casual opinions on the people and scenery of this country are ludicrous. A desperate honesty that throbs through his confession does not absolve him from sins of diabolical cunning. He is abnormal. He is not a gentleman. But how magically his singing violin can conjure up a tendresse, a compassion for Lolita that makes us entranced with the book while abhorring its author!

> John Ray, Jr., PhD., in the "Foreword" to *Lolita,*
> by Vladimir Nabokov

The court room and the judge and the condemnation for life were mere shadows of a much huger and more real drama of which I was the hero and the victim. Human love is the gateway to all knowledge, as Plato understood. And through the door that Julian opened my being passed into another world.

When I thought earlier that my ability to love her *was* my ability to write, my ability to exist at last as the artist I had disciplined my life to be, I was in truth, but knew it only darkly. All great truths are mysteries, all morality is ultimately mysticism, all real religions are mystery religions, all great gods have many names. This little book is important to me and I have written it as simply and as truthfully as I can. How good it is I do not know and in a sublime sense I do not care. It has come into being *as* true art comes, with absolute necessity and with absolute ease. That it is not great art I daresay I

am aware. What kind of thing it is is dark to me as I am dark to
myself. The mechanical aspects of our humanity remain obscure to
us until divine power has refined them absolutely, and then there is
no anxious knower any more and nothing to be known. Every man is
tiny and comic to his neighbour. And when he seeks an idea of
himself he seeks a false idea.

Iris Murdoch, *The Black Prince*, p. 337

The most cursory reading of Iris Murdoch's *The Black Prince*
(1973) evokes echoes of Nabokov's greatest novel, *Lolita* (Paris, 1955;
New York, 1958), and causes a curious coupling in the mind of these
similar, dissimilar experimental novels. It is not my purpose in this essay
to conjecture influence or to conjure up the tedium that characterizes so
many sadly inefficient "comparative" studies. Rather, I wish to use
these two extraordinary novels as a springboard for a necessarily brief
discussion of the problems of literary realism within the novel, and the
relationship of that realism to the experimentation which has become
the natural direction of the genre in the twentieth century.

Generally, we have taught ourselves to see the novel as having a
two-pronged development. First in interest for the contemporary reader
is the anti-realistic experimental novel which proceeds from Cervantes'
Don Quixote, through Sterne's *Tristram Shandy,* to its greatest triumph
in Joyce's *Ulysses,* and finally to such lesser but highly significant
writers as Nabokov, Queneau, Beckett, the French new novelists, and
the anti-novelistic Argentinian Borges, whose short story is a whisper or
a skeleton to be rendered fully novelistic by an act of the responding
imagination. The other form of the novel stems from an instinct for
verisimilitude, and has its base in both the heroism of the epic and the
extended narrative forms of mediaeval romance. Basically, its
eighteenth-century predecessors are Defoe and especially Richardson,
whose *Clarissa* remains one of the most impressive books in English
literary history. The great hey-day of realism was, of course, the
nineteenth century in England, Russia, and to some degree, France and
America. Certainly, specialized and naturalistic realism is the gift of
France and America—Zola, Balzac, Dreiser and his American
followers—and it is with a certain degree of conscious effort that we
remind ourselves that the greatest verisimilar novels come from much
better writers for whom the idea of the *tranche de vie* was not a limiting
principle—George Eliot, Dickens, Tolstoi, Proust, James.

One might clarify the distinction between modes of experimentation and modes of realism by pointing out the intellectual gamesmanship
(Johan Huizinga's theory of "play" in *Homo Ludens* is important here)
which preoccupies the experimentalist, as opposed to the allegiance to
the quotidian of the realist writer. Although it is correct to say that the
experimentalist is largely concerned with form and its extensions, the
most interesting writers of this sort tend to be obsessed with

metaphysics and to use fiction as a vehicle for the exploration of the nature and possibilities of art. It is, doubtless, because of this quest that experimentalism has so seized the contemporary imagination. The conventional or realist writer, on the other hand, is equally obsessed, but by other less abstract concerns. Character, action, plot and, above all, "truth" and "reality,"[1] are his centres and he sees his fictions as serving society or, as in Tolstoi's or George Eliot's case, history. The conventional novel is very consoling—one thinks of the sheer pleasure of reading a Jane Austen novel—and an excellent instrument for ordering a recalcitrant universe. The conventional novel, in spite of many exceptions, has tended toward the closed, as opposed to the more open experimental ending and usually has its antecedents in the ancient notion of comedy (concluding with marriage), although the closed tragedy is also a possibility. Hence its great popularity in the nineteenth century, even amid Hardyesque bleakness.

In terms of readership and literary criticism, the novel has become and remains the most studied and fascinating genre of the twentieth century. Critically the dichotomy of experimental, open-ended, anti-realist versus conventional, closed, realist, has been received as basic, and not only critics but novelists themselves tend to line up on one side or the other, even though it is quite clear that, as in all cases of labelling, the terms are not as simply and absolutely opposed and separated as the rather clumsy instrument of literary criticism would suggest.

It is, in fact, a primary problem in consideration of the novel that most readers are trained (one might even apply behaviourist vocabulary and say they are conditioned) to expect realism or verisimilitude. The difficulty may be even more primal and have to do with basic human response to stories, which we tend to receive simply and literally; the play of the mind at its more subtle levels is a sophisticated and unnerving development which challenges truth, belief, reality and our relationship to them. Thus the experimental novel is never consoling, although it may flatter the intellect; in terms of popularity, then—and we must always keep before us the incontrovertible fact that the novel is essentially a *popular* genre—the conventional or realist novel is the one which is aimed at, and best received by, the greatest segment of the reading public, however diminished that public may be in our era. Generally, then, the conventional novel will appeal to the general reader, the experimental to the *literati*.

With this in mind, I have found it ideally convenient to use Vladimir Nabokov and Iris Murdoch as illustrative centres for a discussion of the

---

[1] Nabokov claims that such words as reality should always be put in quotation marks. "Reality" and "truth" are terms only conventional, verisimilar writers will use: Murdoch, one should add, is devoted to them. See Vladimir Nabokov, *The Annotated 'Lolita'*, ed. Alfred Appel, Jr. (New York: McGraw-Hill, 1970), p. 324, note 6/4. See also "On a Book Entitled *Lolita*," p. 314.

problems of realism within experimentalism. Nabokov sees himself as an experimentalist, a direct descendant of Sterne and Joyce, although he disclaims direct or particular influence;[2] Murdoch sees herself as—or rather aspires to be—a realist writer in the tradition of Dickens or perhaps James. Certainly their critics would label the one an experimentalist, the other a realist, although Murdoch suffers under the additional burden of her philosophical training and publications, and has also been accused, by limited and oppressive reviewers, of being merely a philosophical novelist.

The initial reception of both *Lolita* and *The Black Prince* was clouded by the literalism of the reviewers and by the reputation of the authors. For both Nabokov and Murdoch, these serious and masterly novels occur at an advanced stage in their distinguished literary careers; both were experienced writers, in their fifties at the time of publication (Nabokov fifty-six, Murdoch fifty-three), and had many books to their credit, but here the resemblance ends. By 1955, when the Olympia Press in Paris first published *Lolita,* Nabokov had been in America for fifteen years, was teaching the European novel at Cornell, and was only dimly known in the United States as a writer with a limited, côterie following. Most of his previous publications had been in Europe, and the bulk of them were in Russian. The manuscript of *Lolita* had been turned down by four American publishers[3] on the basis of indecency, smuttiness, pornography, before Girodias published it in Paris under Olympia Press's quasi-pornographic imprimatur. Its real success came with its American publication by Putnam in 1958. Its status as a best-seller was established largely because of literal readings of Humbert Humbert as merely a sexual pervert, perversion always outselling intellect or literary merit. But in spite of some outraged reviewers, *Lolita* was almost instantly recognized by the literary establishment as an experimental novel of a very high order indeed. Thus the book has had a dual critical reception, balanced between naïve or short-sighted literalism and a knowledgeable recognition of the Nabokovian genius.

Murdoch's *The Black Prince* (1973), almost twenty years *Lolita*'s junior, presents us with a very different background of publication and reception. From the appearance of her first novel in 1954, *Under the Net,* Murdoch has turned out a novel almost every year. This one, *The Black Prince,* was her fifteenth, and was received as one more in a series of enormously entertaining books. Her audience was already fixed to a degree; Murdoch is a writer who calls out extreme responses of ardent discipleship or violent dislike, but her readers, by the time of *The Black Prince,* felt a deep sense of familiarity with her world. In spite of some

---

[2] *The Annotated 'Lolita',* p. 395, note 200/3.
[3] Vladimir Nabokov, "On a Book Entitled *Lolita,*" in *The Annotated 'Lolita',* pp. 315-16.

mild experimentation in the past (the elements of Beckett in *Under the Net*, the Gothic displacement of *The Unicorn*, the contrived, almost Shakespearean ironic closure of *Bruno's Dream*, the murder-mystery/detective-story forefront of *The Nice and the Good*), she had been generally a realist, a conventional novelist, a reliable narrator. Her other first-person narrators, Jake Donaghue in *Under the Net*, Edmund Narraway in *The Italian Girl*, Martin Lynch-Gibbon in *A Severed Head*, were handled skilfully but without the inclination to throw the reader's response off balance, to disorient his point of view, which is usually included in the concept of experimentalism. In other words, Murdoch's audience was prepared for the status quo and reacted accordingly. The newspaper reviewers blandly put forth their Murdoch-as-usual blurbs (the then anonymous *TLS* reviewer came closest to some sort of technical insight in describing this as her *Hamlet*, but he did not carry this to the logical conclusion the analogy would imply, since *Hamlet* is surely the most vexed, daring, high-risk experiment Shakespeare tried), and unfortunately the few books on Murdoch's opus which include discussions of *The Black Prince* tackle it rather wearily, even confusing characters' names.[4]

Whereas *Lolita* suffered from public underexposure to Nabokov's range and talent, *The Black Prince* was too generally misapprehended because of Murdoch's established reputation and the consistent and monolithic nature of her fictional world. I would like to argue that it is her best novel, and technically her most daring and interesting one, for in it she combines her longing for realism and for the quotidian freedom of characters within a realistic world with experimental devices which expand her fiction into a serious inquiry into the nature of truth and its relation to art. In other words, her experiment is to effect a coalescence of the conventional and the experimental, to try to see whether she—or rather the art of the novel—can have it both ways; in doing so, she is, I think, trying to advance the potentiality of the novel within its historical and literary backgrounds. Like all realist authors, she is committed to the novel's mission to the bourgeoisie or the common reader, and she therefore writes of believable characters in believable contemporary London circumstances. She is also, as she has pointed out in her essays in theory of the novel, especially in "Against Dryness,"[5] convinced that the task of art is to transcend reality, to take its reader from limited existential concepts of "sincerity" to what can best be described as transcendent Platonic ideas of truth, an idea with which Nabokov will not juggle. The difficulty, the lies, the tricks of this quest can best be relayed through the medium of experimentalism.

⁴ Frank Baldanza, in *Iris Murdoch* (New York: Twayne Publishers, 1973), confuses Julian Baffin with Christian, Bradley's first wife. A serious mistake.

⁵ Iris Murdoch, "Against Dryness," *Encounter* 16 (January 1961), 16-20.

II

Before we can see very clearly what Murdoch has attempted, it is helpful to see what a master experimentalist like Nabokov has achieved. Both *Lolita* and *The Black Prince* show their line of descent from Lewis Carroll's *Alice in Wonderland,* with Humbert Humbert, the narrator of *Lolita,* inheriting an extreme form of Carroll/Dodgson's attraction to little girls, while Bradley Pearson, the narrator of *The Black Prince* takes on a strange form of Carroll's prudish, nineteenth-century puritanism. Both narrators are involved in January-May relationships (January-April in the case of Lolita) in which it is understood that there is something peculiarly disgusting to society in such sexual interest. Both participate in the ageless tradition—from Propertius, Catullus, Horace, Dante, Shakespeare—which sees art and love as intensely interdependent, and which asserts that the purpose of the work of art is the enunciation and subsequent immortality of the loved one. Although Nabokov says that he has no moral in tow,[6] the point of the book is to work from the trap of solipsism—H.H.'s total, selfish absorption in his perversion, "nympholepsy"—to the outward generosity of a love which transcends the perversion of this self-concentration. In his last interview with Lolita who is about to reject him and who will shortly die in childbirth, Humbert Humbert is able to indicate his progression:

> ... and I looked and looked at her, and knew as clearly as I know I am to die, that I loved her more than anything I had ever seen or imagined on earth, or hoped for anywhere else. She was only the faint violet whiff and dead leaf echo of the nymphet I had rolled myself upon with such cries in the past; an echo on the brink of a russet ravine, with a far wood under a white sky, and brown leaves choking the brook, and one last cricket in the crisp weeds ... but thank God it was not that echo alone that I worshiped. What I used to pamper among the tangled vines of my heart, *mon grand péché radieux,* had dwindled to its essence: sterile and selfish vice, all *that* I canceled and cursed. You may jeer at me, and threaten to clear the court, but until I am gagged and half-throttled, I will shout my poor truth. I insist the world know how much I loved my Lolita, *this* Lolita, pale and polluted, and big with another's child, but still gray-eyed, still sooty-lashed, still auburn and almond, still Carmencita, still mine.[7]

And the concluding sentences of the book summarize the function of art as an instrument asserting the permanence and significance of love in the face of time and death—the time that disallows Lolita's role as nymphet to be eternal, and the death that will seize her before the book can be published. Frail, physical Lolita will perish, but H.H.'s art, prompted

---

[6] "On a Book Entitled *Lolita,*" p. 316.
[7] Vladimir Nabokov, *Lolita* (New York: Putnam, 1958), pp. 279-80. All quotations are from this edition.

by love, will endure: *ars longa, vita brevis,* once again: "I am thinking of aurochs and angels, the secret of durable pigments, prophetic sonnets, the refuge of art. And this is the only immortality you and I may share, my Lolita" (p. 311).

Fortunately, Nabokov is not enslaved by his idea, and what makes *Lolita* such a dazzling book is its literary scope, its moment-by-moment verbal brilliance, its Joycean fecundity, its purely Nabokovian play. In the spirit of experimentalism, Nabokov is deeply absorbed in form, and the game he plays requires more than all of the intelligence of the reader. As a writer, Nabokov is an elitist (Alfred Appel, Jr. claims that he and Borges are the most mandarin of contemporary fictionmakers)—almost maddeningly so, in that, although most of his references can be tracked down, several are non-allusive,[8] and are perversely put in to confound the elitist reader who is also playing this game of intelligence. In the enclosed world of his narration, presented alike to the "reader" and to the "gentlemen of the jury" who are to judge him indirectly for his debauching of Lolita and specifically for the murder of Quilty, Humbert Humbert meets only one like mind, one equal—his double, his *alter ego,* Quilty, the dramatist, the artist, the pervert. This dark, shadow double can scatter clues, literary references, grotesque puns with an expertise which H.H. recognizes as his own and which again asserts the self-concentration of the book. The reader, on the tail of H.H. and Quilty, is basically excluded from the game, in spite of H.H.'s several addresses to him; the significance of every name, list, turn of event is only caught on re-reading, on checking back with a gasp of amazement as significance floods what had appeared to be a straightforward, non-connotative moment (e.g., *Who's Who in the Limelight,* the list of Lolita's classmates, Charlotte's statement that H.H.'s watch is waterproof, the mention of the dentist next door).

Although H.H. appears to be ultimately interested in addressing a Quiltian *alter ego* rather than his reader or ostensible jury, there is another relationship concurrently exercised, that between Nabokov and the reader, who is nudged into consciousness of the real authorial presence by the recurrent anagram of Nabokov's name—Vivian Darkbloom. The effect of this secondary relationship which is rather coyly presented is to remind us that this is a fiction, that H.H. is only a vehicle for Nabokov's talent, and that the whole book is a *jeu,* an *oeuvre*—that it is, in short, emphatically *not* verisimilar or realistic.

John Ray, Jr., PhD., the putative editor of H.H.'s tale and author of the "Foreword" (the most telling paragraph of which I have quoted as one of the headnotes or epigraphs of this essay) is a typical academic, professor and critic, whose stupidity can be counted on. In using him,

---

[8] Alfred Appel, Jr., in *The Annotated 'Lolita',* is a reliable sleuth in differentiating the referential from the non-referential.

Nabokov, always lively in condescension, indicates the purblind nature of established literary criticism: of course, Ray will concentrate on psychoanalysis (Nabokov's hatred of Freud is everywhere documented) and moral lessons (nothing could interest Nabokov less). And even more crucially, Ray will misunderstand Nabokov's point about Humbert Humbert, taking him literally as a disgusting pervert rather than seeing him as a means of embodying the destructive absolute of solipsism. From his early statement during his first sexual play with the still innocent (of him, at least) Lolita, H.H. shows his capacity to ignore her, to satisfy himself without realizing her:

> With the deep hot sweetness thus established and well on its way to the ultimate convulsion, I felt I could slow down in order to prolong the glow. Lolita had been safely solipsized. (p. 62)

But H.H. develops to a final self- and perversion-denying acknowledgement that he loves the post-nymphetic Lolita, that he is able to *see* her, recognize her being, and love her rather than himself. *Lolita* is an illustration of human transcendence, of the vital idea of metamorphosis from time and selfishness to timelessness and eternality—to, in short, the ultimate achievement of great art in its triumph over human limitation.

To receive the fiction of *Lolita* on a literal level, as Ray does and as too many readers have unfortunately done, to allow oneself to read it not as a game but as a realistic novel where the story line and surface event are seen as verisimilar reportage is to limit the experience of the novel and to impede advancement beyond flimsy surface meanings. As I indicated earlier, the purely experimental novel is in active contradiction to the realistic work, and tends to be more abstract, metaphysical, and concerned with self-conscious recognitions of the nature of art. Its larger intentions are theoretical rather than practical, and in detail it tends to be more witty, ironic and parodic than the conventional novel, and very much centred on wordplay. Nabokov's scorn of the critic who would make a "realistic" judgment of H.H. shows the degree to which he sees his work as separated from the mainstream of the bourgeois novel and its wide practical appeal. Nabokov writes for the intellectual mandarin who can be vastly amused at the irony of surfaces, knowing that they are surfaces only, and for the reader who can, moment by moment, with awe and congratulations, follow the complex manoeuvrings of an infinitely talented writer. And in the process, that highly qualified reader will be reminded freshly and astonishingly of the real nature and purpose of art: Nabokov demands much and delivers much.

It would be wrong, having made a point of the anti-realistic stress of *Lolita,* to pass over its very real pleasures, particularly since they contribute to its status as a highly successful, thoroughly representative experimental novel. Many of them are elements that are shared with

Murdoch's *The Black Prince,* such as the feeling of literary backgrounds and antecedents (Murdoch's novel is also highly allusive and could bear an annotating of the sort that Alfred Appel, Jr. has done for *Lolita*), the presentation of a literary autobiographical manuscript as a defence against murder charges, the sense of an enormous chess game in the mediaeval tradition which so characterizes Nabokov's style (Bradley Pearson also worries in midstream that "in my chess game with the dark lord I had made perhaps a fatally wrong move"[9]), the haunting of destiny (represented by a fellow wittily named Aubrey McFate in *Lolita*), and the identity of art with the loved ones, Lolita and Julian, to mention only a few and obvious examples. But there are many other purely Nabokovian elements, including the genius of the mixed form—autobiographical narrative, plus journal entries, the sense of murder-mystery/detective-story in the Gustave Trapp/Quilty/H.H. contest, the ironically connected play-within-the-play of Quilty's *The Enchanted Hunters,* the collapse into determinism when H.H. has finally killed his *alter ego*: "This, I said to myself, was the end of the ingenious play staged for me by Quilty" (p. 307).

Perhaps the most interesting achievements, however, are the transmission of American popular culture of the late forties and early fifties, and the ingenious handling of death. In *Lolita,* European (H.H.) and American (Lolita) culture encounter each other with connection but mutual abhorrence. The controversy over Nabokov's point of view is very predictable, Europeans claiming that *Lolita* is anti-American, Americans asserting the opposite.[10] Certainly in the depiction of Lolita herself, the vulgarity of Americans and the shabby nature of American popular culture are exploited to the full, and in the description of H.H.'s and Lolita's trips across the United States, the dreariness of stores, gas-stations, motels, and highway life are very much in the forefront. But Nabokov also carefully tells us that the problem lies in H.H.'s selfish misapprehension:

> And so we rolled East. I more devastated than braced with the satisfaction of my passion, and she glowing with health, her bi-iliac garland still as brief as a lad's, although she had added two inches to her stature and eight pounds to her weight. We had been everywhere. We had really seen nothing. And I catch myself thinking today that our long journey had only defiled with a sinuous trail of slime the lovely, trustful, dreamy, enormous country that by then, in retrospect, was no more to us than a collection of dog-eared maps, ruined tour books, old tires, and her sobs in the night—every night, every night—the moment I feigned sleep. (pp. 177-78)

[9] Iris Murdoch, *The Black Prince* (London: Chatto and Windus, 1973), p. 212. All quotations are from this edition.

[10] Nabokov himself, in "On a Book Entitled *Lolita,*" claims that accusations of anti-Americanism wound him.

The final point I would like to make about *Lolita* is that it is about death—it reeks of death; there are no survivors. At the end of his narrative, H.H. says: ". . . Dolly Schiller will probably survive me by many years. The following decision I make with all the legal impact and support of a signed testament: I wish this memoir to be published only when Lolita is no longer alive" (pp. 310-11). The fact that we have just read it means that she is dead. Indeed, John Ray, Jr. had told us in the "Foreword" of Dolly Schiller's death in Gray Star, but this is another Nabokovian trick; we do not recognize Mrs. Schiller as Lolita until very late in the book. As we read, then, H.H. is dead of a coronary, Lolita dead in childbirth, Charlotte Haze violently dead, Quilty murdered, even poor, momentary Jean Farlow dead of cancer at thirty-three. Human frailty and evanescence are well established and are fought only with the instrument of art itself: Lolita dies in time, *Lolita* survives joyfully in the immortality of art. A brilliant *coup*.

III

In 1961, Iris Murdoch wrote: "It takes a foreigner like Nabokov or an Irishman like Beckett to animate prose language into an imaginative stuff in its own right."[11] Even in *The Black Prince,* her most experimental novel, Murdoch does not play with language in the witty, fecund way that characterizes her two experimentalist predecessors. For her, the wordgame is serious rather than funny, to be meditated on endlessly, and with infinite moral, spiritual, and artistic results. The best statement she has ever made of her view of the nature of art occurs in this book, and is made in reference to Shakespeare whom she constantly refers to as the greatest artist, the closest to godhead. The narrator, fifty-eight-year-old Bradley Pearson, is talking to twenty-year-old Julian Baffin about *Hamlet,* giving her a lecture which will be instrumental in the maelstrom experience of falling in love with her. I will quote fully, since this is the centre of the novel:

> '*Hamlet* is nearer to the wind than Shakespeare ever sailed, even in the sonnets. Did Shakespeare hate his father? Of course. Was he in love with his mother? Of course. But that is only the beginning of what he is telling us about himself. How does he dare to do it? How can it not bring down on his head a punishment which is as much more exquisite than that of ordinary writers as the god whom he worships is above the god whom they worship? He has performed a supreme creative feat, a work endlessly reflecting upon itself, not discursively but in its very substance, a Chinese box of words as high as the tower of Babel, a meditation upon the bottomless trickery of consciousness and the redemptive role of words in the lives of those without identity, that is human beings. *Hamlet* is words, and so is Hamlet. He is as witty as Jesus Christ, but whereas

[11] "Against Dryness," p. 19.

Christ speaks Hamlet is speech. He is the tormented *empty sinful consciousness of man seared by the bright light of art, the god's flayed victim dancing the dance of creation.* The cry of anguish is obscure because it is overheard. It is the eloquence of direct speech, it is *oratio recta* not *oratio obliqua.* But it is not addressed to us. Shakespeare is passionately exposing himself to the ground and author of his being. He is speaking as few artists can speak, in the first person and yet at the pinnacle of artifice. How veiled that deity, how dangerous to approach, how almost impossible with impunity to address, Shakespeare knew better than any man. *Hamlet* is a wild act of audacity, a self-purging, a complete self-castigation in the presence of the god. Is Shakespeare a masochist? Of course. He is the king of masochists, his writing thrills with that secret. But because his god is a real god and not an *eidolon* of private fantasy, and because love has here invented language as if for the first time, he can change pain into poetry and orgasms into pure thought—'... 'Shakespeare here makes the crisis of his own identity into the very central stuff of his art. He transmutes his private obsessions into a rhetoric so public that it can be mumbled by any child. He enacts the purification of speech, and yet also this is something comic, a sort of trick, like a huge pun, like a long almost pointless joke. Shakespeare cries out in agony, he writhes, he dances, he laughs, he shrieks, and he makes us laugh and shriek ourselves out of hell. Being is acting. We are tissues and tissues of different *personae* and yet we are nothing at all. *What redeems us is that speech is ultimately divine.* (pp. 163-64. The sentences are italicized by me.)

Shakespeare is an important issue not only in the case of Murdoch's art, but in the history of the controversy of verisimilitude versus artifice; in novel criticism, these terms are represented as realism versus experimentalism. Shakespearean commentary is divided between the two, with some critics arguing for his lifelikeness, while others are adamant in claiming that his central subject, his only subject, is the nature of art and artifice. It is interesting that the great realist, Tolstoi, saw Shakespeare's plays as being so anti-realistic as to fail in the necessarily moral imperative of art. In this passage Murdoch is talking about the transcendence of *Hamlet,* its ability to take its creator out of reality into "the presence of the god." The work of art is thus an agent for the creative self—its words deliver the writer through love to the pain of reality (the real god) and truth. Notice how painful this process is as "the god's flayed victim [dances] the dance of creation."

The myth being evoked is, of course, that of Apollo and Marsyas, one that has interested Murdoch throughout her career, and the frame of *The Black Prince.* Its use, however, is intrinsic to and yet separated from the narrative. The experimental elements of the novel are all attached to it, and yet the story, as realistic narrative, is quite complete and apprehensible without it.

Let me first address the conventional story line, which is described in Pearson's manuscript under the subtitle, "A Celebration of Love."

Without the two Forewords and six Postscripts, the autobiographical, realist, first-person narrative functions as a straightforwardly told, nicely constructed tale. It opens with the results of a telephone call to Bradley Pearson from Arnold Baffin announcing that he thinks he has killed his wife, Rachel (with a poker), and closes with the results of a telephone call from Rachel Baffin who thinks she has—and she's right—killed her husband, Arnold (with a poker). Bradley calls the final call a "portentous *revenant*" (p. 324) of what he had earlier referred to as "the strange and violent world of matrimony" (p. 29). Arnold and Rachel Baffin are secondary and even contingent characters, foils to the primary agents of the novel, Bradley Pearson and their daughter, Julian.

Bradley Pearson, the narrator, is at fifty-eight a minor author of two narrow novels, a former tax collector who has retired early in order to clear the decks for the creation of his great *oeuvre* which he believes will now come into being. The creation of a great book will be the central achievement of his life, but its birth is impeded by his own sterility and by contingency—by people, events, and the responsibilities of related-ness which keep getting in his way. His ex-wife, Christian, comes back from America, eager for adventure; her tawdry, homosexual, touch-ingly serviceable brother, Francis Marloe, zeroes in on him; his sister, Priscilla, leaves her debased husband, comes to Bradley for protection, and ultimately commits suicide; Rachel Baffin falls in love with him; Arnold Baffin involves him in his life. Throughout all of this faintly hilarious, often tragic stuff, Bradley keeps trying to escape, to find the solitude and disinterested silence from which he believes his art will emerge.

His two major relationships are with Arnold Baffin, a prolific, successful, best-selling writer whom Bradley "discovered," loves, and jealously hates, and Julian, Arnold's twenty-year-old daughter of unim-pressive qualities, with whom Bradley falls in love suddenly, wildly, and absolutely. The story of this jealousy and this love is the subject of the book, although, true to her principles, Murdoch forces Bradley into a realization of the reality of the contingent as part of one's destiny. Early in his tale, Bradley had reported that ". . . in that lurid evening light, a superstitious feeling that if I did not make my escape before Sunday something would grab me" (p. 28). Something does, but it is a godlike force which pushes him into relatedness, into a cycle of love and death and a dreadful participation which ultimately produces not a tight, crafted, disciplined, cool work, but the present manuscript, full of pain but capable of transcending agony in the "bright light of art."

The manuscript, the work of art, is written after Bradley has been imprisoned for life, accused through the betrayal of Rachel of murdering Arnold; Julian, the focus of his art and love, is lost to him, herself also a betrayer. Unlike Humbert Humbert's narration, this is a realistic forefront, a story transmitted to an audience who judges the tale according to the rules of verisimilitude and social experience. In relaying the story, Murdoch is fulfilling her mission of appealing to a wide audience, of telling a story well. She is not, however, satisfied to leave her task there, and it is in her developments and departures that this novel participates in the experimental mode.

It is first of all necessary to point out that this novel is full of conversations, theories, explications and reviews of literature and art. Because Bradley so absolutely identifies himself as an artist, and because of his friendship with the successful, despised Arnold, the plot situation is set up for theoretical discussion. Arnold condescends to Bradley's jealous narrowness, to his neurotic insistence that he has, by crafting carefully and publishing practically nothing, kept his gift pure. Bradley despises Arnold's prolific, second-rate production which Julian describes thus:

> 'I do love the way you talk, you're so precise, not like my father. He lives in a sort of rosy haze with Jesus and Mary and Buddha and Shiva and the Fisher King all chasing round and round dressed up as people in Chelsea.' (p. 107)

Bradley eschews experience and the gossipy observation of people; Arnold adores both and claims them to be essential to the novelist. With many clever swipes at her critics, many of whom have accused her, as Bradley does Arnold, of too much fecundity in publication, Murdoch uses *The Black Prince* (who is Julian, *B*radley *P*earson, and Hamlet) as a means of pointing out that both ideas are wrong. Bradley is unsuccessful because he has not gone through the pain of participation and the total, absolute transformation of love; Arnold fails because he settles for the warm, cosy feeling of mediocrity. He dodges the pain of participation or the loving, imaginative identification which would allow him to see Rachel and avert her violent, unforgiving hatred. Even when Bradley learns to love Julian and is transformed by it ("Happy love undoes the self and makes the world visible," p. 299), his attention to Priscilla, to Rachel, to Francis is inadequate, and tragedy follows. His love for Julian can create the work of art which exists to celebrate her, but it also celebrates Priscilla's death and acknowledges the pain and terror of life:

> That this is a place of *horror* must affect every serious artist and thinker, darkening his reflection, ruining his system, sometimes actually driving him mad. Any seriousness avoids this fact at its peril, and the great ones who have seemed to neglect it have only done so in appearance. (This is a tautology.) This is the planet where cancer reigns, where people regularly and automatically and almost without comment die like flies from floods and famine and disease, where people fight each other with hideous weapons to whose effects even nightmares cannot do justice, where men terrify and torture each other and spend whole lifetimes telling lies out of fear. This is where we live. (pp. 298-99)

The Marsyas myth which gives focus to the experimental aspects of the novel is a myth of the tragedy and agony of mortal participation in the divine. As a central concept, it could have resulted in what Murdoch described in a 1968 interview as "a sort of closed novel, where my own obsessional feeling about the novel is very strong and draws it closely together."[12] She opposes this to "an open novel, where there are more accidental and separate and free characters. I would like to write the second kind." *The Black Prince* succeeds in being the second kind by the freedom toward responsibility and the ingress of love which it allows to Bradley, its central character.[13] As in the introduction of Vivian Darkbloom (Nabokov's anagram for himself) into *Lolita,* the Apollo-Marsyas background is presented with a certain coyness. The specific idea of Marsyas is seen in the description of *Hamlet* quoted above, where the greatest artist is presented as the flayed, suffering, but dancing mortal who has dared to enter the lists of the gods. Pain and the dance of achievement concur, but Marsyas who boldly challenged the god Apollo to a musical competition has been defeated, flayed, and hence killed by him. In the indirect references of the forewords and postscripts, Apollo uses his little known classical name of Loxias, is mentioned as a great musician who murdered a colleague, and shares Bradley's imprisonment. The step is quite daring and absolutely anti-realistic.

Apollo is P. Loxias, the entrepreneur and editor of Bradley's book, the "dear friend" of the frequent addresses which he encourages Bradley to use as part of his novel's formal structure. He also becomes the instrument of transferring the narrative from realistic believability into that off-centred uncertainty which is so typical of experimental fiction. As a narrator, Bradley is extremely trustworthy, aware of the inadequacy of words ("As I now read this Foreword I see how meagrely it conveys me. How little can words convey except in the hands of a genius" [p. xviii]), and wary of the pitfalls of dishonesty, solipsism and belief in easy excuses like the hand of destiny. Both of the Forewords—by P. Loxias the friend and Bradley himself—encourage the reader to believe in the honesty and reliability of Pearson, but Loxias as editor encourages the writing and organizes the publication of four postscripts by significant, surviving characters, all of whom betray Bradley—Christian, Francis Marloe, Rachel, and Julian. The result of

---

[12] W. K. Rose, "Iris Murdoch, Informally," *London Magazine* (June 1968), p. 66.

[13] Rubin Rabinowitz, in "Iris Murdoch," in *Six Contemporary British Novelists,* ed. George Stade (New York: Columbia University Press, 1976), does Murdoch a disservice in claiming that her novels are too patterned and bound by philosophical contexts, and underestimates her achievement seriously when he says of *The Black Prince:* "Once again Murdoch succeeds in establishing the authenticity of an emotional experience only to throw it away with a tricky twist of the plot" (p. 324). The revision of his earlier Columbia monograph seems to have tired him out.

these postscripts is not only an ironic commentary on interpretation, a sort of *Pooh Perplex* criticism of criticism, but a sudden and quite alarming calling into question of the reader's reliance on the narrator's honesty. Francis' Freudianism seems appallingly feasible; Christian's bland statements that Bradley overstated and missed the point, and Rachel's vindictive reduction of his literary and social stature raise the question of his inadequacy and of the possibility of his lying; Julian's prim, quasi-aesthetic essay reminds the reader of the futility and self-interest with which writers—Bradley, Arnold, and the newly poetical Julian—argue their case. The retrospective doubt is unnerving and is redeemed, not by our memory of what Bradley in his new wisdom tells us so eloquently in his postscript, but by Loxias' final word.

That word assures us that the god of art needs the human mortality of the artist; one remembers that on the very first page of the novel, in his "Editor's Foreword," he had identified himself as Bradley's *alter ego*. Here he goes further:

> I am glad to think how much I comforted his last days. I felt as if he had suffered the lack of me throughout his life; and at the end I suffered with him and suffered, at last, his mortality. I needed him too. He added a dimension to my being. (p. 364)

Earlier, in his own postscript, Bradley had written that "the black Eros whom I loved and feared was but an insubstantial shadow of a greater and more terrible godhead" (p. 337). To say merely that this godhead is Apollo as a minor aesthetic agent is to underestimate the transcendence which Murdoch has aimed at and so superbly attained.

As a writer, Murdoch has always shown enormous fascination with religious vocabulary and experience as it touches on—or fails to touch—a secular, contemporary, bourgeois world. In *The Black Prince* that vocabulary, through the daring medium of Apollo, takes on a fullness of significance which she has not achieved elsewhere in her largely non-experimental novels. In this densely written, ruminative novel, religious vocabulary dealing with demons, angels, gods, saints, sacraments and transfigurations occurs constantly and the central episode, in which Bradley falls in love with Julian and is transformed by it, transfigures him momentarily into a saint (Christian: "Brad's become a saint. . . . I guess it's the transfiguration" [p. 192]). Of course there has been much talk of saints before this, and Julian is, we are told very directly, the namesake of Julian of Norwich whose mystical vision of the world elevated it from a place of horror to a universe where "all shall be well and all shall be well and all manner of thing shall be well." Bradley, writing with the sad knowledge that the intensities of love, art, and mystical transfiguration are temporary for creatures who live in time, has given us definitions of sainthood: "I suppose almost everybody diminishes someone. A saint would be nobody's spoiler" (p. 5) and "A saint would identify himself with everything'' (p. 81). The moment of falling in love allows sainthood to happen, and the god sanctions this as a subject for the supreme fiction.

For Murdoch, love leads to art, and both indicate the presence of the god, the dark Eros, the ultimate religious experience. Only through these intensities can human limitations be overcome and selfishness and solipsism defeated. Pearson, realizing this, dies gently with an acceptance of the pain of *Der Rosenkavalier* (like *Hamlet,* a central aesthetic document in the case). But how, finally, can this resolution, achieved largely by anti-realism and by calling down a god into a realistic text, be seen in terms of the quotidian which Murdoch also serves? How, in other words, does the anti-realistic aspect mesh with the realistic? Oddly enough, by asserting that the unreal is real, that the transcendent and the fictional are both real, tied to the world by specific objects. Essentially what Murdoch is saying is that her own reality is less than those things she has created. An experimentalist to the end, she once again disarms our security by making real a fictional bronze statue, a gilt snuff box, and two characters—her symbols for the real and the transcendent:

> I hear it has even been suggested that Bradley Pearson and myself (P. Loxias) are both simply fictions, the invention of a minor novelist. Fear will inspire any hypothesis. No, no, I exist. Perhaps Mrs Baffin, though her ideas are quite implausibly crude, is nearer the truth. And Bradley existed. Here upon the desk as I write these words stands the little bronze buffalo lady. (The buffalo's leg has been repaired.) Also a gilt snuff box inscribed *A Friend's Gift.* And Bradley Pearson's story, which I made him tell, remains too, a kind of thing more durable than these. Art is not cosy and it is not mocked. Art tells the only truth that ultimately matters. It is the light by which human things can be mended. And after art there is, let me assure you all, nothing. (p. 364)

Like Nabokov, she has achieved a major sleight of hand through which the subject of art becomes convincingly eternal; in the contest between art and solipsism, art wins. But unlike Nabokov, she joins anti-realism to realism so that the intensity of art and love can both participate in our ordinary, quotidian human life, and transcend it.

Malcolm Lowry:
Statements on Literature and Film

PAUL TIESSEN

I

The label, "cinematic," since its earliest appearance as a critical term around 1920, has become a cliché in discussions of twentieth-century literature in general, and of work by novelists such as Malcolm Lowry in particular. Lowry himself, in reflecting his belief that "the novel, of all the arts, is the one most allied to the film,"[1] was one of the very few writers of fiction to have contributed to theoretical discussions related to the uses of that term. His discussions of relationships, similarities and differences, between novel and film have been both extensive and vigorous. In "Preface to a Film-script" and *Notes on a Screenplay for F. Scott Fitzgerald's Tender Is the Night,* two post-humously published companion essays which include in places comparative observations on literature—especially the novel—and film, Lowry[2] confirmed the importance of discussing novel and film in the same critical context. In his bringing personal attitude and far-reaching insight to bear on the topic, he contributed unique perspectives to both the criteria of judgment and the categories of critical response that any discussion of the "cinematic" in fiction might involve.

It was about a quarter-century after the screening of the world's first film programme, several years after the establishment of Charlie Chaplin's international reputation, and about a year after the advent of Expressionist film in Germany, when reviewers and critics, confronted with the innovative techniques of the modern novel, began to use the

[1] Malcolm Lowry, "Preface to a Film-script," p. 4. Even though in his manuscript Lowry wrote "cut" beside this specific comment, it is consistent with other comments made or implied in the same manuscript.

[2] While Margerie Lowry contributed to these writings, and was always regarded by Lowry as co-author of the film-script, "Tender Is the Night," the dominant voice throughout is Lowry's.

word, "cinematic," as well as related terms, such as "cinematographic," to convey through implied metaphor some idea of the form
and the content of experimental prose. The narrative works of James
Joyce, along with those of Dorothy Richardson, were among the first
widely regarded as having been influenced by the cinema, that revolu-
tionary new medium for narrative expression. Since 1920 the word,
"cinematic," has many times been used to point to some apparent
analogy between literature and film. When the term has been too literally insisted upon, however, its use has become often mechanical,
arbitrary, or even absurd. Technological differences basic to the two
narrative art forms preclude the fruitfulness of literalist comparative
approaches. However, metaphorically-based references founded on the
nature of film and applied to the critical response to literature have been
at times illuminating.

Stephen Spender's 1965 introduction to Lowry's *Under the Volcano* initially established the meaning of the film-metaphor in the context of Lowry's work. Finding the techniques of the novel to be "essentially cinematic," Spender wrote that "the most direct influence on this
extraordinary book is not . . . from other novelists, but from films, most
of all perhaps those of Eisenstein. The movies—that is, the old, silent,
caption-accompanied movies—are felt throughout the novel." Spender
spoke also of the use of "flash-backs," "cutting," and "abrupt shifts
from extended scenes to close-ups" in the novel. Words seen on post-
ers, Spender said, "arise naturally enough—whenever one of the
characters catches sight of them: a movement of the camera eye glancing at a printed notice."[3] In book-length studies of Lowry's work published in the early 1970's, Daniel Dodson as well as Douglas Day spoke
of Lowry's "cinematic eye"; Richard Hauer Costa of a "cinematic"
scene in *Under the Volcano*; Anthony Kilgallin of *Under the Volcano* as
"one of this century's most cinematographic novels." Muriel Bradbrook suggested that

> the cinema's combination of intimacy with distance, no less than the
> way in which a film is built out of innumerable versions of each
> incident, taken, re-cut and reformed by the art of *montage*,
> powerfully suggests both Lowry's aim and the craft method which
> he employed in the composition of his works. He learnt from the
> cinema the art of suggestion, of collocation without comment, and
> transposed it into his own medium.[4]

[3] Stephen Spender, "Introduction" to *Under the Volcano* (Philadelphia, 1965), pp.
xiii, xiv.

[4] Daniel Dodson, *Malcolm Lowry* (New York, 1970), p. 9; Douglas Day, *Malcolm
Lowry* (New York, 1973), p. 325; Richard Hauer Costa, *Malcolm Lowry* (New York,
1972), p. 70; Anthony Kilgallin, *Lowry* (Erin, Ontario, 1973), p. 131; Muriel Bradbrook,
Malcolm Lowry (London, 1974), p. 67. See also Paul Tiessen, "Malcolm Lowry and the
Cinema," in *Malcolm Lowry: The Man and His Work,* ed. George Woodcock (Van-
couver, 1971), pp. 133-43.

Certainly Lowry frequently used his knowledge of what might be called the film-experience to formulate the experiences of his characters in *Under the Volcano,* where each seems almost to be entranced by an omnipresent, frequently oppressive world of visual images. At times Lowry tried to use these very visual stimuli to re-create for the reader the actual, physical sense of certain of his characters' sensual experiences and, hence, of the emotions that these experiences evoked. The literal, rather than the literary, image—which, in Lowry's work, might include actual words, as in letters, signs, advertisements, or perhaps some readily reproduced visual object, like the black hand in *Under the Volcano*—was given form in the real world of the reader, who was thus subjected to the very visual environment that was so often related to the mental torment of the characters. Physical, spatial, and, in part, temporal relationships between reader and image, and character and image, became parallel. As is so commonly the case with film, when character and viewer can literally be made to see the same image (though, to be sure, from different perspectives, in different contexts), the reader and the character could be said to share an experience. The central role of actual, visual stimuli in Lowry's technique might rightly remind one, then, of the function of the motion picture camera. Lowry was attempting to simulate the experience of film, where the viewer's response is rooted in the actual stimulation of the sense of vision. Similarly, Lowry's persistent attempts at the precise physical rendering of the appearance of visual objects which could not be reproduced typographically, indicate his desire to attain, here too, as great a sense of visual immediacy as written description would allow.

II

Only about two-and-a-half years after the publication of *Under the Volcano,* Malcolm Lowry abandoned other work in progress and began to write a film-script, based on F. Scott Fitzgerald's *Tender Is the Night.* The 455-page script was finished in about nine months.[5] This script-writing interlude, which lasted from July 1949 to April 1950, was a most joyous time in the last, often sorrowful decade of Lowry's life. Immersing himself in the project, he said he felt "possessed" by it.[6] To Frank Taylor, who knew Lowry's *Under the Volcano* well (since he, along with Albert Erskine, had been publisher of the Reynal and Hitchcock edition of the novel) and who was now a producer at MGM, Lowry wrote that he had in mind "one of the greatest and most moving films of all times."[7] Lowry knew many movies, and his remark was not made

---

[5] The film-script, housed at the University of British Columbia, has not been produced as a film or published as literature.

[6] Malcolm Lowry in Paul Tiessen, "Introduction" to *Notes on a Screenplay for F. Scott Fitzgerald's Tender Is the Night* (Columbia, 1976), p. vii.

[7] Ibid., p. xiii.

casually. It was a good novelist's task, his duty, to try to contribute to the development of film art by writing an exemplary script, he felt. He cited "the passion and scholarship and artistic devotion"[8] which writers like Joyce and Proust put into their work as models for the serious script-writer. Certainly those qualities seem to have characterized Lowry as he undertook the project, for he said—and his statement is striking and important for an understanding of Lowry the man as well as Lowry the artist—that he had never "felt so creatively exhilarated since writing the better parts of the *Volcano*."[9]

When Lowry sent the finished film-script to Taylor he sent also a covering letter which included, among its opening remarks, the comments, "there was a sort of preface to it and is: and there are copious notes."[10] That "sort of preface" and those "copious notes," already mentioned above, have only recently been published, in 1974 and 1976 respectively. These companion pieces will be referred to here as the "Preface" and the *Notes*.[11]

The "Preface" itself was never finished, and the published version, based on various manuscript drafts which are partly typewritten and partly handwritten, is necessarily in a fragmented form. The *Notes* are easier to read; they are from a completed typescript. The editor remarks, nevertheless, that they have a "distinctly oral quality and are punctuated more like speech than like written material" (N, 81). These writings are really epistolary in nature, addressed, as they were, to Taylor, whom Lowry spoke of as a member of the "family" (N, xix).

The following three sections of this essay represent an attempt to draw together the diverse statements Lowry made here and there concerning the visual image, the written word, and the rhythm of sound, in both literature and film. Although personal in nature, these statements are intellectually and emotionally consistent with thought and feeling expressed elsewhere by Lowry. Furthermore, these statements represent work which is, to use Lowry's own reference to his film-script, "essentially creative" (N, xiii). They come out of Lowry's experience of having combined practice with theory; out of what Margerie Lowry referred to as Lowry's "Learning a Lot About the Novel in tearing this one [*Tender Is the Night*] to pieces and recreating it" as an imagined film

[8] Malcolm Lowry, "Preface to a Film-script," p. 9.

[9] Malcolm Lowry in Paul Tiessen, "Introduction" to *Notes on a Screenplay*, p. xiii.

[10] Malcolm Lowry in *Notes on a Screenplay*, p. 1.

[11] Malcolm and Margerie Lowry, "Preface to a Film-script," *White Pelican* 4/2 (Spring 1974), 2-20, intro. and ed. Paul Tiessen; Malcolm Lowry and Margerie Bonner Lowry, *Notes on a Screenplay for F. Scott Fitzgerald's Tender Is the Night*, ed. Matthew J. Bruccoli, intro. Paul Tiessen (Columbia, South Carolina, 1976). Hereafter references to the *Notes*, or to my "Introduction" to the *Notes*, will be made parenthetically within the text as in this example: (N, 21). References to the "Preface" will be similarly made, as in this example: (P, 11).

(N, xiii). They grow out of passionate emotion, brilliant insight, and what seems at times like naive conviction. They reveal a belief in the potential greatness, and uniqueness, of both literature and film, a belief certainly not articulated, and by and large not held, by novelists of Lowry's time. Such novelists, Lowry said of his contemporaries, "love not the film" even though they may have "learned from it" (P, 6).

III

Several factors seem to have contributed to Lowry's turning to film as he struggled for a means of expression after the completion of *Under the Volcano*. He came to insist on an affective, even "ennobling" role for narrative art. He expressed a need for art to make an audience not only feel deeply the experiences of his fictional characters but also be inwardly enriched by them. His faith in the film image's ability to move man seemed to surpass his faith in the ability of the literary image to do the same. He noted that "the appeal of the movies is far more directly to the senses [than is the appeal of the novel]" (P, 10), and it was this appeal that had come to attract him to the newer medium. He felt, too, that he was expert at communicating in terms of sensual images, whether in the novel or in film. He even saw himself as unique among the novelists of his time in this regard, and lamented that other novelists-turned-script-writers could not "think visually and aurally" when it came to working for the film. Implicitly referring to his own strengths he said, too, that "these writers cannot make you see and hear in their novels either" (P, 6).

Speaking of parallel visual and narrative contexts in the novel and the film, Lowry noted that the film medium, by virtue of its very nature, would normally confer with greater ease more power or force or meaning upon any visual image, and elements associated with such an image, than would the print medium of the novel. Without qualifying his observation, he presented the argument that character depiction and development or, as in the case of his illustration, a central aspect of characterization, such as the character Nicole Diver's madness, is "far more vivid and convincing in a film [than in a novel] since we see it actually in operation" (P, 16). It was his explicit assumption that "the value of objects and of people in relation to them ... is a hundredfold greater on the screen than in a book" (N, 15). In film individual images could be presented instantaneously before the eyes of the viewer, and so be "fully realised," any number of times, at any point in the viewing (N, 15). Thus complete scenes, and any emotions which might be associated with them, could be evoked at various points in the film even though only portions of those scenes would be repeated (N, 32).

It was "realism" of the kind unique to film that provided Lowry with another point of distinction between film and novel. Film had the advantage of access to a form of realism—a realism which, he hinted, was linked to the "objectively real," or to the "so-called outer world" (N,43)—which, in the presenting of individual images, did not require "ten pages of condensed naturalistic technique at a blow each time they appear" (N, 15). Seemingly more emotionally than objectively, Lowry suggested that the naturalistic presentation of visual images in the novel remained "impossibly crude" relative to their presentation in film where, he said, they might be "even profound" (N, 15). It is true that Lowry always found in concrete images the bases for virtually endless symbols and correspondences. He wrote in the *Notes,* " 'what is above is like what is below,' mystics say—what is going on in my coffee cup has its parallel in Arcturus" (N, 34).

Lowry was not disturbed if his use of an image, and even some of the possible symbolic meanings of the image, would be "absolutely obvious to a five-year-old messenger boy" (N, 69). There were, he felt, countless layers of meaning. He was prepared to discuss at length the subtlety of his use of the images of his proposed film. The comment he made on one occasion—"there was a certain complexity in the way all this was instinctively arrived at" (N, 69)—might convey something of the nature of the argument he was prepared to make in his defense of the film image.

One of the several images from the film-script which Lowry actually did isolate for purposes of relatively lengthy discussion was that of the automobile, an image which, he said, "merely looks conventional" (P, 16). He was forced into the discussion by his need to justify the substitution of an automobile motif for the deleted incest motif in his version of Fitzgerald's story. In its most important narrative function, an automobile becomes the means—or what Lowry punningly called the "vehicle" (N, 12)—for giving expression to Nicole's illness and her recovery. In the film-script it is a car accident, in which Nicole, as driver, kills her father, as passenger, which Lowry calls the "precipitating factor" (P, 16) of her illness.[12]

In terms of the formal structure of his work, Lowry could easily enough have found ways of integrating the incest motif into the work as a whole, even though he was dissatisfied with Fitzgerald's handling of it. After all, in his concern for proportion and balance, integration and completeness, he did frequently extend or alter many portions of the original if he thought that such portions were "untrue," "narrow," or

[12] Lowry wrote that in the film "the primary cause of Nicole's insanity has to be at the same level of the action as the rest, be welded in it, and part of it, and solved within it, and an important part of the film's resolution. This is where the car motif comes in" (N, 12). Lowry's determination to "surmount the hurdle of the incest motif," to substitute for the "forbidden hot sauce of incest" a "gasket sauce" of his own (P. 14), might have been influenced by some anxiety on his part about the power of the Catholic League of Decency (P, 12).

"half-written," for example (N, 14). But in this case he felt that even though the incest motif would not be visually suggested, any verbal reference to it would make it too overbearing in the context of the film as a whole. "It is questionable," he said, "whether even a verbal suggestion in a film would not cast a shadow of such appallingness that it would outlaw any subsequent humour [in the film]" (P, 16). Lowry seemed to feel that the incest motif would not have as disproportionate an impact on the reader of the novel as it would have on the viewer of the film. He granted that it "goes on echoing dolorously in our minds throughout the book" (N, 12), yet suggested that while the presence of incest tends to shock, it does not destroy the overall effect of the book. Perhaps Lowry's feeling that one's identity with characters is stronger in film than in the novel, that elements quickly take on a hundred times their usual level of impact, explains his distinction between the effects of this motif in the two media. He was led to suggest that "the forms of evil which [film] is able to show alluringly, ... in keeping with good art, unlike in writing per se, are ... very few" (p, 10).

The automobile functioned well in the film-script as a "multi-form visual symbol" (P, 16). In this image's symbolic suggestiveness, Lowry said, "the film ... gains in complexity of interpretation" while it remains at the same time "perfectly simple on the surface" (P, 16). His explanations of the symbolic, and also of what he saw as the buried symbolic meanings of the image are presented in an inimitably cumulative statement pervaded and controlled by an eagerness of tone characteristic of Lowry's defenses of favourite topics. Thus he spoke of the car "as a symbol of [Nicole's] neurosis and sickness," and of the "psychological implications of car as adolescent phantasy, sexual characteristic, father, patricide," of "car as guilt, car as fear of life, car in terms of riches, car thus doubly a factor that stands between Dick and Nicole, [—'the Isotta for one thing is the patent symbol of Nicole's wealth, in addition to her neurosis, and hence ... stands between Dick and Nicole' (P, 16)—] up to, as Fitzgerald has it, car as a vehicle of attempted murder, and finally an emblem of cure, something that has been mastered—(in addition to a host of other buried symbologies that a psychiatrist would see in it)" (N, 12). All this, Lowry insisted, could be presented "filmically" (N, 12), as incest could not.

A car accident could be presented in film in such a manner that the viewer would be sensually overwhelmed, with visual images and editing technique evoking tactile sensations, while remaining at the same time, it should be noted, outside the event. "We ... will have had the whole shock and seen how it happened" (P, 16), said Lowry of the advantages of his use of the incident. On the one hand, then, the viewer has a subjective view of the event through the eyes of the characters about to crash their speeding roadster head-on into a huge, speeding truck. There

is the "shock" of the crash, and, finally, "we begin to regain consciousness, as it were." On the other hand, the viewer almost simultaneously,
in intermittent shots, has the benefit of a high-angle "God's eye view
that sees the future"[13] just before the crash actually occurs. Camera
angles serve to provide two modes of perception, then, as Lowry's film
technique produces a metaphor for what is dominant in all of Lowry's
work: ironic vision.

IV

Of the various possible means of expression in novel and film
perhaps the one which functions most similarly in both (and so can be
said to overlap) is the written word. While in the use of the written word
one exploits the obvious similarities not present in many other novel-
film comparisons, it is again important to note that differences in technological contexts inevitably create differences in the immediate experiences of the written word in a book, and the written word in a film.
Striving again for a means of involving the viewer in the world of the
character, Lowry proposed a film technique which involved the written
word fulfilling what he felt was a "decidedly unusual function for a
talking picture" (N, 29). One illustration of this technique can be found
in his use of words contained in two telegrams delivered to Dick Diver.
The preparatory phase of Lowry's technique involved having the viewer see and read, with Dick, the words as they appear in the telegrams
themselves, shot in close-up. Subsequently, however, Lowry had the
words take on a kind of animated life of their own as they were made to
appear in a jumbled way somewhat like anxiety-ridden subtitles near the
bottom of the screen. By having them appear in fragmented phrases,
constantly separating and re-forming, Lowry intended that the words
should act as mirrors of Dick's inner, and at this point in the story,
tormented world. "It is not the sound of the words that matters either,"
he said; "it is the effect of the *look* of them upon Dick and our identification with the process in Dick's brain" which is important (N, 30).

At the same time Lowry saw ways in which silent, written words
appearing upon the screen could, like the automobile-image, involve
more than just the visual sense of the viewer. He likened the effect of
such words, accompanied, to be sure, by music (N, 29, 30), to that of
words experienced at heightened moments in other contexts: "at moments of crisis [as in Dick Diver's case], . . . one sense literally takes
over part of the function of another: senses deceive, you can hear with
your eyes, psychologists tell us . . . : the words [on the screen] are silent
and unspoken, yes, but nonetheless to us [in the audience] used to a
continuum of sound in relation to words, are a sort of function of

---

[13] Malcolm and Margerie Lowry, "Tender Is the Night," unpublished film-script,
pp. 139, 140.

sound . . . in the same way too that aural hallucinations are sometimes partly the function of the eye" (N, 29). The same process can sometimes occur, he said, "even when reading a poem" (N, 29). In literature or in film, Lowry suggested, words could be used evocatively, powerfully, as "visual weapons" (N, 30).

In the multi-sensory forcefulness of these silent words, Lowry again saw a means of linking viewer and character, as has already been noted. He said of the proposed effect of his technique that, "in short, it is intended to be an approximation to an actual process, and we are liable, through identification with Dick, to come closer, so to speak, even than the 'Dick upon the screen,' strange though this sounds, to what he feels" (N, 30).[14]

Lowry admitted that, given traditional views concerning the use of the written word on the screen, his innovation might be "a little art form totally without a future, the beginning and end of it in short" (N, 29). It was as though he was bringing a "cinematic" literary device into film, and using it there as a cinematic device. He was aware that it was customary to regard the written word as an intrusion upon the medium of film, whether the film was silent or not; that it was customary to regard it as a "liability or weakness, in fact a limitation of the form" (N, 29). At the same time, he insisted that his experiment was a significant departure from and advance over the use of the written word even in the silent film. He could not, he said somewhat sarcastically, think of "one example in ten thousand of words ever having been called upon to play a visual function intelligently in a silent picture, a single place-name being about the limit of their explosive dynamism, which still sometimes pertains in sound films where a parchment still unscrolls an expository evocation at the beginning and end sometimes" (N, 29). Lowry's use of explosively dynamic words is a characteristic of his novels and the proposed film alike, but the advantages of the film context in this regard are obvious, given the mechanically regulated, relentless movement of the film itself.

V

Like other artists and critics concerned with film even indirectly, Lowry felt that film had been "coming to maturity" in the mid-1920's, that it had, for one thing, successfully moved away from its initial theatricality toward cinema expressed in terms of cinema (P, 9). He held a view common among many serious observers of film: that the advent

[14] Speaking of his use of the news headlines circling the *Times* building in New York, headlines prominent also in *Under the Volcano,* and delighting in the possibilities in the film-script of a "benign diabolism" (N, 35) resulting from the comic or ironic juxtaposition of headlines, or parts of headlines, Lowry suggested that an "important part of the soul of a country, as well as of the age, has come to be expressed in the sky signs of its great cities" (N, 36).

of sound was, at least temporarily, disastrous for the artistic development of the medium. With sound technology came an emphasis on the spoken word and, hence, "the reappearance of the horrible tyranny of the theatre" (P, 9). Lowry felt that the director of film should be like a writer who attempts to transcend the limitations of linguistic expression. The director was, said Lowry, "really a sort of super-writer" for whom virtually everything in the film should be "sublimated or subsumed in the faculty of vision" (P, 9). Too often in the director's attempts to use words, lamented Lowry, he allowed them to "drag him down" (P, 9). Lowry seemed to feel that any spoken words used in film could, at least potentially, too easily bring about some narrowing of echoes, analogies, correspondences, or symbolic meanings suggested by the visual idiom. If only a writer could think visually and aurally, he said with seeming paradox, "the sacrifice of words would not seem so great" (P, 6).

Lowry believed that "a film—or any other work of narrative art —would not hold together without [some kind of rhythm], for it is related to momentum" (N, 50), and it was in the visual techniques of film that Lowry often found a rhythm or, as he said, a "tempo," a "speed," a "lucidity" based largely on "cutting" (N, 52, 53), a rhythm which the presence of the spoken word too often served only to counteract. As has already been suggested by Lowry's use of the written word in the two telegrams received by Dick, the visual rhythm of film was, he felt, quite easily capable of incorporating the written word, the caption, and the subtitle. While having, to be sure, found few good examples of the use of the "old subtitles" in film, he did suggest about their use in silent films, for example, that one might "find a case for them simply on the grounds of their being visual" (N, 52).

It was Lowry's concern for rhythm which led him to criticize certain uses of the spoken word in the sound film. In such film, contrapuntal rhythms were, for Lowry, ideally created through the use of visual techniques together with music, or with any musical use of sound, including words. He saw most uses of the direct or voice-over narrator commenting on the main action while remaining outside that action, and the use of poetry spoken aloud, as particularly alien to the visual rhythm of the film, which for him was, of course, the primary rhythm.

Lowry emphatically stated, concerning the narrator, that "there are about fifty reasons . . . why this device often injures a film, . . . [why] its usage seems, save in rare cases, or very sparingly, artistically indefensible on the screen"[15] (N, 51). He listed some of those fifty reasons:

> the narrator, apart from his ancestry, that sour and much-abused gift of Joseph Conrad, and Orson Welles and the radio, is direct and

[15] Lowry made exceptions for the use of the narrator when "the aim is pure instruction—or the same on a higher level as in the more poetic type of documentary" (N, 51).

mundane, and as distinct as if the theatre manager were to get up and make a speech: he is indefensible in a film unless he or she is personally part of the plot—as in ... *Citizen Kane,* say—because, speaking from another plane of reality altogether, he is reminding you directly that he is telling you about the work of art in question, even if thereby he furthers the story: this is not merely being reminded you are present at one, nor is it listening to the story at third or fourth remove as in Conrad in order to get another perspective on that story—(for Marlow, in the *Heart of Darkness,* I feel, got into *Citizen Kane*)—it is as if, finally, a novel should be continually interrupted by excerpts from its blurb or preface, or as if even, on turning a given page, a mysterious gramaphone record in the author's voice should suddenly give you a précis of the next five chapters. (N, 52)

Any consideration Lowry may have given to the possibilities of using the technique of the narrator for the creation of irony was eclipsed by his concern for integration; here, the integration of techniques. His discussion of the narrator reminded him of a possible but, he said, false analogy evoking the use of the Greek chorus in the theatre. Lowry replaced the false analogy with one that provides startling insight into his use of the camera eye in film and, by implication, in his novels and short stories: "in a film," he said, "the camera should be the chorus" (N, 51). For Lowry, the camera, unlike the narrator, was, like the chorus, a "part of the play" (N, 51).

In the attempts to use poetry in film Lowry saw another specific instance of the difficulty of combining the rhythm of the spoken word with visual rhythm: the rhythm of movement on the screen, the rhythm of the cutting. Attempts to bring together poetry and film were not only mutually annihilating artistically, but also mutually parodying. Thus he suggested that "there is little future for the poetic drama or Shakespeare in movies" (N, 51).

Lucidly and succinctly he suggested that "poetry is perhaps too visual and dynamic a medium to make good company for the camera, and the result is [that poetry] tends to compete with [the camera] in a field in which the former does not seem to belong" (N, 51). The camera's "field" is that of a "special reality," said Lowry, one of a "realism" such as has been mentioned above, and of "motion," and these qualities, with few exceptions, are, he said, "enemies of poetry in poetry's terms" (N, 51). For Lowry, then, attempts to utilize poetry in film again create problems of integration; the camera, in effect, "is reduced to functioning outside the whole in an irrelevant manner, or in a manner at best untrue to the special reality the director is trying to maintain" (N, 51). Of the Lowrys' film-script he reminded Taylor: "we ... have only prose" (N, 73).

Lowry's stress on the nature of rhythm in film being defined primarily in terms of movement and editing, "by the camera itself in the

rhythmical succession of shots, and the continuity of the film, etc."
(N, 51), was accompanied by his consideration of the use of "sound and
music," of music "absolutely charged with the voltage of the [film]
itself" (N, 51), in the creation of complementary rhythms. If spoken
words could be employed as much for their sound as for their sense, they
too could function as part of the musical accompaniment, for even the
voice, when it is used for speaking, he said, "very often is presumably
not much more than a higher function of sound"[16] (N, 51).

A musical rhythm should help to bind together the picture as a
whole, said Lowry, and thus function in a way he felt was "extremely
rare in sound movies" (N, 48). Specifically in the case of Lowry's
proposed film, one of the binding and integrating rhythms was to be
provided by musical variations, often as from a ship's engine, upon the
well-known round, "Frère Jacques," which, he said, followed, like
other musical portions of the film, "autochthonous and native form"
(N, 53).

In his use of this round, what Lowry at one point anxiously referred
to as "this hallucinating idea" (N, 44), he again utilized an element
which became, though in different ways, a significant part not only of his
proposed film but also of some of the literary work of his last decade: for
example, "Through the Panama," "The Present State of Pompeii,"
"Forest Path to the Spring," and October Ferry to Gabriola. In literature the round functions as what he called "an onomatopoeia for a ship's
engine." In film "it is both more and less" than this. "Anyhow," he
playfully asked, "who wants an onomatopoeia in a sound film?"
(N, 44).

While delighting in the uniqueness of his technique, in that "it bears
no essential resemblance . . . to anything of a similar nature that has been
attempted in films and literature" (N, 44), he did single out what he
regarded as its unique strength in film: "obviously," he claimed, "it
does not work so well unless you actually hear it" (N, 56). Again,
Lowry felt that the argument of "realism" was an important one, and
film had the advantage of being able to present what he called an
"absolute realism, a super-expression of a ship's engine" (N, 47). And
it might be added that film had the advantage of having the realism
already discussed above, the realism of the visual image, of a camera
which, said Lowry, would at certain points during the presentation of
the round, "Frère Jacques," be "shooting smack into the engines
themselves" (N, 45).

[16] At the same time, however, words in the context of music, for example, often
played an important thematic, often ironic, role in the proposed film. For example, on one
occasion Lowry wrote, "at this moment we are listening intently to the words of the song,
finding some significance in them. . . . Let us listen then to its words. . . . Let us listen
carefully" (N, 19-20). Lowry was aware, however, of the "appalling" results in a serious
film of music commenting on and, in effect, parodying, though unintentionally, the action
(N, 23).

VI

The preceding overview of various of Lowry's scattered statements in the "Preface" and the *Notes* concerning literature and film points to a re-orientation in Lowry's definition of himself as an artist. The "Preface" and the *Notes* themselves convey strongly the sense that in the last decade of his life Lowry saw in the film medium the best means by which he personally might be able to express his artistic vision. Always he had had faith in the "cinematic" presentation of image and technique in the context of literature, but the film-script, the major work completed by him after the publication of *Under the Volcano,* marks a deliberate movement to his new preference for the use of cinematic techniques in the context of film itself. There images and techniques function abundantly, vibrantly, immediately, yet, at the same time, evocatively and symbolically. The mechanically-determined spatial and temporal distinctiveness of film gave Lowry precise control over his audience, as well.

As the work on the film-script came to an end, Lowry spoke of having "seen, directed, produced, written, walked in and out of this film some twenty-nine times" (N, 18). It existed outside of himself, as an objectified whole, a continuous and discrete unit of the absolutes of time and space, or, if one considers the film in terms of its many individual shots, many such units of time and space, appealing directly to the senses. It is significant that Lowry was able to "walk out of" and, in the end, away from this work, for that was a process he was not always able to accomplish with his novels and short stories, especially toward the end of his life. In *Dark as the Grave Wherein My Friend Is Laid* Sigbjørn Wilderness "tried hard to stand right outside himself, . . . to see the situation as objectively as if he were watching a film with [himself as the actor]."[17] It was the opportunity for such detachment from himself, and from his work, that film offered Lowry.

Lowry was also interested in the film's treatment of life and of man himself. Ethan Llewelyn, protagonist of *October Ferry to Gabriola,* a novel which Lowry had much in mind while he was working on the film-script, perhaps functions as a mouthpiece for Lowry when he says that there were times when "films had more reality to him than life." He went on:

> but novels possessed secretly no reality for him at all. Or almost none. A novelist presents less of life the more closely he approaches what he thinks of as his realism. Not that there were no plots in life, nor that he could not see a pattern, but that man was constantly in flux, and constantly changing.[18]

[17] Malcolm Lowry, *Dark As the Grave Wherein My Friend Is Laid* (Toronto, 1968), p. 166.

[18] Malcolm Lowry, *October Ferry to Gabriola* (New York, 1970), p. 61.

There was an analogy to life in the movement of film, and the images of film. But there was also inevitability: film held the viewer "at the mercy of [its] momentum" (N, 9), Lowry said. When he spoke of the "configured destiny" (N, 21) of Dick and Nicole Diver during the viewer's seeing into their future, in a kind of flash-forward, a moment "which was at the same time a later moment towards which they are tending, and through that moment later to a later moment still, . . . and something terrible has happened that we have already seen, and which is absolutely inevitable, no action of free will can interpose, nor anything we can possibly do hinder its onset" (N, 21), Lowry conveyed a sense of a visual and aural medium which functioned with relentlessness and tyranny: "And against such a predetermined doom, as against one's fate in the nightmare, finally you rebel! How? when the film will always end in the same way anyhow?"[19] Lowry had found in film a double attraction: the sensual image and technique provided an objectively concrete entry into the realm of the imagination; the mechanism of film provided a momentum and a form representative of Lowry's presentation of his characters' inevitable movement toward a fixed end, as much in his script-adaptation of Fitzgerald's novel as in his own *Under the Volcano*.

[19] Ibid., p. 133.

Margaret Drabble
and the Search for Analogy

JANE CAMPBELL

> This search for analogy is not merely a search for equivalence . . . :
> it is also at the heart of the creative process, for in writing novels
> we . . . create not only a book but a future, we bring into being what
> we need to be.[1]

This statement, from an article on Doris Lessing which Margaret
Drabble wrote for *Ramparts* in 1972, may serve as a point of departure
for a study of Drabble's own writing. In the seven novels which she
wrote between 1963 and 1975, the search at the heart of her creative
process can be traced, and it can be seen that in all these novels, as in the
work of many modern and not-so-modern writers, there is a concern
with the nature of story-telling itself, a preoccupation with the difficulties of telling truth in words at all, and an awareness of the limits and
perils of all our narrative activity. Several reviewers, beginning with the
Times Literary Supplement reviewer of the relatively conventional
Garrick Year, have compared her to Iris Murdoch; others have found
resemblances to George Eliot,[2] whom Margaret Drabble herself describes as "what I would like to be"—a "good all-around novelist."[3]
Both these parallels suggest areas of interest which go beyond the usual
material of women's fiction. Like Murdoch and Eliot, Drabble is inter-

---

[1] Margaret Drabble, "Doris Lessing: Cassandra in a World Under Siege," *Ramparts*
10/8 (February 1972), 50-54.

[2] For references to Murdoch, see Review of *The Garrick Year, Times Literary
Supplement,* July 23, 1964, p. 645; Charlotte Georgi, Review of *The Millstone, Library
Journal* 91 (May 1, 1966), 2361; Review of *The Waterfall, Times Literary Supplement,*
May 22, 1969, p. 549. For references to Eliot, see Review of *Jerusalem the Golden, Times
Literary Supplement,* April 13, 1967, p. 301; Review of *The Waterfall, Times Literary
Supplement,* May 22, 1969, p. 549; Anthony Thwaite, Review of *The Needle's Eye, New
Statesman,* March 31, 1972, p. 430.

[3] Nancy Poland, "There Must Be a Lot of People Like Me" (Interview with Margaret Drabble), *Midwest Quarterly* 16/3 (Spring 1975), 263.

ested in alternatives and potential for growth and learning, and in traps and limitations. Like them she is aware of our use of narrative, in art and in ordinary living, as a device for making sense of our lives. She recognizes the truth of Barbara Hardy's observation that narrative is a "primary act of mind transferred to art"; novels thus "tend to be about the larger narrative structure of consciousness, and the values and dangers involved in narrative modes of invention, dreams, causal projection...."[4] Her novels are solidly rooted in life, in the realities of marriage, child care, economics, law, archaeology, social responsibility; they have also, however, been increasingly involved with an exploration of the workings of the imagination as it searches for patterns, and the one area necessitates the other. Margaret Drabble's work is insistently, undogmatically moral in its implications. She has said, "If I am a moral writer it is not because I want to teach anybody anything. I want to think about it, to write seriously about life."[5] She gives Angus Wilson as an example of a contemporary whom she admires. For his part, Wilson has written with understanding about her achievement as a modern realist:

> She presses against the outer edges of the realist mode with such subtlety, plays with the English traditions with such respectful serious teasing... that the simple or the hasty or the prejudiced... see only her competence, sincerity, and readability, and give only ordinary consideration to what we mistakenly class as ordinary work.[6]

In this essay I shall try to explore some of the pressing and teasing which Wilson notes, by looking at the imaginative search for form in her novels. I hope to show that in the four earlier novels the works of other authors are frequently used in order to gain insights into the processes of art, while in the last three the author's imagination works more independently with the knowledge it has acquired.

Even a casual reading reveals that there is a great deal about literature in her novels. As the characters and author search for illumination, other writers' works are used as touchstones or parallels, sometimes as warnings, and as true or false or ambiguous formulas against which the described and lived experiences of her novels are tested. The titles of six of the novels make some allusion to literary works or figures. The first, *A Summer Bird-Cage* (1963), echoes a passage by John Webster about varieties of human entrapment; in this book the young

---

[4] "Towards a Poetics of Fiction: 3) An Approach through Narrative," *Novel* 2/1 (Fall 1968), 5, 7. I owe a considerable debt to this essay and to Barbara Hardy's book, *Tellers and Listeners* (London: The Athlone Press, 1975), in which she develops further the ideas in the essay. (She does not, however, discuss Margaret Drabble's work.)

[5] Poland, "People Like Me," 264.

[6] Review of *Arnold Bennett: A Biography*, by Margaret Drabble, *Times Literary Supplement*, July 12, 1974, p. 737.

Sarah, with her eyes on her sister's mysteriously unattractive marriage, ponders her own future. *The Garrick Year* (1964) is about a theatrical marriage and is named for the company of actors to which the husband, David, belongs, and which has taken the couple away from London, where the wife had hopes of a career; the company, of course, is named for the eighteenth-century actor and author. The title of *The Millstone* (1965) alludes to the Biblical warning against the destruction of innocence, and has, according to Margaret Drabble, a double reference, to a burden and to salvation.[7] Its subject is the birth of an illegitimate child and the awakening of maternal love. *Jerusalem the Golden* (1967) borrows from the hymn by J. M. Neale and ironically describes a young girl's escape from provincial life and her quest for love and glamour; the end of the novel, though open, suggests that she has found a false Jerusalem. *The Needle's Eye* (1972), which has been accurately summarized as being about "the difficulties of being good,"[8] refers to the Biblical statement of the incompatibility of riches and eternal life. Rose, its heroine, has chosen to interpret the text in its hardest sense, rejecting the lax modern explanation that the Needle's Eye was simply a narrow gate in Jerusalem. The most recent of the seven, *The Realms of Gold* (1975), derives its title from Keats's sonnet marking the discovery of riches; the most cheerful in outlook, it deals with the unexpected discovery of values in various places. Only *The Waterfall* (1969) lacks a literary title. It is named for its central symbol, which is both a card trick performed by the heroine's lover and a real waterfall in the Pennines. Like the other titles, this one reflects the ambiguities perceived by the author's imagination, since we must consider whether the gift of love and liberation which James gives to Jane is simply a skilful act or an experience of grace. This title thus continues the exploration of artifice and truth which the other titles suggest.

The novels often tell their stories by evoking other stories. Margaret Drabble has said that *Middlemarch* provided the basis for the relationship of the two sisters in *A Summer Bird-Cage* (in the book, Sarah notes that a reunion with Louise was "like something out of *Middlemarch* or even Jane Austen"[9]). The author has also admitted that a passage in *Jerusalem the Golden,* in which Clara reads about her dying mother's youthful hopes and vows to escape her mother's fate of entrapment in a narrow, unfulfilling environment, has analogies in Arnold

[7] Nancy S. Hardin, "An Interview with Margaret Drabble," *Contemporary Literature* 14/4 (Autumn 1973), 280.

[8] Anthony Thwaite, Review of *The Needle's Eye,* p. 430.

[9] *A Summer Bird-Cage* (Penguin, 1967), p. 171. Further references to this text will be made in parentheses. For *The Garrick Year, The Millstone, Jerusalem the Golden* and *The Waterfall,* the Weidenfeld and Nicolson editions have been used; for *The Needle's Eye,* the edition by Alfred A. Knopf (New York) and for *The Realms of Gold,* the Penguin edition (1977). All references to these texts will be made in parentheses.

Bennett (whose biography Drabble has written) and in Maupassant.[10] The knowledgeable reader will also see the implied parallel between Rosamund, the scholarly unwed mother in *The Millstone,* and the heroine of ''The Complaint of Rosamund,'' a poem by Samuel Daniel and one of the subjects of her research.[11] Both Rosamunds must accept the results of love-making. Rosamund's flatmate Lydia is a novelist and so is Joe, one of the two men with whom Rosamund has been going out, pretending to each that she is sleeping with the other. The process of turning life into art is graphically demonstrated here, when Rosamund finds that she and her baby Octavia have become material for Lydia's latest novel; she is annoyed by the presentation of herself as an escapist, using her ''luxury'' research to evade realities, and feels that there is poetic justice in Octavia's destruction of the only copy of the manuscript. In *Jerusalem the Golden* Clara's Jerusalem is embodied in her friendship with the Denham family, with its aura of culture, tradition and love, and the mother of the family has written a novel called *Custom and Ceremony,* taking its title from Yeats's poem ''A Prayer for My Daughter.'' That poem ends with these lines:

> How but in custom and in ceremony
> Are innocence and beauty born?
> Ceremony's a name for the rich horn,
> And custom for the spreading laurel tree.[12]

In the context of Clara's story, which includes an unceremonious mating with the married son of the family on the floor of his office, the resonance of these lines is ironic. Earlier, when Clara saw two of the sisters in the family together, she was reminded of Christina Rossetti's ''Goblin Market'' (p. 128): that story also, with its elements of threatening evil, eroticism and sacrificial love, provides interesting parallels with the main story.

Like their author, Drabble's characters are in the habit of using literature for ''guidance or help or illumination.''[13] Their lives are concerned with writing in various ways, and literary references come naturally to them. Sarah is a recent graduate of Oxford who as a student prided herself on her essays; her brother-in-law Stephen writes slick, successful novels, and Sarah observes the way in which the social

[10] Bernard Bergonzi, *The Situation of the Novel* (London: Macmillan, 1970), p. 22. He is citing a BBC recording, 1967.

[11] Nancy S. Hardin, ''Drabble's *The Millstone:* A Fable for Our Times,'' *Critique: Studies in Modern Fiction* 15/1 (1973), 22-34, points out the significance of the parallel.

[12] ''A Prayer for My Daughter,'' ll. 77-80, in *The Collected Poems of W. B. Yeats* (London: Macmillan, 1955). The epigraph to *The Needle's Eye* is a misquotation of the opening lines of Yeats's ''The Fascination of What's Difficult.'' Margaret Drabble has said that she had in mind here not so much herself as her characters; see ''Margaret Drabble Talks to Terry Coleman,'' *Manchester Guardian Daily,* April 1, 1972, p. 8.

[13] Hardin, ''An Interview with Margaret Drabble,'' 280.

behaviour of their friends becomes transformed into the situations in his books—not, she thinks, with total truthfulness. Besides her thesis, Rosamund writes reviews; she is used to making relationships between life and books, and as she views Octavia's destructive work on Lydia's manuscript she recalls the parallel case of Carlyle and John Stuart Mill. "My mind had always boggled at what Mill had said to Carlyle, at what Carlyle had said to Mill: well, now I had done it. Now I would find out" (pp. 171-72). Sometimes other works provide the basis for a shorthand character sketch, as when Sarah, pondering her sister's enigmatic nature and strangely mechanical marriage, remembers Louise's wedding flowers, a stiff bouquet of lilies, and applies to them a line from Shakespeare's Sonnet 94, "Lilies that fester smell far worse than weeds" (*Bird-Cage*, p. 72). The narrator explains Clara's enjoyment of the plays of Racine and Corneille:

> Their ways were hers. For one event, five acts of deliberation. But she played alone, because the other people would not play. And she thought . . . that if she ever could find the personages for the rest of her tragedy, then her happiness would be complete. (*Jerusalem,* p. 65)

What she finds is a clandestine affair with a disillusioned, sad man. The reader measures the gap between Clara's self-seeking dream and the reality. In *The Waterfall,* a much more complicated question is examined, and the concern of the reader is directed toward the proper evaluation of Jane's story-telling rather than to the events themselves. Jane's struggle to define the saving qualities of a relationship which is at the same time a routine, even sordid affair is put in terms of Charlotte Brontë's life and art:

> Reader, I loved him: as Charlotte Brontë said. Which was Charlotte Brontë's man, the one she created and wept for and longed for, or the poor curate that had her and killed her, her sexual measure, her sexual match? (*Waterfall,* p. 89)

Jane has to distinguish among three men (as, in a different way, Charlotte Brontë did): James the common adulterer, James the saviour and rescuer, and Malcolm, who at the end of the book is still her husband. Other fictitious heroines—Sue Bridehead, Maggie Tulliver—haunt her, and indicate the discrepancy and the similarity between two eras of woman's experience.

> But love is nothing new. Even women have suffered from it, in history. It is a classic malady, and commonly it requires participants of both sexes. Perhaps I'll go mad with guilt, like Sue Bridehead, or drown myself in an effort to reclaim lost renunciations, like Maggie Tulliver. (p. 163)

She continues:

> Maggie Tulliver never slept with her man [who, like Jane's, was her cousin Lucy's husband]: she did all the damage there was to be done, to Lucy, to herself, to the two men who loved her, and then, like a woman of another age, she refrained. In this age, what is to be done? We drown in the first chapter. I worry about the sexual doom of womanhood, its sad inheritance. (p. 164)

In these examples the experience of literature is used as a help in dealing with the issues of life. The relationship of the literary parallel or echo is, I believe, living and creative. It does not seem to be, as Bernard Bergonzi implies in his provocative book *The Situation of the Novel,* a parasitical relationship betraying the comatose state of modern British fiction. These references are not made for the sake of adding intellectual glamour to the characters or of providing a facile exercise for the well-read reader; rather, they involve the reader with the author in a reassessment of the value of fiction and offer a statement of faith both in the human importance of story-telling and in the continuity of all narrative efforts. Bergonzi finds in such echoes an indication that the form of fiction is "losing its total commitment to originality and the immediate unique response to individual experience."[14] Perhaps what Margaret Drabble is asking us to accept is that originality has never been possible, and that we may find this fact reassuring rather than depressing, since it argues for vitality quite as much as for impotence in the face of the perennial problems.

Certainly her characters find in literature a consolation as well as a challenge. Frances in *The Realms of Gold* recites to herself a speech from Shakespeare, sonnets from Keats (including, the reader speculates, the one from which the title comes) and from Milton, an ode from Horace and a piece of Virgil as a solace in toothache as she had earlier done in childbirth (p. 57). Later, at the burial of her nephew who, having inherited the family tendency to depression, has committed suicide and killed his baby, it is natural that Frances, as an archaeologist, should think of Keats's grave in Rome and the churchyard of Gray's "Elegy" (p. 341). The less mature heroines of some of the earlier novels (as Valerie Grosvenor Myer has pointed out)[15] reach through their experience an appreciation of the meaning of literature which is a measure of their growth in imaginative sympathy. Emma, renouncing romance and dreams of independence to bow to the demands of domestic responsibility, now repentantly weeps "real wet tears" at the early poems of Wordsworth which she had laughed at as a schoolgirl. Now, after the suicide by drowning of Julian, the young man with whom she had imagined herself having an affair, and her rescue of her small daughter from the same river, she sees that "they are as moving as air disasters,

---

[14] Bergonzi, *Situation,* pp. 22-23.

[15] *Margaret Drabble: Puritanism and Permissiveness* (New York: Barnes and Noble, 1974), pp. 128-29.

those poems, they have as high a content of uninflated truth'' (*Garrick Year*, p. 222). Similarly, Rosamund learns to relate her feelings for Octavia to Ben Jonson's love for his son (*Millstone*, p. 147). Her grasp of her subject has been humanized, and she has, at the same time, painfully arrived at a deeper relationship with individual words. The language in which she reports on her feelings for the newborn child is a touching mixture of pedantic restraint and humble recognition: ''Love, I suppose one might call it, and the first of my life'' (p. 118). She has already noted the discoveries about life that she had made during her pregnancy: ''I am sure that my discoveries were common discoveries; if they were not, they would not be worth recording'' (p. 78). Some of them were the facts her idealistic socialist parents had taught her about ''the blows of fate and circumstance'' under which others suffered. She says, ''I had always felt for others in theory . . . but now, myself no longer free, myself suffering, I may say that I felt it in my heart'' (p. 79). From the beginning Margaret Drabble has seen that the imaginative apprehension of clichés can be an act of wisdom. Sarah, appealed to by her sister Louise for help when Louise's husband has discovered her with her lover, concludes that—contrary to what she had believed —blood is thicker than water (*Bird-Cage*, p. 192). When Louise has arrived to take refuge in Sarah's flat, the sisters consider the possibility that ''all the fairy-story things'' like wicked stepmothers, like the novelist's convention of marrying for money (as Louise has just admitted doing) may be true after all (p. 195). Truth and fiction coincide.

The shaping process by which facts of life are made into art is also an ongoing topic in the novels. In the first novel Sarah argues with Stephen about a novel which she admires: Stephen, the professional, says that the book would have been more effective if set in ''a slightly lower social setting'' and Sarah challenges this view: ''He was writing about those people because those were the people he was writing about'' (*Bird-Cage*, p. 59). She is upholding the autonomy of art, although she does so rather simplistically. Later, she uses Stephen's work as a guide to the steps involved in achieving a style and finding plots which will present things truthfully:

> Satire won't do. Worldliness won't do. But until you can do them both you can't do anything. Immaturity is no good, and they made me feel immature, all those people [at a party], even those I could see through: they caught undertones I couldn't, though they didn't even know they were doing it. The thing is that I couldn't start to feel them in my terms because I couldn't really feel them in theirs, and one needs the double background. Perhaps it can be learned by long apprenticeship and dedicated exploration: I hope so. Perhaps it's only me that takes refuge in things like chance, unchartered encounters, cars in the night, roads going anywhere so long as it's not somewhere that other people know better. (p. 128)

In this novel the problems of selection are handled with a fairly light touch; as her work progresses Margaret Drabble shows a much deeper awareness of the question of whether truth can ever be told, of the moral, aesthetic and psychological implications of the choice of what is to be told, and of the sense in which all literature is a form of lying. Rosamund neglects to tell her friends about her experience of holding another woman's child in the clinic she attends before her baby is born: "I realised that I had not taken it in, I had not got it into a state fit for anecdote . . . . I did not find out what it had meant to me until after the birth of my own child" (*Millstone*, p. 82). At the time all she sees is the fact of human interdependence. Earlier, she and Lydia had discussed Hardy's use of coincidence, relating this technique to the role of accident in life. Lydia, after being refused an abortion, has had a miscarriage after being hit by a bus; Rosamund, who has become pregnant as a result of her first sexual experience, has tried to induce an abortion and failed. They consider the question of whether Hardy's novels show a profound or merely a mechanical attitude to life. Despite the fact that the bus accident happened, Lydia says that she could not put that kind of thing into a book: "I am not convinced by it, it hadn't got the stamp of reality on it to me." Rosamund, on the other hand, finds Hardy truthful (p. 75). Other aspects of the relationship of art to life are explored when Rosamund is annoyed to find that Defoe's *Journal of the Plague Year* is fictional, not factual, and then is annoyed at her own annoyance "as I have always maintained that I hold an Aristotelian and not a Platonic view of fact and fiction" (p. 169). Meanwhile, Octavia is ripping up Lydia's manuscript. The interconnections of life and literature in this novel are richer and more amusing than in the two books which precede it or in *Jerusalem the Golden* which follows it, and the power of literature is more deeply felt.

It is in *The Waterfall,* the fifth novel, however, that the difficulties of truth-telling are made the main subject of the novel. Among the seven, this stands out as the "novelist's novel," and I shall examine it at some length. The burden of the narration is shared between a first-person and a third-person narrator, but both are Jane, the central character, and she is sometimes the rhapsodic teller of a tale of rescue and redemption through love and sometimes the detached and even sceptical assessor struggling for insight into this affair, and making her lover James, as one reviewer remarked, "as dismissable as a character in fiction."[16] As the book begins, the third-person narrator speaks and introduces Jane, alone with her small son and newborn daughter after her husband has left her, and James, visiting her and caring for her and beginning to love her. Then Jane breaks in on her own story:

[16] Maureen Howard, Review of *The Waterfall, New York Times Book Review,* November 23, 1969, p. 67.

It won't, of course, do: as an account, I mean, of what took place. I tried, I tried for so long to reconcile, to find a style that would express it, to find a system that would excuse me, to construct a new meaning, having kicked the old one out, but I couldn't do it, so here I am, resorting to the old broken medium. (p. 48)

We perceive now that she was telling the story from the start, share her recognition that her choices of style and form have moral connections, and participate in her attempt to tell the truth. She says:

The ways of regarding an event, so different, don't add up to a whole; they are mutually exclusive: the social view, the sexual view, the circumstantial view, the moral view, these visions contradict each other; they do not supplement one another; they cancel one another, they destroy one another. (p. 49)

Here is an awareness of the other possible stories hovering about the boundaries of the told one, of the necessity of omissions which can become falsehoods, and of the dangerous power of the artist. To tell her love story, a story of "grace and miracles" (p. 52), she has had to leave out her feelings for the baby; she has been unable to give consideration to the points of view of Lucy or of Malcolm; she has made her story, symbolically if not literally, a dialogue, for "the only other parts are non-speaking parts" (p. 89). Although—particularly after the car crash which almost killed James and revealed the affair to Lucy—guilt keeps threatening to overcome her, Jane has chosen not to tell the story of guilt (p. 242). She continues to be troubled by the knowledge that lies are inevitable, especially in a love story: "Lies, lies, it's all lies.... Oh, I meant to deceive, I meant to draw analogies, but I've done worse than that, I've misrepresented"[17] (p. 89). She has tried to describe "a passion, a love, an unreal life, a life in limbo, without anxiety, guilt, corpses..., the pure flower of love itself, blossoming out of God knows what rottenness, out of decay, from dead men's lives, growing out of my dead body like a tulip" (p. 89). She has not been able to describe the conditions of her life with James, and instead has fallen back on language of enchantment. Yet, to the end she insists that the isolated story she has chosen to tell, "that sequence of discovery and recognition that I would call love" (p. 49), has validity. The story James has created for her is true. "When James looked at me, he saw me, myself. This is no fancy, no conceit. He redeemed me by knowing me, he corrupted me by sharing my knowledge," she says early in the novel (p. 54), and at the end "he changed me forever and I am now what he made" (p. 245). Whatever else may be said about the affair, it has released Jane from her

---

[17] See Ellen Cronan Rose, "Margaret Drabble: Surviving the Future," *Critique* 15/1 (1973), 5-20, for a thematic study of the first six novels. It is strange that in an otherwise perceptive examination Rose should say (p. 10) that the first-person narrative begins at this point (p. 89); it in fact begins much earlier (p. 48).

state of neurotic fear, and she can now move freely in the outer, ordinary world.

As Jane is searching for ways of telling a true story, she, a poet, meditates on the truth of poetry. She was first attracted to Malcolm, a classical guitarist and singer, by his song:

> Then wilt thou speak of banqueting delights
> Of masks and revels which sweet youth did make,
> Of tourneys and great challenges of knights
> And all these triumphs for thy beauty's sake:
> When thou hast told these honours done to thee
> Then tell, O tell how thou didst murder me.

The song (by Thomas Campion) is about story-telling, and Jane comments, "it made its own conclusion of our lives: for I did in a sense murder him, and I murdered him in the true lyrical sense" (p. 93). Yet the poets are to be blamed, she thinks, for giving us love and death in images of pure beauty, for real murder is "hideously ugly"; "in vain do the poets try to disguise and excuse and purify these things" (p. 93). Still, the images of art retain their power over us: "Nevertheless, I prefer to think of Malcolm, innocent, passionate, singing of murder, than to think of him with his fingers and thumbs sunk into my shoulders, beating my head against the bedroom wall" (p. 93). In an early short story, "A Voyage to Cythera," Margaret Drabble evoked the images of the daydreaming fancy in the heroine's vision of "some possible other country of the passions" to be described "in terms of myth or allegory."[18] This world, it seems to her, cannot be satisfactorily related to the real world, "the poetry of inspiration being to a certain extent . . . the poetry of ignorance, and the connections between symbols a destructive folly to draw."[19] In *The Waterfall* Jane picks up this theme:

> Perhaps love can't survive a context: perhaps it dies if it admits the outside world or crumbles to dust at the breath of coarser air. But that air is the real air, I know it. I can't make the connections; I can't join it up. And yet love has a reality, a quotidian reality, it must have . . . . (pp. 89-90)

Despite her statement that she cannot make the connections, Jane has made some by the end of the book; yet the problem cannot be finally solved. After the car accident which cut short their planned trip to Norway, their imagined "other country," Jane, staying in a hotel to be near James in the hospital, hears a song on a television programme her children are watching. A serving girl implores her beloved knight as he sleeps:

> For seven long years I served for you,
> The bloody cloth I wrung for you,

[18] "A Voyage to Cythera," *Mademoiselle,* December 1967, p. 149.
[19] Ibid., p. 150.

The glassy hill I climbed for you,
Will you not wake and turn to me?
(p. 211)

Later, she tries to dismiss such artistic configurations, but finds that they cannot be dismissed. We need them:

Why else had those stories been created, those tales of entranced lovers kept alive through the years by faith, those fables of sleepers and dreamers awoken finally by the intensity and endurance of desire? Will you not wake and turn to me? I must have been mad to think these thoughts. And yet madder still to abandon them. (p. 230)

Like Malcolm's song, this one is prophetic. James does wake and turn to her. Jane and the reader are left, however, with the open ontological question of the reality of art. On the one hand, James was real, says Jane, "I swear it" (p. 89); on the other, the story like all stories was a fabrication. The mountain scenery she and James go to see after his recovery is "real, unlike James and me, it exists" on the ordinary level of experience; yet it is also "an example of the sublime" (p. 251). The ending must be open. She could, she sees, have given her story a different ending, could have killed James in the car, as the "moral view" of the events might demand; would that be a "feminine ending"? Or she could have maimed him, as Charlotte Brontë maimed Rochester so that the other Jane could have him. But she loved him too much, and besides, "the truth is that he recovered" (p. 246). Meanwhile they are left with their supporting documents: the hospital's notes on James's case for the insurance company, and Jane's poems of grief for a lost love, written when she thought he was dying. "I had the experience without the loss; for free" (p. 249). Both sets of documents are, in fact, falsifications, since James's, from the hospital, identifies Jane as his wife. Yet both have their own truthfulness. The ending which Jane does provide, "as a finale," is their weekend trip to Yorkshire where they see the waterfall, the symbolic counterpart of James's card trick. It is "a lovely organic balance of shapes and curves, a wildness contained within a bodily limit" (p. 252). There is even a shepherd; it is a pastoral idyll. Yet —typically—this narrator cannot leave the matter there. She gives us another, less elevated image, a mouthful of Scotch mixed with talcum powder accidently swallowed by James that night, and, evoking the methods of more experimental writers, provides both another rejected ending—making James impotent—and the "true" one: after having a clot in her leg she has stopped taking birth control pills. "I prefer to suffer, I think" (p. 255). The ending is open, leaving room for further exploration of the "connections between symbols."[20]

[20] Critics have disagreed about whether the method used in *The Waterfall* succeeds. Maureen Howard in her review says that the "seemingly effortless design" of the card trick is missing in the novel; *The Times Literary Supplement* finds both the moral structure and the narrative method unsuccessful. On the other hand, Myer recognizes that *The*

The Waterfall marks a turning point in Margaret Drabble's development.[21] The last two novels, *The Needle's Eye* and *Realms of Gold,* reveal a movement away from the "escape" or "rescue" plot (noted by William Trevor in his review of *The Waterfall*)[22] and an insistence on the need for compromise and acceptance and for human community in the midst of our inevitable defeats.

These two novels are philosophically more ambitious and symbolically denser, the plots more involved and the casts of characters larger, and the time spans more extensive. The literary references become less self-conscious and more organic. At the same time, the author continues to extend her command of point of view and narrative method. The first three novels had been presented in the first person, with little suggestion of the author's separate, judging presence; the fourth, *Jerusalem the Golden,* uses a third-person narrator, leaving room for objective assessment (although in terms which, I feel, are not quite clearly defined) and for the presentation of the thoughts of Gabriel Denham. *The Waterfall* remains within Jane's mind, but keeps its balance, though precariously at times, among several possible views of the facts. *The Needle's Eye* returns to a third-person narrator; it is about the workings of imagination in ordinary life, and, for the first time, no major character is involved professionally with literature. (Offstage, there is Simon's mother, whose chatty radio talks for housewives have made her a minor celebrity and enabled her to pay for her son's education; Simon, once embarrassed and angered by what seemed to him to be the falseness of her optimistic stories of everyday hardships, comes to see that their truth lay "in the fact of expression" [p. 120].) The narrator enters the minds of Rose, the rich girl who has tried to create for herself a life of poverty and grace, and of Simon, who watches her with fascination and love. In *The Realms of Gold,* the third-person narrative plays with the method, inviting the reader to share the fun. It is as if the author, having explored the demands of her profession, is content in this novel to take for granted the openness of the form of fiction and the paradoxes of narration.

The philosophical issue that is probed most seriously in these two novels is that of free will with the related questions of determinism, luck,

---

Waterfall is "a novel partly about the difficulties of writing a novel" (p. 123) and says that the "apparent shapelessness" is "transcended by an art which creates a coherent and beautiful pattern out of incoherence and contradiction" (p. 23). As I hope I have shown, I agree with Myer, although I would quibble with her statement of the question posed by the novel: "Which is more important, art, the product of the imagination, creating a second reality, or life itself?" (p. 143). It seems to me that the question concerns rather the discrepancy between two views of life.

[21] A short story, "The Crossing of the Alps," *Mademoiselle,* February 1971, pp. 154-55, 193-97, is an interesting transitional step in the development from *The Waterfall* to *The Needle's Eye.*

[22] *New Statesman,* May 22, 1969, p. 738.

choice and chance. In an interview given after the publication of *The Needle's Eye*, Margaret Drabble spoke of her attraction to the view that "whatever you do is all written up for you," yet she also admitted that "I have very naive conceptions about these things," and that "what has appalled me about the world is that some people have good luck." She did not, of course, attempt to solve this problem, but suggested, in the same interview, that "one must maintain virtue by one's acts while hoping for grace"; grace she defined in secular terms as "being in harmony with the purpose of life."[23] Her growing interest in the complexities of these ideas is attested to by her progressively more sophisticated handling of plot in successive novels.

In the first novel the author was already thinking about the logic of plots; Sarah has a friend who writes "imitation-French" novels, "all about pursuing ways of life to the absurd or the logical" (*Bird-Cage,* p. 75). But the plot of Sarah's own story is haphazard and rambling. In *The Millstone* the plot is used to provide a moral shape for Rosamund's life, to educate her in participation through suffering, and she, the most intellectual of all the heroines, speaks of her feeling that she is submitting to a predetermined fate: "I was trapped in a human limit for the first time in my life, and I was going to have to learn how to live inside it" (p. 66). She detects a purpose behind her pregnancy: "Really, it was a question of free will; up to this point in my life I had always had the illusion at least of choice, and now for the first time I seemed to become aware of forces not totally explicable, and not therefore necessarily blinder, smaller, less kind, or more ignorant than myself" (p. 77). In *The Waterfall,* the arduous construction and reconstruction of the plot is related to Jane's longing to build a new morality; she "could not resist" James's recognition of her true self, and therefore "if I need a morality, I will create one: a new morality, a new ladder, a new virtue" (p. 55). Neither construction is neatly accomplished in the end. How much of her redemption by James's love was foreordained? Her life and her nature are a "fated pattern," one which she must walk in until death, "but sometimes, by accident or endeavour (I do not know which,in writing this I try to decide which) one may find a way of walking that predestined path more willingly. In company, even" (p. 172). Looking back over the story, she observes that "although the whole affair was so heavily structured . . . that I felt, at times, that I could see the machinery work, that I was simply living out some text book pattern of relationship," it has no ending (p. 248). In this novel Margaret Drabble's handling of plot takes on a new maturity.

In *The Needle's Eye* Rose, a rich man's daughter, has been obsessed since childhood by Bunyan and by the Bible's warning; she sets out to create her own morality, and achieves for herself and her children (and vicariously for Simon) a life which satisfies her, avoiding the

[23] Hardin, "An Interview with Margaret Drabble," 285, 284.

burdens of her wealth and the violence and quarrels of her life with her husband Christopher. She lives with her illusion of freedom. We see the author resist the obvious temptations, sensational and sentimental, which the plot offers: of a happy love story for Rose and Simon, of the feared abduction of the children by their father, of Rose's escape to Africa to work for the natives whom she has already, disastrously, tried to help with her unwanted money, and finally, of the continuation of Rose's chosen life. The ending which is provided is one of mundane but nevertheless heroic sacrifice, as Rose, exhausted, chooses an unhappy reunion with Christopher for the children's sake. It is an ending of compromise, partly freely chosen, partly imposed by fate. Yet, at the end, Rose is still living in her beloved shabby neighbourhood, still creating.

The appalling fact of good luck, of hereditary neuroses evaded, Hitler's gas ovens escaped, and true lovers united, is the motivating force of the plot of *The Realms of Gold.* It is high-spirited and comic—"I dislike a book without jokes," said Sarah in the first novel (*Bird-Cage,* p. 8), and this book has jokes in abundance, from the pun when Frances wonders what kind of man, long ago, betrayed her aunt Con into madness: "seducer, con man" (p. 308) to the large joke of the narration itself. Frances, the archaeologist, enjoyed as a child the idea that God had created everything "for fun" (p. 107); in the novel the author operates quite openly, with self-directed humour, as God.[24] She calls attention to her interventions, primly refusing to carry coincidence too far (two characters happen to be eating shepherd's pie and frozen peas at the same time in different houses, but only one has cauliflower as well; "There is some limit to life's coincidences," says the narrator [p. 317]). The machinery so intently scrutinized in *The Waterfall* and so sadly and gently invoked in *The Needle's Eye* is treated playfully now. The postcard which Frances sends to her lover Karel (whom she has rather whimsically dismissed from her life) to tell him she loves him goes astray in a postal strike—the modern version of Hardy's device in *Tess of the D'Urbervilles*—and the author says that this is not a coincidence: it would have been "more of a miracle," in these times, if the postcard had arrived on time (p. 224). Karel receives the card at last and goes to meet Frances in Africa, narrowly missing a plane which explodes, killing all passengers. After many complications caused by Frances' involvement in two family deaths, both illustrating the family neurosis (the result, it seems, of both heredity and environment),[25] which Frances, through

[24] See Suzanne Juhasz, Review of *The Realms of Gold, Library Journal* 100 (October 1, 1975), 1844.

[25] Margaret Drabble said after finishing *The Needle's Eye* that she wanted to "tackle hereditary depressions that run through three generations of a family" and also spoke of her feeling that certain environments are more conducive to good qualities than other environments; she described the United States and northern England as inhospitable environments (Hardin, "An Interview with Margaret Drabble," 289).

luck and Karel's love, escaped, the lovers are together and happy. They are even permitted to marry, since Frances is already divorced and Karel's wife discovers that she herself is lesbian. Their lives are further enriched by a newly discovered cousin of Frances', David, a geologist, and his bachelor flat in London, which surprises Frances by its self-contained elegance, provides the last image in the novel. It, like the first image, of an octopus living in a transparent box, is an example of containment, of the efficient and beautiful use of space, and these two form a frame for a series, including Frances' buried cities, graves, rooms and cottages, all working together with the plot to offer a demonstration of the fitness of things.

In the last two novels of the seven discussed here, the literary references are less ponderous than in some of the earlier ones. Rose's misquotation of Rossetti's "Woodspurge" in *The Needle's Eye* is introduced casually; it simply reinforces her search for value in ordinary places—in this case, for a rare flower of urban waste areas, the London rocket (p. 217). Frances, thinking of Karel and the reunion she hopes for, compares Hunter, who has told her of his meeting with Karel and Karel's statement that he loves her, to Antony's messenger, and herself to Cleopatra. "Husband, I come," she quotes to herself (p. 52), and we know that while she respects herself she does not take herself completely seriously.

Yet *The Realms of Gold* is also the most serious of the seven. Decay and death provide some of the most persistent imagery; there are the deaths, within the book, of Frances' nephew Stephen and Aunt Con, and, in the background, of Frances' sister, by suicide, of Karel's family, in Nazi Germany, of the passengers in the plane he missed, and of the people of Frances' lost cities. Because of its chief character's professions—archaeologist, historian, geologist—it covers a wide span of time and space, and this effect of expansiveness is supported by many instances of the weathering process in animate and inanimate things: teeth, rocks, ancient buildings, statues, the pond life of a ditch, human loves. The reader's awareness of suffering and depletion as the generations move on is not less strong for being established in such matter-of-fact ways. The fact of her great good luck in her profession, her health, her children and her meeting with Karel is constantly in Frances' mind ("I owe it to fate, to chance, to Karel," she reflects [p. 69]). There is a sense of the arbitrary quality of all stories in life and yet a belief in the possibility of making sense of the world. David has learned that "it was only ignorance that concealed the pattern" in the rocks he studies (p. 187). The mysteries of imagination are celebrated: Frances and David share the kind of feeling for their subjects which enables them to imagine discoveries before they make them. Frances thinks of her intuitive gift with awe: "It was difficult to know what to imagine next, when one had so much" (p. 35). And the failures as well as the triumphs of imagination are recorded: Aunt Con, dying alone and starving; Stephen, resisting the weathering process to which the others submit, with his wish to die "whole, intact, undestroyed" (p. 349); Karel's wife Joy, unstable and masochistic. Nevertheless, riches accrue, and even Janet, another cousin of Frances', gains hope that she may escape from at least some of the boredom and bleakness of her marriage. At the conclusion the narrator comments, "A happy ending, you may say. Resent it, if you like" (p. 356).

Besides making a closer examination of free will, determinism and luck through an assured management of plot, these last two novels show the processes of creativity from the inside, and thus demand a more active participation from the reader. The relation to literary models of the past is less obvious and the relation of governing stories and images is at the same time more complex. Though original in tone and attitude (a reviewer of *The Millstone* pointed out that Margaret Drabble "writes unromantically stories that have often been told sentimentally")[26] the earlier stories are more predictable and less satisfying. In *The Garrick Year* we foresee that Emma will settle down to the work of her marriage. In *Jerusalem the Golden* the image of the seed scattered on stony ground, which Clara takes as a challenge to survive, and the fable of the two weeds, one of which chooses to live a long time in obscurity while the other wills itself to die in glory, together predict the terms of Clara's life. We are aware of the moral that there is a price for everything; we are left uneasy only because the complexity both of the governing story of escape and of the fable and the image of Jerusalem has not been fully explored. Again, *The Waterfall* is a turning point. In it, and in *The Needle's Eye* and *The Realms of Gold,* we watch the imagination choose its symbols. This process is carried on through what Angus Wilson calls "the mysterious elements in ordinariness."[27] A contrast with an early novel can be helpful here. Part of the dissatisfaction we may feel with the conclusion of *The Garrick Year* comes from the predictable separation of the ideal landscape and the actual one which must be chosen; there is the landscape of fantasy, one of "pure intensity" with "no rivers, no children" (p. 205) in which Emma imagines a love affair with Julian, and there is the final landscape of flawed pastoral, with a snake clutching at a sheep's belly (p. 223). In *The Waterfall* the two come together: Jane, at the end of her story, thinks of herself as "a landscape given to . . . upheavals" which James has made blossom (pp. 244-45). *The Needle's Eye* shows the making of legends, but they are ordinary legends made of

---

[26] R. G. G. Price, Review of *The Millstone, Punch,* October 6, 1965, p. 512.

[27] Review of *Arnold Bennett,* p. 737. Cf. P. J. Kavanaugh's description of *The Needle's Eye* as "remarkable for its description of those sudden accesses of grace, arising from simplicity, that we no longer have a common vocabulary to describe" (Review of *The Needle's Eye, Manchester Guardian Weekly,* April 8, 1972, p. 4).

everyday things. The moral terms of the legend of Rose, in which Simon's imagination participates, are recognized by Simon's comparison of his exclusive Oxford college with Rose's inclusive world (pp. 300-301). There are many images of her world: the chicken in the old armchair in a vacant lot to which Rose and her friend Emily and their children take Simon, which delights them all; the sea anemones, on a bitterly cold day, which Simon and his daughter Kate enjoy; the dog show which Simon, Rose, Emily and the children visit at the end of the book. The most striking and memorable image is that of the lion in front of the Alexandra Palace. Rose's imagination illuminates this lion, after comparing it, in its crudity and shabbiness, with the lions of her father's estate, which are heraldic and expensive. This lion is "one of many" and she prefers it: "She liked the lion . . . . Mass-produced it had been, but it had weathered into identity. And this, she hoped, for every human soul" (p. 369). Rose's character, as it unfolds itself to Simon, is itself story. As Joyce Carol Oates has perceptively said, Rose "does not really know the vocabulary that will define her"; she is engaged in an existential enterprise of creating values by which she can live.[28] The reader must take part in the search for analogy. The language of glamour in the earlier books is supplanted by language of grace, of a hard-won beatitude found, with luck, in ordinary living. In both of the two latest novels, other possible views of the central situation are suggested- —particularly in *The Needle's eye,* in which legal documents, newspaper accounts, even Simon's father-in-law's opportunistic mail order catalogues, invite scepticism or dismissal of Rose's life. There is more room in these novels for critical controversy, and more productive ambiguity.[29] The imagination of the characters, struggling to survive with grace, increasingly finds comfort in chance happenings like Frances and Karel's discovery of the frogs singing in the pipe:

> Hundreds and hundreds of frogs were sitting down that pipe, and they were all honking, all of them, not in unison but constantly, their little throats going, their mouths open . . . . Karel and Frances stared, awestruck, amused: the sight was repulsive and at the same time profoundly comic, they loved the little frogs and the big

[28] Joyce Carol Oates, Review of *The Needle's Eye, New York Times Book Review,* June 11, 1972, p. 23.

[29] There is a good deal of disagreement, for example, over the interpretation of Rose's chosen life of poverty and her return to Christopher. *The Times Literary Supplement* finds this ending "not only a further concession but a defeat" (March 31, 1972, p. 353); Thwaite finds the reconciliation and compromise at the end admirable and reminiscent of the ending of *Middlemarch*; Oates sees Rose's chosen life as one of integrity and her return to Christopher as a sacrifice. Kennedy Fraser (*New Yorker,* December 16, 1972, p. 149) calls the book dull and lacking in passion and imagination, and objects to the way in which Rose's surroundings are "constantly wheeled out . . . to testify to her spiritual progress." E. C. Rose views Rose's insistence on her virtuous path as an "arrogant denial" of the current of life (p. 15).

ones.... And every time she [Frances] thought of them, she felt such pleasure and amusement deep within her, a deep source of it, much deeper than that pipe. (*Realms of Gold,* p. 25)

The frogs form part of the love story, and they are a link with the other images of containment, and with the themes of acceptance, imagination and play.

Margaret Drabble's development is not completed. Her work until 1975 has impressed us with its patient, loving probing of the possibilities of her craft. If she is sometimes sceptical about the novel, hers is surely a healthy scepticism, arguing not for rejection but for commitment.[30] Always firmly placing herself in the tradition we call realism, she is one of those whom David Lodge describes as responding to the "pressures of scepticism on the aesthetic and epistemological premises" of this tradition.[31] Her response, as I hope I have shown, has been a continued exploration of the methods of literature. We may again apply to her some words she wrote about Doris Lessing: describing her as "one of the very few novelists who have refused to believe that the world is too complicated to understand," she added, "Her devoted application to the understanding of life is not likely to produce improbable or irrelevant conclusions."[32]

[30] Cf. François Bonfond's article on the first four novels, "Margaret Drabble: How to Express Subjective Truth Through Fiction?" *Revue des Langues Vivantes* 42 (1974), 54. In view of Margaret Drabble's "essentially subjective concept" of reality and her questioning of the nature of the fictional form and its relationship to reality, Bonfond states that it is doubtful whether her technique is adequate to her purpose. In support of his argument Bonfond cites Rosamund's rejection of Lydia's portrayal of her—an illustration which is also used by Bergonzi (p. 204) as an example of "the notion in some modern novelists that the literary transformation of experience is a form of mystification or lying."

[31] *The Novelist at the Crossroads* (Ithaca: Cornell University Press, 1971), p. 19.

[32] "Doris Lessing," 54.

"Any Modern City": The Urban Canadian Fiction of Richard B. Wright[1]

JAMES DOYLE

From the earliest appearances of nationalism as a literary theme in English-Canadian literature, Canadian writers have tended to look to rural and small town settings for the distinctive or characteristic features of their national identity. When they have looked to the city, especially in the twentieth century, they have tended to discover an urban and technological image of life which in externals is not significantly different from that of the United States. Morley Callaghan, for instance, is noted for his deliberate fictional exploitation of the bland and characterless qualities of Toronto, which he frequently represents merely as an unnamed city on the Great Lakes, distinguished from Buffalo or Cleveland only by recognizable street names and allusions to the proximity of the northern cottage country. There have been efforts to exploit in fiction the local colour of some Canadian cities: Hugh MacLennan, in *Barometer Rising* (1941), tried to evoke the unique atmospheric concoction of Scots Calvinism, imperialist sentiment, and incipient nationalist fervour of wartime Halifax; and even Callaghan, when he turned to Montreal for *The Loved and the Lost* (1951), discovered a bizarre inner-city underworld of strikingly defined ethnic, social, and racial elements. But in general, the urban Canadian novel is often distinguishable from its American counterpart only in the representation of minor external details. In considering this phenomenon, Northrop Frye has offered an explanation which is more useful to the explication of Canadian literature than the obvious and simplistic deduction that Canadian society and culture are merely satellites in the American orbit. The

[1] An earlier version of this paper was read at the Canadian Association for American Studies Conference, 1977.

Canadian city and the artistic representation of it are part of what Frye
has called the "international modern," a term which he applies to a
content and style of art predominantly concerned with such things as
skyscraper cities and the "tremendous technological will to power"
characteristic of the twentieth century. The United States, Frye
acknowledges, has probably contributed more than any other country to
both the conditions which have made this art possible and the idiom of
the art itself. But ultimately, as Frye says, "America is a province
conquered by the international modern much more than it is a source of
it."[2] The Torontonian of the 1970's suffers from a sense of lack of
identity as he looks about him at the dehumanized computerized technology of his skyscraper city, but so does his reflective counterpart in
New York, or Chicago, or London, or Berlin.

This failure of identity, as it particularly affects representative
middle-class individuals living in Toronto in the 1970's, is the main
concern of the first two published novels of Richard B. Wright (b. 1937).
In *The Weekend Man* (1970) and *In the Middle of a Life* (1973), Wright
presents a familiar image of the Canadian city as a sprawling urban
jungle in which the human intellect and spirit are bruised and battered,
hammered into numb conformity, or provoked to impotent hysteria or
catatonic passivity by relentless social and economic pressures.[3] Thus
baldly summarized, Wright's image of Toronto sounds like merely
another cliché of American urban fiction. And indeed, the cliché of
modern urban living is precisely the point at which Wright begins. Early
in *The Weekend Man,* his sardonic narrator describes the suburb of
"Union Place" where he lives and works:

> ... Union Place is a part of metropolitan Toronto; a large suburb
> which has wandered east of the city along the lakefront and then
> northward to meet the Macdonald-Cartier Freeway. It's much like
> the environs of any modern city: flat farmland which has been paved
> over and seeded with trim brick bungalows, small factories and
> office buildings, service stations and shopping plazas, all of it since
> 1950. In the last few years they've changed the zoning by-laws and
> now at least three or four dozen high-rise apartment buildings have
> climbed to the sky. Several more are now a-building and I spend
> many lunch hours watching the steelworkers crawl about on the
> girders of a new one at the corner of Mirablee and Napier Avenue. I
> myself live in one of these towering boxes; on the eighteenth floor of
> Union Terrace. ... (p. 5)[4]

[2] Northrop Frye, "Conclusion," *Literary History of Canada,* ed. Carl Klinck et al.
(Toronto: University of Toronto Press, 1965), pp. 846-47.
[3] Wright's third and most recent novel, *Farthing's Fortunes* (1976) obviously reflects
the author's urge to strike out in a completely new direction. A vigorous but eclectic
picaresque historical novel, it is not immediately relevant to the present discussion.
[4] All quotations from the novel refer to Richard B. Wright, *The Weekend Man*
(Toronto: Macmillan, 1970).

Not only is Wright's Toronto explicitly described as virtually indistinguishable from any modern city: it is easy to demonstrate that Wright deliberately derives much of his subject matter and techniques from certain urban novelists of the United States. *The Weekend Man,* with its indecisive protagonist who withdraws into a fantasy world of TV movies and emotional indifference strongly resembles in tone and characterization the early chapters of *The Moviegoer* (1961), by Alabama novelist Walker Percy, an indebtedness which Wright himself has acknowledged.[5] Wright has also expressed great admiration for Saul Bellow, and *In the Middle of a Life* is very reminiscent of *Herzog.* Both Bellow's Herzog and Wright's Fred Landon are late middle-aged urban North Americans whose youthful intellectual and imaginative ambitions have stagnated or disintegrated, whose marital relationships have degenerated into almost semi-farcical confusion, who dream of escape towards some sort of romantic pastoral ideal of which the actuality involves disappointment and incipient despair (in Bellow's novel, the false ideal is in Cape Cod; in Wright's, it is in the cottage country north of Toronto); and finally, both protagonists spend much of their fictional existence in frantic but ultimately aimless automotive odysseys, searching for some kind of relief for the pressures of their desperate existence.

It is difficult to exonerate Wright from the charge of being derivative. American reviewers took him to task on this charge, complaining for instance that the protagonist of *The Weekend Man* is like "a younger Herzog or Henderson, but without the intelligence or vitality that earns either his right to boredom or his right to regeneration."[6] Certainly Wright's characters lack the explicitly defined academic background of Herzog: they are not professors of philosophy or literature, but only moderately well-read average men whose ideas and beliefs have been formed by the media of mass culture. Wes Wakeham draws wry and sardonic inferences about such twentieth-century obsessions as the fear of mass annihilation while watching old science-fiction movies or programmes like "Run For Your Life"; Landon, on a slightly higher and more active intellectual level, has tried to write for television, concentrating his efforts on domestic melodramas about modern life. Herzog, on the other hand, has spent years attempting to write a definitive critical study of Romanticism, by means of which he once hoped to penetrate to the roots of the moral and metaphysical dilemmas of modern man. This effort has degenerated into a frantic and compulsive note-jotting, comprising the chaotic record of thought fragments which pass through his mind as he moves within the increasingly oppressive limitations of his social and domestic situation, and which serve mainly

[5] See Shirley Gibson, "Life to Wright" [an interview with Richard B. Wright], *Books in Canada* 5/12 (December 1976), 10.

[6] Lee T. Leman, "Some Fashions in Fiction," *Prairie Schooner* 45 (Fall 1971), 270.

as a pathetic reminder of the distance between thought and action, between the cultural heritage of western civilization and the sometimes petty and ludicrous circumstances of ordinary life. It might be argued, of course, that it is better to have struggled vainly, like Herzog, with the more sophisticated forms of one's cultural heritage than never to have struggled at all. But there is some compensation for the intellectual shortcomings of Wright's heroes in the imaginative energy which they repeatedly reveal. Wes Wakeham, for instance, draws upon the store of trivia he has accumulated from his persistent television viewing to make comments on the people and events within his immediate experience, comments which are convincing by virtue of the concise and vivid pictures they evoke. Mrs. Bruner, the efficient and beefily Teutonic secretary in Wakeham's office "looks like James Mason's mistress in some movie about the fall of Berlin" (p. 6). As he listens to the crisp, impatient voice of his estranged wife on the telephone, Wes imagines her "... drawing on leather gloves... and looking a bit like Joanne Woodward in one of those scenes where Joanne is trying to get rid of some creep so she can rush off to meet Paul Newman on the steps of the Natural History Museum" (pp. 18-19). Wes's good-natured and perpetually bemused father-in-law, "... with his moon face and Joe E. Brown mouth... looks like a comic from some Hollywood musical of the early forties, one of those birds who was always taking pratfalls while his good-looking straight man buddy was getting the girl" (p. 29).

Wes's perpetual tendency to relate the spectacle of his experience to the spectacle of movies and television has the inevitable effect of suggesting that the two spheres of existence are directly related and of equal importance. Wes has obviously tried to cultivate a detached and almost indifferent attitude to life, as if his personal and business relations were parts of an adventure series or an old movie. When a colleague tries to interest him in certain problems of the current business situation, Wes listens politely but indifferently, as he would to the dialogue of one of his television programmes. "He paused and flipped up the collar of his topcoat, waiting for me to say something. I had no thoughts on the subject" (p. 23). To the less reflective observers in Wakeham's environment, his behaviour appears to be the eccentric and egotistical self-pity of one who feels superior to the ordinary mortal whose primary desire is for a measure of comfort and security. But the reader who agrees with (for instance) Wakeham's estranged wife Molly and sees him as merely a self-centered rebel against the rat race is missing the point. Wright tries to make his exact point clear—and to encourage sympathy for his protagonist—by having Wes narrate his own story, and at various points in the novel, by having Wes spell out explicitly the moral and metaphysical issues involved:

> Molly believes that the only reason I am not successful is because I am willfully opposed to worldly success. In her eyes I am

> a thwarted idealist who has difficulty coming to terms with life as it
> is lived in our day and age. This is not so. I am not opposed to
> worldly success and am no more a thwarted idealist than a pygmy's
> uncle. The truth is that I am not a success because I cannot think
> straight for days on end, bemused as I am by the weird trance of this
> life and the invisible passage of time. (p. 209)

Wes's active thoughts are mostly directed towards creating for
himself a workable system of belief which will enable him to cope with
this weird trance of life and invisible passage of time. This system,
created out of verbal fragments from popular culture and his own
idiosyncratic terms and concepts, is centred on the idea of the
"weekend man," a sort of modern Everyman who "has abandoned the
present in favor of the past or the future" (p. 9). As Wakeham makes
clear, everyone is in one way or another a weekend man: everyone is
constantly looking forward to whatever slight "diversions" may come
along to alter the drab continuum of experience, or looking wistfully
backward to the few supreme moments of excitement that memory has
to offer. These diversions do not necessarily have anything to do with
happiness or good fortune: the greatest diversion of Wes Wakeham's
life, as he recalls in flashback, has been the Cuban Missile Crisis of 1962,
when under the shadow of imminent nuclear holocaust he found himself
"tingling with aliveness."

> All the emptiness and sadness of our days has been blown away by
> the great black wind which now sweeps across the sky. It scours the
> air and leaves it bitter and sharp as ammonia. Everything has
> meaning and nothing can be ignored. (p. 122)

As the Cuban Missile Crisis episode makes clear, however, this search
for "diversion" is a counsel of almost hysterical desperation. The bleak
plight of modern man is underscored in the situation of Wes Wakeham,
who is so sunk in numbness and despair by the apparent meaninglessness of life that he looks forward with almost enthusiastic excitement to
the possibility of nuclear holocaust. And when the crisis passes over
without disaster, he is almost disappointed.

Wes is able to contemplate this spectacle of imminent disaster with
some objectivity and ironic detachment because it comes to him on the
television screen and therefore appears as remote, unreal, and absurd as
an old movie he has recently seen about an invasion of giant ants. But
this remote spectacle has had a parallel in his own experience. As the
author reveals in another flashback episode, Wes's sense of malaise can
be at least partially related to the stunning effect on him of his parents'
death by car accident some years before. This personal disaster, and the
recurrent spectacle of imminent universal catastrophe have effectively
deprived him of a capacity for faith and optimism. To make matters
worse, he has encountered further personal disappointment and tragedy
in his marriage relationship, and in the birth of a mentally retarded son.

In addition to these various images of depression and despair within the consciousness of Wes Wakeham, the author presents a related pattern of image, symbol, and allusion which virtually surrounds his experience. The action of *The Weekend Man* takes place in the week before Christmas, and the author predictably exploits the traditional cultural associations of the season. From his own point of view, Wes Wakeham is waiting passively and stoically for a "diversion"; but from a larger perspective, he is in effect waiting for the birth of Christ—or perhaps, the Second Coming. As in the poem of W. B. Yeats, the Second Coming may be a cataclysm, a horror, and perhaps a purifying force, ushering in a completely new age. Significantly, Wright takes as an epigraph for his novel a quotation from Yeats; not from the "The Second Coming," however, but from a brief poem entitled "Death," written on the assassination in 1927 of Kevin O'Higgins, Minister of Justice in the Irish Free State.

> Nor dread nor hope attend
> A dying animal;
> A man awaits his end
> Dreading and hoping all;
> Many times he died,
> Many times rose again.
> A great man in his pride
> Confronting murderous men
> Casts derision upon
> Supersession of breath;
> He knows death to the bone—
> Man has created death.[7]

Wright's epigraph consists of only the last two lines of the poem. It is not the hope of resurrection, but the familiarity with death that is the omnipresent fact of existence as far as his main character is concerned. The knowledge of death—of his parents, of himself, of all humanity—is constantly present to transform his existence into a bleak and meaningless prospect. And the hope of some kind of redemption or resurrection is only a remote and extremely ambiguous possibility on the periphery of his experience. Throughout the novel, this remote possibility is conveyed through light imagery. Repeatedly, Wes Wakeham is presented both literally and figuratively as being immersed in darkness and waiting for light. Most often, however, the light comes to him from the cheap and garish Christmas decorations on stores and houses, or from the headlights of automobiles, those mechanical monsters which Wright uses in common with a legion of other twentieth-century writers to epitomize the isolation and confinement of modern man. This artificial light also seems to suffuse certain episodes in the novel when Wakeham

[7] W. B. Yeats, "Death," *Selected Poetry,* ed. A. Norman Jeffares (London: Macmillan, 1963), p. 142.

experiences a kind of pseudo-happiness, involving transitory or temporary relief from anguish and despair. A brief, mildly pleasant sexual liaison with a sympathetic woman whom he has met casually at a Christmas party is presented amid the bland setting of her modern high-rise apartment in suburban Toronto, where the "bluish lights of television sets" can be glimpsed through the picture windows of houses, and the "running lights of tractor-trailers" and the "revolving blue light of a snow plow" can be seen on the freeway in the distance (p. 142).

In contrast to this kind of artificially illuminated episode, one of the most significant encounters in the novel takes place in a "sun room" (p. 166), part of a residence school for retarded children, where Wakeham visits his young mentally defective son. The cultural implications surrounding this encounter are inevitable and obvious: one thinks, for example, of Benjy in Faulkner's *The Sound and the Fury,* a grotesque imbecilic Christ figure whose coming heralds the meaninglessness of life. But just as in Faulkner's novel the idea of idiot-as-Christ-figure is offset by the love between Benjy and his sister Caddy, so Wakeham feels genuine love and compassion for his son, feelings which almost stir him out of his lethargy and despair. The child, associated with the sun rather than with the artificial light which pervades so much of Wakeham's experience, conveys both meaninglessness and potential meaning. Perhaps the life of modern man is arid and pointless, but meaning may emerge out of the very situations of conflict and tribulation which predominate in life. The ambivalence of this possibility, and of the imagery which conveys it, is underscored at the end of the novel, when Wakeham finds himself silently contemplating the sky on Christmas Eve, as he waits for a morning which may bring a change in his situation—or a continuation of the same empty existence.

> Overhead the sky is flooded with stars. On such a night as this I used to position my telescope just so, aiming it at Ursa Major and extending an imaginary line through the two end stars of the Dipper. This way I could get a fix on the North Star, that ancient guiding light of other lonely mariners who have passed this way. Perhaps in the new year on another fine night I will take out the telescope and have another look. Right now it is enough to gaze upward and bear witness to all this light, travelling from its fiery origins with a perfect indifference, across the immensities of space and time, to strike the retinas of my eyes at this moment—to bear witness to this remarkable light and wait for sleep and try to remember what it is I was supposed to do. (p. 247)

The theme of hope, of looking up toward the light with expectancy and determination, is thus fused in this concluding episode of *The Weekend Man* with the theme of dread. The result of this fusion is a kind of mental and physical paralysis, combined—as the concluding words of the novel make clear—with something like momentary amnesia. Faced with the irresolvable contradictions of modern life, finding himself on the brink of what may be either a second coming or a meaningless ending, Wes Wakeham can neither think nor act.[8]

This state of paralysis is frequently related in the novel to a social and national context as well as to a metaphysical and cosmic one. Besides being balked by the dilemmas of twentieth-century urban life common to most of western civilization, Wes Wakeham finds himself faced with a distinctively Canadian problem. In the course of the novel the company he works for—which, significantly, is a publishing company specializing in educational materials—is taken over by an American company, a monolithic corporation specializing in electronic systems and equipment. The results of this development are familiar: some of the younger, more energetic members of the firm, completely uncritical adherents to the American faith in material progress, are exhilarated by the prospect of possibilities for advancement. Some of the older, less forward-looking members of the firm, as one young junior executive gleefully speculates, are bound to fall by the wayside; and Wes Wakeham withdraws into his usual semi-paralytic stance of apathy and scepticism, only to find himself ironically singled out as a likely prospect for advancement as a result of his accidental discovery of a potentially successful grammar textbook written by an old school friend.

But Wright's thesis, as Wes's accidental success suggests, is that the constant technological change and economic development epitomized in the American takeover of Canada form a completely arbitrary and unpredictable process. By an almost ludicrous chain of events, Wes Wakeham finds himself a welcome member of the mammoth international electronics corporation which has bought out the publishing firm he was working for. But by an equally arbitrary alternate chain of events, he might as easily have found himself unemployed. The latter situation is the premise of Wright's second novel, *In the Middle of a Life,* the protagonist of which is in certain ways a kind of middle-aged Wes Wakeham. Fred Landon is a forty-two-year-old Toronto greeting card salesman whose company has been bought out by an American conglomerate which has dismissed some of the older and ostensibly less productive employees. The action of the novel covers a few days in Landon's life as he makes the rounds in search of a new job, while simultaneously trying to cope with various personal crises.

[8] In the preceding discussion of *The Weekend Man,* I have tended to emphasize Wright's use of Wakeham as a serious medium for ideas on such subjects as identity failure and modern anxiety. In so doing, I have neglected the fact that Wright also sees his character ironically, a fact of obvious importance to the structure of the novel, but which would be essentially digressive in the argument presented here. The element of irony in the novel is admirably discussed in Sheila Campbell, "The Two Wes Wakehams—Point of View in *The Weekend Man,*" *Studies in Canadian Literature* 2/2 (Summer 1977), 289-305.

Instead of suffering paralysis of the will and sitting as Wes Wakeham does for hours staring at television or forcing himself through the motions of a meaningless daily routine, Landon trudges doggedly onward through unemployment, marital problems, and arguments with his teenage daughter, determined to live out his life, frustrating though it may be, as best he can. His experience with spiritual paralysis, the author reveals in flashback, belongs to a youthful episode in which he dreamed of establishing himself as a playwright, but which ended, after a modest and ultimately deceptive initial success, with Landon sitting for hours before his typewriter in his attic retreat, unable to put down on paper anything but meaningless gibberish. Having failed in the search for order through art, Landon turns to the only alternative available, and resolutely sets out to find meaning in the routine of middle-class life. As he discovers, however, the order of life is only indirectly revealed, through the constant tension between ambivalent or antagonistic ideas and experiences. Faced with the chilling prospect of unemployment in middle age, he eventually finds another job—as salesman for a seedy real estate firm, where prospects for the future include being turned out on the street if he is unable to "move property." Having finally disengaged himself from a hopelessly unhappy marriage, he strikes up an affair with a congenial and sympathetic woman—an affair which is plagued, however, by emotional and economic uncertainty. His relations with his daughter show signs of improving—but suffer a clumsy and absurd setback when the daughter is arrested for possessing marijuana. Life, Landon ponders ruefully from his median position, seems to be a series of hopes and rewards alternating with kicks and blows, through which the individual can only plod doggedly onward, and occasionally take refuge in fanciful and ironic dreams of escape.

Landon's dreams often arise directly from the characterless "international modern" spectacle of Toronto which is constantly under his observation. Obliged to live in a second-rate apartment building in the neighbourhood of the University, Landon looks out on the partially completed new research library. The brave new world of package-processed education suggested by this "bulky gray pile of cement and glass" (p. 34) has no relevance to him, and he finds himself indulging in nostalgic fantasies of a time when some of the older buildings were new:

> Thus reflecting, he would sight through a circle made by thumb and forefinger, holding it before one eye like a photographer. And there, sure enough, were the high box-shaped automobiles on their narrow tires and the open trolleys, red wood and toylike, rattling along the tracks with their bells and blue-vested conductors. (pp. 34-35)[9]

[9] All quotations from the novel refer to Richard B. Wright, *In the Middle of a Life* (Toronto: Macmillan, 1973).

Besides attempting to escape the pressures of modern urban life by nostalgic or whimsical forays backward in time, Landon makes escapist excursions imaginatively in space. During a severe winter storm, Landon volunteers to drive a neighbour to the hospital to see her dying mother; and as he manoeuvres the woman's incongruously large car through the treacherous streets, he momentarily indulges in a fantastic dream of taking the car

> ... Across the dominion with his neighbour. Over the northland with the tips of fir trees lashing in the wind. And beyond them, the frozen tundra reaching out to the rim of the planet and the distant northern sea. Through that exploded pre-Cambrian rock, now buried deep under snow, and past the forests to prairie country. Yahoo! Past towns and way stations he had glimpsed through sleepy eyes from the windows of trains. And somewhere out there a blinding snowstorm, fueled by seventy-mile-an-hour winds, roaring across one thousand miles of tableland. But still no match for this big landship. Climbing the Rockies with the fat tires gripping each tremendous curve. He'd have those tires checked before tackling Roger's Pass. And climbing, ever climbing, until at last, they began their descent to the sea. The Pacific Ocean! Gateway to the Orient!
> (p. 49)

Throughout the novel, Landon is continually making excursions of imagination or memory, reviewing the crucial events of his own life, or creating whimsical fantasies to relieve his sense of frustration with the profuse forces of dehumanization that constantly seem to emanate from the concrete and steel jungle of Toronto. Yet in spite of his penchant for long self-indulgent forays into fantasy or nostalgia, Landon is not a dreamer or an escapist in the sense that Wes Wakeham is. The difference in attitude between the two protagonists is underscored by the epigraph to the second novel. For *In the Middle of a Life,* Wright takes as an epigraph a line from Dylan Thomas: ''Praise to our faring hearts,'' the concluding words of an early poem entitled ''Our Eunuch Dreams.'' Thomas' poem, like Yeats's (and like most of Thomas' work), turns on the all-pervading fact of death. Pointing out the clumsy and pathetic attempts of human beings to suppress their awareness of death, Thomas refers to the cinema, that ''lying likeness'' of reality, where ''one-dimensional ghosts'' pursue fantastic, phantasmagoric, and ultimately sterile dreams, which only succeed in reflecting the fact of death. Thus summarized, the poem would seem relevant to the pessimism of *The Weekend Man.* In the final stanza, however, Thomas urges an exuberant attitude of acceptance, an acceptance not only of the fact of death, but of the fantasies which make the nightmare life in death endurable, and an acceptance which in its enthusiasm shades over into proud, almost rebellious defiance:

> For we shall be a shouter like the cock,
> Blowing the old day back; our shots shall smack
> The image from the plates;
> And we shall be fit fellows for a life,
> And who remain shall flower as they love,
> Praise to our faring hearts.[10]

In his own quiet and mildly ironic way, Fred Landon of *In the Middle of a Life* is a "shouter." His inward exclamation of "Yahoo!" as he takes the great "landship" over the Rogers Pass of his imagination is his way of registering his determination to accept the conditions of life, and perhaps even to defy the universe to do its worst.

The metaphor of the journey is an inevitable part of the idiom of this kind of modern fiction, and in Wright's novels as in so many others the metaphor is explicitly related to the automobile. The car accident involving Wes Wakeham's parents has previously been mentioned; from time to time throughout *The Weekend Man* other situations involving the automobile lead directly into meditations or dramatic revelations about the plight of modern man. The plot of *In the Middle of a Life,* however, is much more explicitly related to a series of automobile journeys. In addition to the drive to the hospital, there is the swift and incongruous drive which Fred Landon takes with his prospective employer out to the suburbs of Toronto, where they hope to sell a house. The episode ends in understated but ominous ambiguity: Fred gets the job, but they fail miserably in their attempt to sell the house, a development which does not speak well for Fred's economic prospects. Of greater thematic importance, however, is the final automobile journey of the novel, in which Fred takes his new fiancée north to the small town in the Georgian Bay cottage country of Ontario to meet his relatives.

From time to time in Canadian fiction, particularly fiction set in Toronto, the Georgian Bay region is used as an epitome of the ideas of innocence and freedom traditionally associated with the return to nature, the search for Eden or Arcadia, and similar images of an existence supposedly simpler and purer than that characteristic of the modern city. This pattern is evident, for instance, in Morley Callaghan's *They Shall Inherit the Earth* (1936), where members of the Aikenhead family flee the depression-ridden turmoil of Toronto northward to the region which evokes memories of ostensible happiness and innocence. Callaghan's novel fulfills the ironic expectations of this kind of plot: the Aikenhead journey results in a series of quarrels, an accidental drowning, and an alienation among the characters which is more intense than ever. Similarly in *In the Middle of a Life,* Fred Landon's journey to "Bay City" with his fiancée results in unsatisfactory encounters with

---

[10] *Dylan Thomas: The Poems,* ed. Daniel Jones (London: Dent, 1971), p. 90.

his relatives and the ludicrous incident of his daughter's arrest for possession of marijuana. These incidents are not, however, the primary medium of the "you can't go home again" theme. Fred is not surprised by the unsympathetic reception of his relatives, and even his daughter's escapade is not entirely unexpected. The experience which vividly and succinctly illuminates his situation—not only of the current place and moment, but of the entire "middle of his life" context—is his rediscovery of a group of tourist cottages once owned by his grandfather. The decayed motor court and the modern motel which has superseded it are both named the Blue Moon, a name which in its pathetic triteness suggests tired illusions and a sentimental withdrawal from reality into a manufactured dream world comparable to the cinematic images of Thomas' poem. The modern motel, a bland and impersonal manifestation of North American junk culture, has almost obliterated all traces of Landon's grandfather's place:

> . . . Slowing down, Landon could see that only a couple of the larger cabins remained, partly hidden away among the pines. The Blue Moon was now an L-shaped concrete block motel with a large sign in the shape of a new moon hanging over the entrance. (p. 240)

Moved by sentimentality and nostalgia, Landon strolls over to inspect the cabins more closely, and finds—as he expects—only evidence of decay. The whole episode is comparable to the conclusion of *Herzog,* where Bellow's character, after weeks of compulsive and erratic travelling, settles in the rotting shambles of his summer cottage in Massachusetts. The "ruined cottage" is, of course, a familiar romantic symbol of disillusionment and failure. In Bellow's novel, it points to both the bankruptcy of Herzog's intellectual ideals and to Herzog's stubborn resolution to persist in his search for form and meaning in life, for in the closing pages of the novel he is apparently determined to clean up and restore the cottage. Whether he will succeed or not remains an open question, for the novel ends in silence and immobility, with Herzog (rather like Wes Wakeham at the end of *The Weekend Man*) in a momentary state of lassitude and indifference. The conclusion of *In the Middle of a Life* is different, however. Landon yields to the sentiment and nostalgia of the moment—and in a larger sense, to the illusion that the past can be restored or recaptured—and registers at the Blue Moon with his fiancée. But subsequent events of the day jolt him out of this mood. After his daughter's arrest and his subsequent involvement in the business of bail arrangements, phone calls to lawyers and so forth, the prospect of a romantic night at the Blue Moon seems ridiculous. Without further thought, he heads back to the city, ready to carry on with whatever obligations and struggles may await him.

In the Middle of a Life is thus, in effect, a novel on the theme of resolution and independence. If the prevailing metaphor of *The*

Weekend Man is paralysis, the prevailing metaphor of Wright's second novel is movement: assertive and defiant movement onward and outward, like the journey of the "landship" in Landon's dream vision. In his two novels, Richard B. Wright has thus presented two complementary views of the situation of man in the modern world: one predominantly indecisive, if not absolutely pessimistic, and another predominantly optimistic. Both novels create a decidedly unpleasant picture of Toronto as the bland and spiritually destructive expression of the "international modern" way of life, although *In the Middle of a Life* makes some tentative suggestions towards coping with this way of life. Richard B. Wright offers no suggestions as to how the process of industrialism and mechanization represented by the modern city can be impeded or reversed, however. His two novels are primarily concerned with the dramatization of two individual kinds of response to these processes, and it is as character studies of modern urban man that they are preeminently successful.